THE ORGAN HANDBOOK

THE
ORGAN
HANDBOOK

By HANS KLOTZ

Translated by Gerhard Krapf

CONCORDIA PUBLISHING HOUSE

SAINT LOUIS

Concordia Publishing House, St. Louis, Missouri 63118

© 1969 Concordia Publishing House
Library of Congress Catalog Card No. 69-11068

This volume is a translation of Das Buch von der Orgel,
by Hans Klotz, 7th edition, published by Bärenreiter-Verlag,
Karl Vötterle KG, Kassel-Wilhelmshöhe, Germany, 1965.

MANUFACTURED IN THE UNITED STATES OF AMERICA

TRANSLATOR'S PREFACE

The present volume is the translation of a well-tried, practical work equally important for the amateur and for the professional organist. Written by one of the foremost representatives of the *Orgelbewegung,* it offers a concise, yet comprehensive presentation of all aspects of the art of the organ. Although prepared for German readers, it is directly applicable to the American scene with but a few necessary adjustments of minor significance (indicated in footnotes).

A translation of a work of such scope must rely on considerable assistance. The translator is particularly indebted to:

Hans Klotz, the author, who very freely gave counsel and advice;

Lawrence I. Phelps and Karl Wilhelm, who gave invaluable assistance in problems of nomenclature;

Paul Bunjes, who gave excellent advice, saved me from several errors, provided a consistent technical nomenclature, and edited the entire manuscript in preparation for publication;

John McLaughlin, for many helpful suggestions regarding English usage;

James Wyly, who read the typescript and volunteered some much appreciated suggestions;

R. Michael Fling, who revised and augmented the bibliography;

Carroll Hanson, who spent much time on special research relating to some technical aspects.

I am further indebted to Miss Sarah Hanks for her untiring efforts in typing my manuscript and for many excellent suggestions concerning style and form; to the Graduate College of the University of Iowa for material assistance; and to Mr. Edward Klammer of Concordia Publishing House for his encouragement, patience, and care in preparing the format.

GERHARD KRAPF

Iowa City, Iowa
September 12, 1966

PREFACE TO THE FIRST EDITION

This *Organ Handbook* is designed as an easily comprehensible introduction, not only for the benefit of organists and aspiring organists but also of amateurs who are interested in organs. It should be of aid to the architect concerned with aspects of organ building as related to church architecture; to pastors and members of committees concerned with the purchase, rebuilding, or maintenance of an organ; to the aspiring organ builder wishing to gain a general understanding of his rather complex profession. For these and similar concerns, the *Organ Handbook* provides practical advice and guidance. It has not been limited to a mere enumeration of facts. Indeed, a certain amount of specific information on seemingly quite specialized aspects has been given, for example, structure and tonal design, advice on placement, purchase, and maintenance (for the benefit of architects, pastors, laymen, and organists), and, finally, history and liturgical functions of the organ and various aspects of the interpretation of old and new organ literature.

As a matter of principle, contemporary organ companies have not been mentioned by name in order to avoid giving the impression of favoritism. Recent years have made extraordinary demands on the organ builder's art; a considerable number of new areas had to be conquered. As a result, slider chests, tracker action, and hitherto largely unknown labial and reed stops are being built by present-day German builders; they also have developed modern consoles of superb quality. These accomplishments bear witness of the profession's accomplishments far better than books could.

I am indebted to many for their kindly interest, counsel, and assistance in the completion of this book, particularly to Dr. Carl Elis, Göttingen, to my wife, and to the Bärenreiter-Verlag. I take this opportunity to express my gratitude to all.

HANS KLOTZ

Aachen, August 1937

PREFACE TO THE SEVENTH EDITION

In this new edition several sections have been revised, and the indexes have been newly compiled. For valuable aid, in the form of counsel as well as of active assistance, I am grateful to Mme. M.-C. Alain, St. Germain-en-Laye; to Messrs. K. Borman, Dipl.-Ing., Munich; M. Drischner, Kirchenmusikdirektor, Goslar; C. H. Edskes, Groningen; G. Eumann, Duisburg; A. Hoppe, Kirchenmusikdirektor, Verden; H. Klöpping, Cologne; Dr. H. Meyers, Luxemburg; Prof. R. Reuter, Münster; R. Scheidegger, Basel; E. Schiess, Bern; Dr. W. Supper, Esslingen; Dr. M. A. Vente, Utrecht; Dr. J. Wyly, Elmhurst, Ill.; and to several leading organ builders who have requested not to be listed by name. Special thanks are due to the Bärenreiter-Verlag.

HANS KLOTZ

Cologne, Whitsuntide 1965

CONTENTS

LIST OF PLATES

CHAPTER 1

The Construction of the Organ

Organ builders and organists are often subjected to queries concerning their instrument; these range in character from the disconcertingly naive to the exasperatingly complex. Any attempt to answer such questions conversationally leads inevitably to inordinately long colloquies in which the querist is informed that an organ contains approximately 85 times as many pipes as stops; that the pipes in the façade are often "real" speaking pipes; that most organs have two or three keyboards for the hands (some even four or five) and one for the feet. Such truisms cannot satisfy genuine curiosity. The following is an attempt to pinpoint the essentials of the structure and functions of the organ.

The Basic Mechanism of the Organ

It is common knowledge that organ tone is neither sung nor bowed but whistled in the literal sense of the word. If air is blown into the pipes, they will speak. The sounds may vary; they may be high or low in pitch, loud or soft, bright or dark, depending on the size, material, etc. of the pipes. The function of supplying wind to the pipes is assigned to the bellows. In order to prevent the simultaneous sounding of all pipes when the bellows are activated, the admission of air into the pipes is regulated by pallets. They are connected to the keys of the keyboard. When keys are depressed, the corresponding pallets are opened, and the pipes speak. In Figure 1 the basic mechanism of all organs is illustrated: [1]

---

[1] All sketches in this book are schematic, intended to illustrate essentials only. Please observe the following:

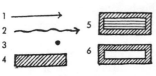

1 indicates the direction of moving organ parts; 2 indicates the direction of the wind; 3 indicates a fulcrum, or pivot; 4 indicates a cut-away area; 5 indicates a cut-away view of a chamber, running from left to right; 6 indicates a cut-away view of a chamber, running from front to back [i. e., transversely].

It is suggested that the reader consult Fig. 67 (folded insert attached to inside back cover), in addition to the figures appearing in the text, for further illustration of the technical aspects discussed in this chapter.

Fig. 1. Scheme of an organ

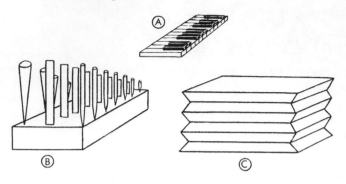

Letter A shows a keyboard, playable with the hands. It is called a "manual" (*manus, la main* — hand). A keyboard for the feet is called a "pedal" (*pes, le pied* — foot). Manuals usually encompass 4 to 5 octaves (C — a''' is a common range), and the pedal usually encompasses 2 to 2½ octaves (C — f' is a common range).[2]

Letter B shows the pipes mounted on the "wind chest." The word "wind" denotes the air stream delivered by the blower. The sketch shows three different ranks of pipes. Each rank begins in front with the large, low-pitched pipes and ends with the small, high-pitched ones on the far side of the chest. Each set of pipes produces a specific tone color and is called a "stop." Ordinarily a stop has one pipe for each key. The manuals have 58 keys, assuming a compass of C — a'''; the pedal has 30 keys with a compass of C — f'. Usually, an organ exhibits between 20 and 40 stops; those in village churches, more likely, between 10 and 20 stops. There are also large organs with 80, 100, 150, and 200 stops. "Stop knobs" facilitate the drawing or canceling of stops at the organist's discretion. The stop knobs are located close to the keyboards (see Fig. 11 and Plates XI and XII). As a rule the stops belonging to a given keyboard are mounted on one wind chest. Thus a three-manual organ has at least four wind chests: one for each manual and one for the pedal. Keys and wind chests are harnessed by the "action."

Letter C shows a bellows, in this case a simple ribbed, multiple-fold bellows. This appliance furnishes rather irregular wind;

---

[2] Manual compass of the American organ varies from 56 notes (C — g''') to 61 notes (C — c''''), while the pedal varies from 30 (C — f') to 32 notes (C — g'). [*Translator*]

therefore it has been obsolete for some centuries. Bellows and wind chests are joined by the "wind trunk" and "conductors."

The Blowplant

Let us first trace the development of various appliances used for the generation of wind.

The Spanbalg

The imperfect ribbed, multiple-fold bellows was first replaced by the socalled *Spanbalg* (single-fold bellows).

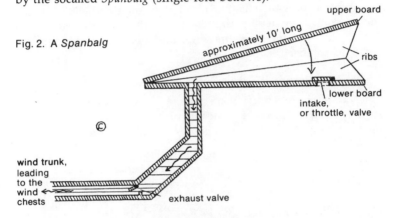

Fig. 2. A *Spanbalg*

Fig. 2 shows a *Spanbalg*. The German word *Span*—no longer in use—means "board." Literally translated, the appliance could be called a "board bellows"; however, because of long and persistent usage, the term *Spanbalg* seems to be universally accepted. It is constructed of wooden boards, ribs, and strips of leather. The boards are so hinged together as to allow for easy folding of the bellows. The cocked bellows slowly folds under the weight of the upper board and surmounted weights which it may carry, forcing air into the wind trunk that leads to the "pallet box." From there, as will be pointed out subsequently, the air proceeds through the open pallets into the "tone channels" (see Fig. 6) and from there, if a stop is drawn, to the pipes.

Let us examine the operation of the bellows. When the bellows unfolds, the intake, or throttle, valve by influence of the higher pressure of the surrounding atmosphere, opens while the exhaust valve closes for the same reason. The purpose of the intake valve is to admit air into the bellows, which, upon compression by the folding bellows, is then forced into the wind trunk through the exhaust valve. When the bellows begins to fold, the intake valve closes, thus directing the forced air into the wind trunk and preventing its return to the atmosphere. When the bellows is being filled, the automatic closure of the exhaust valve prevents the depletion of wind from the trunks (see pp. 17f.). Fig. 2 shows the positions of the valves while the bellows is folding, that is, when air is being compressed and expended into the wind trunk. The *Spanbalg* furnishes far more steady wind than the multiple-fold bellows (shown in Fig. 1), but it does not produce a consistently steady wind pressure. In the initial stage of the *Spanbalg's* cycle, the pressure is somewhat lighter than in the later stages because the upper board increases the wind pressure as it passes through an arc to approach its point of rest.

The Box Bellows (Kastenbalg)

Naturally, no efforts were spared in perfecting the bellows so that it could produce a steady pressure during all stages of operation; eventually the box bellows was developed.

Fig. 3. A box bellows

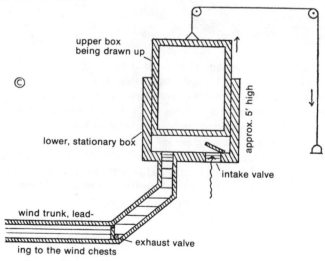

upper box being drawn up

©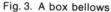

lower, stationary box

approx. 5' high

intake valve

wind trunk, lead-

exhaust valve

ing to the wind chests

Fig. 3 shows the positions of the valves while the bellows is being charged. They function in the same manner as those of the *Spanbalg*.

During the operation of either a *Spanbalg* or a box bellows, the feeding of air into the wind chest is, of course, terminated whenever the bellows is being filled. Assuming that it would need to be filled every 30 seconds and allowing for an interval of 1½ or 2 seconds for this operation, the playing of the organ would have to be interrupted every half minute for about 1½ or 2 seconds. Consequently the organist would be compelled to make "grand pauses" some 30 times within a quarter hour of performance, besides timing them to coincide precisely with the action of the bellows.

Fortunately this is not necessary. At least two bellows are always in use whenever the organ must rely on either a *Spanbalg* or a box bellows. The *Calcant* (the person in charge of operating the bellows) alternately cocks one and then the other. While the first is being filled, the second one expends wind through the wind trunk.

Because the box bellows required rather hard work on the part of the *Calcant* and because it could be attached to a motor only with great difficulty, efforts were soon made to replace it with a better mechanism.

The Feeder Bellows with Reservoir

The device that eventually replaced the box bellows is still used occasionally in present-day organ building; it is the feeder bellows *(Schöpfbalg)* with receiver, or reservoir *(Magazin)*.

Fig. 4. Reservoir with feeder bellows

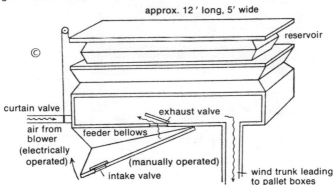

This blower mechanism can be manipulated with relative ease by the *Calcant*, and the wind supply is consistently steady. The feeder bellows is cocked and compressed exactly like the *Spanbalg*.

However, rather than directly transmitting its compressed wind to the wind trunk, it feeds the same into a receiver called the reservoir. This is a large, attached compartment that delivers its wind with constant pressure. Intake and exhaust valves function automatically in exactly the same manner as those of the *Spanbalg* and box bellows. (See above, pp. 13f.)

The Electric Blower Mechanism

Since about 1900, feeder bellows that had to be operated by hand have been replaced by electrically powered blowers. The blower supplies constant wind to the reservoir; a curtain valve regulates the flow of wind from the blower (see Fig. 4): the curtain valve and the upper board of the reservoir are connected by a string running over a pulley. When the reservoir is being filled, the upper board rises and—by releasing the tension on the string—allows the curtain valve to close gradually, thus progressively diminishing the flow of wind from the blower. As the wind supply in the reservoir is gradually used up, the upper board is lowered and—by a reverse procedure—the curtain valve is gradually opened, and wind from the blower is again admitted.

The Schwimmer

Present-day organ builders generally use several so-called "Schwimmers"—preferably attached to the pallet box—rather than one large reservoir.

Fig. 5. *Schwimmer*

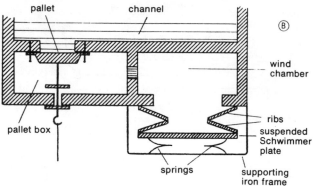

As the wind chamber receives wind directly from the wind trunk, the Schwimmer plates are pressed downward to enlarge the wind chamber and render its volumetric contents flexible and subject to control by the springs. The plates react to the slightest alteration in wind consumption by moving upward, thus regulating even minute changes of wind pressure. (See Fig. 5.)

We have briefly discussed the various types of blower mechanisms. Their history is rather simple. A certain degree of perfection has been attained with respect to steady wind supply and ease of operation. The development seems to have come to a satisfactory conclusion.

Wind Pressure

Wind pressure may vary. It is measured by a gauge or manometer (see Fig. 6, upper left). A "75 mm. wind pressure" indicates displacement of water levels in an open glass S- or U-tube by 75 millimeters.[3] Formerly wind pressure was measured in degrees: 30°, 40°, etc.; one foot comprises 12 inches, one inch, 10 degrees (1'=12"=120°; 1"=10°). The historic measures in feet varied from place to place: one foot equals 27.8 cm. with Praetorius (Brunswick measure); 32.5 cm. with Dom Bédos (Parisian measure); 28.2 cm. with Töpfer (Weimar measure); the foot in Saxony equaled 28.3 cm.; in Hamburg, 28.6 cm.; in England, 30.5 cm., etc. Formerly wind pressure of approximately 50 to 75 mm. was used; later it was increased greatly, up to 120 mm. and beyond. In recent times, attempts to use low wind pressure have been rewarded by great improvement of the tone quality in the speech of the pipes.

Wind Chest and Harness

Having discussed these rather elementary matters, we now turn to a more involved subject: the wind chest and harness, or action. The wind chest's function is to distribute the wind among the several channels and to conduct it into the pipes as directed by the organist. The harness, or action connects the keys to the chest.

The Box Chest (Kastenlade)

The oldest wind chest is the box chest (Kastenlade). In this type of chest all pipes are mounted on a single, large box, provided with a pallet for each pipe. The pallet will open only if the corresponding stop knob is drawn and the corresponding key is de-

---

[3] In American organ building, wind pressure is measured in inches. [Translator]

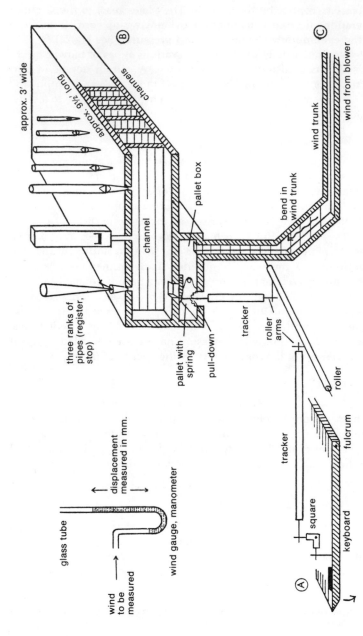

Fig. 6. Tone-channel chest (tracker key action). Upper left: wind gauge, or manometer

pressed. This system was used in 1697 by Casparini, by Röver in the 19th century, and again at the turn of the century. The box chest is an essential feature of unification. (See pp. 118ff.)

The Tone-Channel Chest (Tonkanzellenlade)

Far more important is a type of wind chest which, even at the present time, is still the best: the "tone-channel," or "key-channel," chest in either of its forms — the "spring chest" *(Springlade)* or the "slider chest" *(Schleiflade)*. Figure 6 shows a diagram for a tone-channel chest. Letter A shows the key action. Each key is connected with the wind chest by means of a square, a "tracker," a "roller" with two "roller arms," another tracker and a "pull-down." All key trackers move freely side by side; all rollers are mounted in or on a frame known as a *"roller board."*

Letter B shows the wind chest. The pull-down is attached to the bottom of the pallet. When the key is depressed, the pallet is opened; the pressure wind of the pallet box — fed by the blower — is admitted into the channel and thence into the pipes. When the key is released, the pallet is closed by a spring; the wind is thereby denied access to the channel, and the pipes fall silent. The upper part of the wind chest consists of a number of channels running transversely across the chest. Each key has its corresponding channel. Our figure shows three pipes mounted on each channel. Since all pipes on one channel belong to the same key (and therefore to the same pitch, or tone), this type of channel is called a "key channel" or "tone channel" *(Tonkanzelle)* in contradistinction to another type called a "stop channel" *(Registerkanzelle)*. (See pp. 24ff.)

Meanwhile, we will have noticed the chief characteristic of the organ: Each tone sounds with unchanging volume and timbre for as long a time as its key is held depressed. Although the process of exciting a pipe, i. e., its initial speech, may be influenced by opening the pallet through a firm or gentle touch on the key, its sustained volume and timbre cannot be modified. Thus an organist has to content himself with the sound to which the pipes have been voiced. On first reflection, this may seem rather confining. However, the possibility of controlling the attack [4] by means of

---

[4] Tone origination is a decisive factor of indigenous tone quality. This can easily be demonstrated with the aid of a tape recorder: Blend in on a sustained forte-piano tone *after* the attack. It is difficult to recognize it as characteristic piano sound.

expressive, organistic articulation in the form of a staccato, portato, legato touch, etc., renders this inflexibility a distinct advantage: it is precisely this condition which brings articulation into sharp relief.

We have already mentioned the necessity for drawing and canceling individual stops. Let us examine the "stop action."

The Slider Chest (Schleiflade)

Underneath each rank of pipes, the "slider chest" exhibits a long strip of wood, known as a "slider" (Fig. 7), which runs lengthwise [i. e., longitudinally] through the chest (not shown in Figure 6, which otherwise exactly resembles a slider chest). The

Fig. 7. A slider

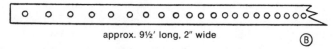

approx. 9½' long, 2" wide (B)

slider is the essential component of a mechanical stop action.[5] It has as many holes as the stop has pipes. These correspond exactly with the "toe holes," or "bores" in the "top board" and with the holes in the "table." The slider is fitted between the top board

Fig. 8. Stop action in the slider chest

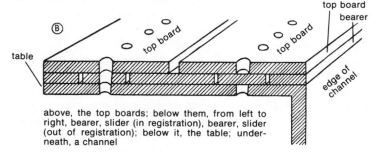

above, the top boards; below them, from left to right, bearer, slider (in registration), bearer, slider (out of registration); below it, the table; underneath, a channel

and the table, so as to be reasonably airtight yet easily movable. Between each of the sliders, and running parallel with them, are fastened solid boards called "bearers."

---

[5] For another type of mechanical stop action, see Fig. 10, Stop action in the spring chest.

If the slider is so positioned as to match hole with hole, (i. e., in registration), the pipes will speak when keys are depressed, i. e., when wind is admitted to one or the other of the channels; the stop is drawn. If the slider is so positioned as to block the holes (i. e., out of registration), the pipes will not speak, regardless of the amount of wind the channel may receive; the stop is canceled. The sliders are connected to the stop knobs. These are handles, located at the sides and/or above the manuals, and they are easily operated by the organist. (See Plate XI and Fig. 11.)

Fig. 9. Weatherproof slider mechanisms

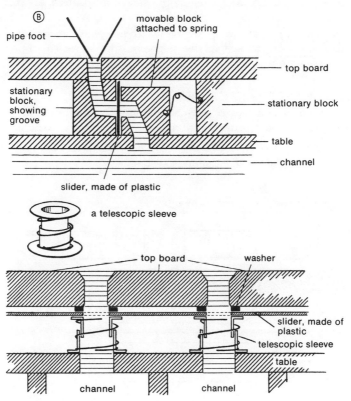

A slider chest must be built with the greatest of care, lest the sliders work themselves loose and permit pipes to sound that are not supposed to sound ("cipher"); it can also happen that sliders swell up and stick so as to make it impossible to draw a stop. But such faulty slider action can be prevented. Fig. 9 shows two types of mechanisms designed to produce a fault-free slider action. The upper drawing shows a slider [generally of plastic] in vertical position. Rather than being mounted horizontally between top board and table, it is mounted vertically between two blocks with matching grooves for the passage of the wind. One of these is stationary; the other is movable and presses against the slider with sufficient pressure to seal the grooves without binding the slider. The drawing at the bottom shows the more recent telescopic sleeve mechanism.[6] A packing washer is inserted between top board and slider, and a telescopic sleeve is inserted between the slider and the table. The packing washer is glued to the top board, the telescopic sleeve to the table. The expanding spring which envelopes the telescopic sleeve presses the slider snugly against the packing washer.

The Spring Chest (Springlade)

The second type of key-channel chest is the rarely found but very desirable "spring chest." It is built exactly like a slider chest,

Fig. 10. Stop action in the spring chest

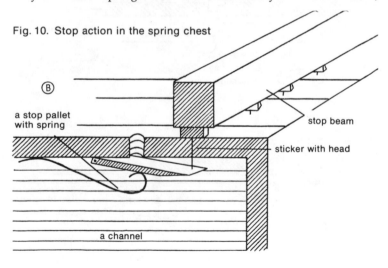

Ⓑ

a stop pallet with spring

stop beam

sticker with head

a channel

---

[6] This is commonly used by American builders of slider chests. [Translator]

with the exception of the stop action. Stops are drawn or canceled by means of the following mechanism. Underneath each pipe appears a pallet with an attached spring. Long, sturdy pieces of wire, the "stickers," leading through small holes in the top board, touch the pallet with their lower ends. The sticker heads are overlaid with a long strip of wood, the "stop beam," which is connected with the stop knob. When a stop knob is drawn, the stop beam and with it all stickers belonging to the stop are pressed down. The stickers open the pallets under the entire rank of pipes; the register is drawn. The pipes will now speak when, by depression of the keys, the key pallets in the pallet box are opened, thereby admitting wind from the pallet box into the corresponding channels. The stop knobs of spring chests have to be secured by means of notches in the shanks both in "off" and "on" positions (see Fig. 11) in order to counteract the pull caused by the weight of the stop beam (when in "off" position) or the pressure of the action of the stop pallet springs (when in "on" position). The great number of these little springs probably accounts for the name "spring chest." In a more sophisticated type of spring chest,

Fig. 11. Stop knobs of a spring chest

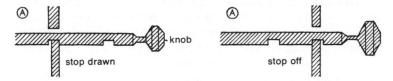

stop drawn · knob   stop off

the stop pallets of each channel are imbedded in a heavy oak beam, approximately 2"×1⅓"; mechanical faults can easily be corrected, as this beam slides out like a drawer.

For some time the question whether the spring chest or the slider chest represents the older type of wind chest, was subject to lively debate. According to widespread opinion, the spring chest was considered the older; the slider chest was thought to have gradually displaced it. Today we know that this contention is incorrect. Both types probably originated independently, perhaps even contemporaneously; both gained popularity, the slider chest remaining somewhat more common than the spring chest until the middle of the 18th century. In the Swiss canton Ticino and in Italy spring chests were manufactured up to the advent of the pneumatic action, as is evidenced by the organs in Loco (1837), Losone (1856), and Soazza (1894). More recently spring chests were installed in the Nieuwe Ooster Begraafplaats in Amsterdam, Netherlands (1938); the Freie Evangelische Gemeinde, Jan van Loonslaan Street, Rotterdam, Netherlands (1953); the Katholische Pfarrkirche St. Michael in Weiler in den Bergen, Schwäbisch-Gmünd, Germany (1962); the Staatliche Aufbaugymnasium in Schwäbisch-Gmünd, Germany (1964). Spring chests for several small German organs, built 1962—64, are located in the Martin Lutherkirche, the Dreifaltigkeitsfriedhof, and the Pädagogische Hochschule, all in Schwäbisch-Gmünd; in the Evangelische Kirche of Belsen near Tübingen; and in five instruments in churches of the Diocese of Rottenburg. During the period of classical organ building spring chests were used particularly in the Netherlands and in Italy.

The slider chest and the spring chest are the best types of wind chests (see pp. 24ff.). The reason for discussing other types of chests in the following pages is that many organs unfortunately do have such chests.

Stop-Channel Chest (Registerkanzellenlade)

We have stated earlier that the channels in the key-channel chest run transversely across the chest and that all pipes belonging to a given key are mounted on top of the corresponding key channel (see Fig. 6). The name "stop-channel chest" implies the opposite arrangement: here all pipes belonging to a given stop are mounted on top of the channel which runs longitudinally along the chest.

The Cone-Valve Chest (Kegellade)

In Fig. 12 letter A shows keys, trackers, and squares in a cone-valve chest. The fulcrum is located in the center of the keys rather than at the tail end as shown in Fig. 6. There the keys formed one-armed levers, i. e., second-class levers, here they function as two-armed levers, i. e., first-class levers.

Letter B shows a stop channel (Registerkanzelle). In the case of the tone-channel chest (see Fig. 6) one pallet serves all pipes of one key. Here each individual pipe has its own pipe chamber, controlled by individual valves from the stop channel. Owing to the conical shape of these valves, this chest is called a cone-valve

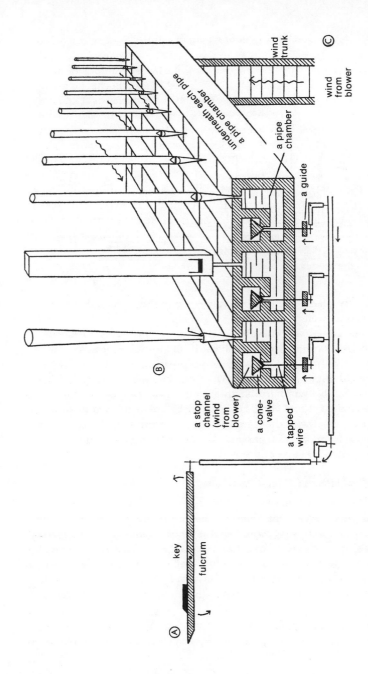

Fig. 12. Cone-valve chest (mechanical action)

25

Fig. 13. A tone channel (slider or spring chest)

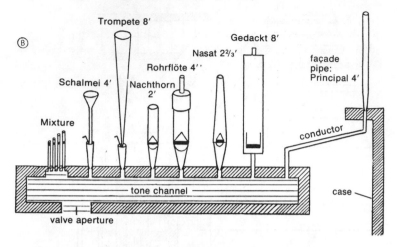

chest. In place of the cone valve, differently shaped valves can be used as well.

The cone-valve chest functions thus: Depression of a key opens the corresponding row of valves. If all stop channels are charged with wind from the blower, wind pressure will be admitted to excite all pipes of the key. The stop channels are directly connected to the wind trunk; this connection can be controlled by valves called "stop ventils." Located between the wind trunk and the stop channels, they are connected to the stop knobs for easy manipulation by the organist. Thus only pipes of drawn stops speak when a key is depressed.

Evaluation of Wind-Chest Types

We have acquainted ourselves with the two prototypes [7] of wind chests: the tone-channel chest and the stop-channel chest. Which of the two is more reliable and tonally more satisfactory? Reliability is merely a question of quality workmanship; reputable builders will always manufacture reliable chests. The essential and decisive consideration is the wind chest's effect on the tone quality of the pipes: Experience has demonstrated that the tone-

---

[7] The American reader may wish to include the pitman chest, the ventil chest, the electro-pneumatic-tracker chest, and the direct-electric chest. [*Translator*]

channel chest produces a nobler speech, purer intonation, better blend, and a clearer ensemble effect in polyphonic organ music than does a stop-channel chest. The sound of the organ as produced by the tone-channel chest is, from every point of view, better than that of a stop-channel chest. Let us briefly examine these four conditions:

Nobler speech. Each pipe is excited by wind admitted to it by the opening of a pallet, or valve. This operation always carries with it a certain explosive effect. In the tone-channel chest, the entire height and length of the rather large channel provides an expansion chamber between the pallet and the foot of the pipe. The mass of air within the channel absorbs the explosive effect of the onrushing wind; it acts as a cushion between the pallet and the pipe. Thus the pipe speaks calmly and nobly. In the stop-channel chest, however, each pipe is fed by a valve located in close proximity to it. The absorbent air mass, such as found in the channel of the tone-channel chest, is lacking. The explosive effect of the air pressure is therefore audible in the speech of the pipe; it becomes hard. There is an additional consideration. If compressed air is suddenly released, a moment of lowered pressure follows the initial rush of wind; this in turn is followed by renewed, but slightly reduced high pressure, then by a lower pressure, and so forth; thus "beats" result. These beats are completely absorbed by the channel in the tone-channel chest and the pipes are not affected thereby. In the stop-channel chest, however, the beats are often disconcertingly audible in the speech. Especially the upper ranges of reed stops and of wide-scaled labial ranks are adversely affected.

Purer intonation. In the tone-channel chest, as will be recalled, all pipes belonging to one key are mounted on the same channel. They are related because they mutually share the same channel wind; the vibrations of their air columns are transferred to the channel and are matched there.

Better blend. This same interrelation of the pipes common to a given key contributes to the blend of several stops into a uniform sound. In the stop-channel chest, where pipes belonging to one key are mounted on different channels, this interrelation is lacking. Therefore they do not match in intonation and will not blend as well and as completely as in the case of the tone-channel chest.

Clearer ensemble effect. Let us assume we have drawn two stops (Gedackt 8' and Principal 4') and play the tones d, a, and f'-sharp simultaneously. In the tone-channel chest the two pipes d of the Gedackt and of the Principal blend well, and their intonations match perfectly. The same is true for the two pipes a and the two pipes f'-sharp. Each individual tone is clean in intonation and uniform in tone color — a great advantage. (On the other hand, the tones d and a blend imperfectly because they are mounted on different tone channels; the same is true for a and f'-sharp and for d and f'-sharp, respectively.) The listener can clearly discern the three tones sounding simultaneously. In subsequent playing, all voices will be clearly and precisely discernible — again a desirable feature.

A different condition prevails in the stop-channel chest. The two pipes of the Gedackt and Principal for the note d are mounted on different channels. Consequently they do not blend as well and their intonation is not as well matched as in the tone-channel chest — a distinct disadvantage. The same is true for the keys a and f'-sharp, respectively. The three pipes d, a, and f'-sharp of the Gedackt, however, are mounted on one channel; they blend well with one another. The same is true of the three Principal pipes. Therefore the three tones d, a, and f'-sharp will hardly be discernible as individual tones. In subsequent playing, especially of polyphonic textures, the voice leading will not be clear — again, a distinct disadvantage.

The tone-channel chest's manifest advantage over other types shows itself in the area which is of the first importance in organ building — the area of tone production. It is particularly noteworthy that the musically educated layman usually prefers the sound of organs with slider or spring chests.

Albert Schweitzer was one of the first to point clearly and emphatically to the superiority of the tone-channel chest. One of the merits of the organ builder Cavaillé-Coll (1811–1899) was that he never changed over to stop-channel chests but preferred to hold fast to the artistically superior principle of the slider chest. In German classical organ building, the tone-channel chest in the form of slider or spring chests dominated the field for centuries; the most eminent builders used them. In recent years the best of our contemporary German organ builders have once again produced a number of outstanding instruments with slider chests. This speaks more forcefully for the excellent qualities of the classical wind chest than lengthy theoretical discussions.

Fig. 14. Barker lever at rest

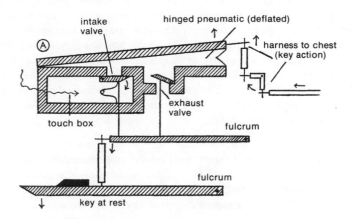

Fig. 15. Barker lever in operation

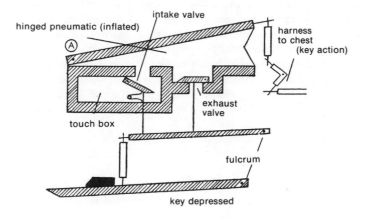

The Barker Lever (Barkerhebel)

In the types of wind chests described so far, key and stop actions were set in motion mechanically. The power for mechanical motion was furnished by the organist himself. We shall now discuss the invention of the "Barker lever," which partially relieves the organist of this expenditure of energy. In 1833 David Hamilton constructed a mechanism (subsequently called Barker lever) which supplied the necessary power to the key action at the expense

29

of only light finger pressure on the part of the player. The advantage of this invention consists not merely in the physical comfort to the organist but primarily in the fact that it enabled organ builders to design instruments in which wind volume, number of stops, scaling of pipes, and commensurate sizes of valves could be chosen according to exclusively artistic considerations, while the resultant problem of a cumbersome and heavy action was virtually obviated. Hamilton harnessed the organ wind itself to propel the key action. Figures 14 and 15 illustrate the disposition and function of the Barker lever.

A small wind chest, called a "touch box" is mounted above the keys. It receives wind from the blower through a branch of the wind trunk. The blower has to feed wind into the large wind chests as well as into the small touch boxes. Hamilton mounted a number of small bellows on top of the touch box, in fact, one for each key. When a key is depressed the intake valve is opened, and the wind from the touch box inflates the corresponding pneumatic, which in turn pulls the trackers. These trackers are constructed in the same manner as those of the mechanical slider, spring, and cone-valve chests described earlier. Their function is to open the pallet in the pallet box. Depressing a key also effects the closing of the exhaust valve. Its function is easily understood. Upon release of the key, the wind supply to the pneumatic is canceled, and the exhaust valve is reopened simultaneously. The pneumatic is immediately deflated, its air escaping through the exhaust valve; the pallet in the pallet box is closed, and the pipe ceases to speak. Without the opening of the exhaust valve the pneumatic could not fold with sufficient dispatch.

The Tubular-Pneumatic Cone-Valve Chest

A good organ is expensive; therefore efforts have constantly been made to reduce manufacturing costs, which resulted in the development of the tubular-pneumatic action. Fig. 16 shows a touch box with primary and secondary valves, mounted above the keyboard. One lead tube per key leads from the touch box to the wind chest (see Fig. 17). In the wind chest, a "pouch" is placed under each pipe valve. The pouches for the several stops of each key receive wind through a key-action channel when the key is depressed. Each valve in the touch box is connected with its corresponding pouches in the wind chest by a lead tube approximately ¼" in diameter. When the valve in the touch box is opened

Fig. 16. A tubular-pneumatic touch box (pressure system)

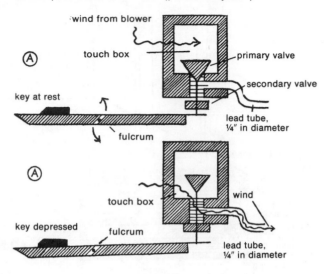

in response to a light touch on the key, the touch box releases wind through the lead tube into the key-action channel and thus to the pouches. These, in the process of being inflated, open the pipe valves. Thus in the pneumatic cone-valve chest, mechanical key action (see Fig. 12) is replaced by pouches and lead tubes (see Fig. 17) that connect the touch boxes with their corresponding key-action channels in the chest. (See Fig. 16.)

The Relay

The construction illustrated in Fig. 17 soon required some improvement. It became apparent that the wind on its way through the long lead tubes to the wind chest lost so much of its force by viscosity as to impair the reliable functioning of the pouches and pipe valves. Efforts to correct this malcondition resulted in the design of the "relay" (see Fig. 18) which was intended to recharge the force of the wind just before entering the wind chest. The relay is essentially a repetition of the touch box appliance. Rather than having to activate the entire row of pouches and pipe valves, the wind, coming from the lead tube, opens only a single compound valve, the "relay valve." The relay valve releases new wind (with full pressure), which inflates the pouches, by which the pipe valves are opened. Frequently a second relay, called a "booster

Fig. 17. Cone-valve chest (tubular-pneumatic)

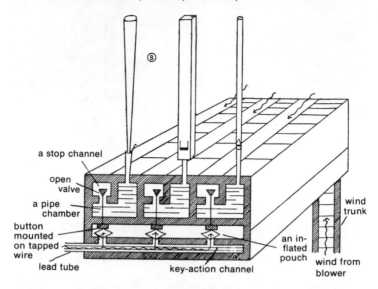

relay," is needed to insure a reliable action. Although this appliance may seem relatively cumbersome, it does effect greater promptness in the action.

The Tubular-Pneumatic Tone-Channel Chest

As we have seen, the stop-channel chest was adapted with relative ease to a tubular-pneumatic action. Adaptation of the tone-channel chest to tubular-pneumatic action is more involved. The touch box of the tubular-pneumatic tone-channel chest is constructed identically to that of the tubular-pneumatic cone-valve chest (see Fig. 16). In the tubular-pneumatic tone-channel chest each lead tube connects a chamber of the touch box with a corresponding pouch under the pallet box, similarly as in the cone-valve chest. Everything else, however, is totally different: When a key is depressed, the pouch under the pallet box is inflated, whereby a "pilot valve" is activated. The function of this pilot valve is illustrated in Fig. 19. When the key is at rest (see upper drawing), the wind pressure of the pallet box

    1. depresses the pilot valve in the "subfloor" of the pallet box in order to close the aperture to atmosphere;

    2. neutralizes the pneumatic.

Thereupon a spring (not shown) closes the pallet valve and lifts the upper plate of the pneumatic. When the key is depressed (see drawing at bottom), the pilot valve closes the aperture to atmosphere in the "floor" of the pallet box, and the wind pressure of the pallet box

1. deflates the pneumatic and opens the pallet valve attached to it;

2. enters the tone channel and excites those pipes whose sliders (not shown) are in registration.

The pressure on the pneumatic is greater than that on the pallet, since the surfaces are unequal. The wind of the deflated pneumatic

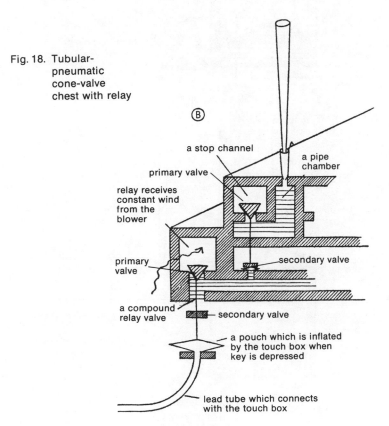

Fig. 18. Tubular-
pneumatic
cone-valve
chest with relay

Ⓑ

a stop channel

primary valve

a pipe
chamber

relay receives
constant wind
from the
blower

primary
valve

secondary valve

a compound
relay valve

secondary valve

a pouch which is inflated
by the touch box when
key is depressed

lead tube which connects
with the touch box

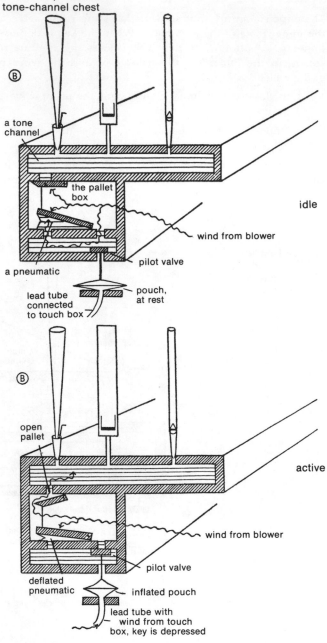

Fig. 19. A tubular-pneumatic tone-channel chest

Ⓑ

a tone channel

the pallet box

idle

wind from blower

a pneumatic

pilot valve

lead tube connected to touch box

pouch, at rest

Ⓑ

open pallet

active

wind from blower

pilot valve

deflated pneumatic

inflated pouch

lead tube with wind from touch box, key is depressed

Plate I

Positiv, built in 1963 (one manual, 5 stops). Tonal design in the style of Scherer (designed by Alfred Hoppe); keyboard in the rear; Regal 8′ mounted within arm's reach of player. The Holzflöte, mounted in front, is partly concealed by a screen consisting of an inscription cast in tin.

Plate II

Organ of the Frauenkirche in Nuremberg, Germany; built around the middle of the 15th century. Rückpositiv in front, Hauptwerk in upper center. Between the two and quite small, appears the Brustwerk.

escapes to the atmosphere through the opening provided by the pilot valve in the subfloor of the pallet box. When the key is released, the aperture in the floor of the pallet box is reopened by the pilot valve, and the pneumatic is neutralized. The spring (not shown) closes the pallet.

The Membrane Chest (Membranenlade)

Turning our attention once again to the stop-channel chest, we shall now inspect the "membrane chest" (see Fig. 20), which exhibits a simplified pipe-valve mechanism and constitutes a less complicated application of tubular-pneumatic action than that of the cone-valve chest. When wind pressure from the relay acts on the "membrane valves" these will prevent access of wind to the "stacks," i. e., to the pipes, which consequently remain silent. To excite the pipes, the relay wind must be canceled by exhausting the key channel so that the membrane valves will not be pressed against the lower openings of the stacks. In this way, the stop-channel wind is admitted to the pipe through the stack, and the pipe is excited. This type of construction is called an "exhaust system." Its characteristic feature is the inverse use of wind pressure to close rather than to open the valves. The opening of the

Fig. 20. A membrane chest (tubular-pneumatic)

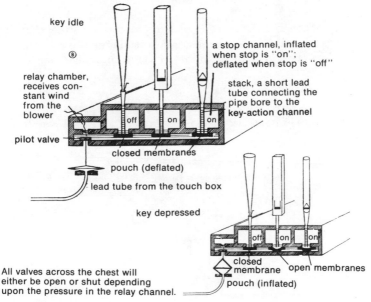

key idle

⑧

a stop channel, inflated when stop is "on"; deflated when stop is "off"

relay chamber, receives constant wind from the blower

stack, a short lead tube connecting the pipe bore to the key-action channel

off   on   on

pilot valve

closed membranes

pouch (deflated)

lead tube from the touch box

key depressed

off   on   on

closed membrane   open membranes

pouch (inflated)

All valves across the chest will either be open or shut depending upon the pressure in the relay channel.

37

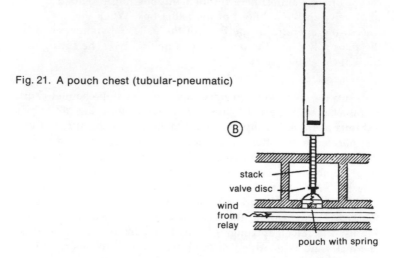

Fig. 21. A pouch chest (tubular-pneumatic)

stack
valve disc
wind
from
relay
pouch with spring

valves is effected by exhausting the wind from the key channel. The exhaust system may be viewed as the ultimate achievement of tubular-pneumatic action.

The Pouch Chest (Taschenlade)

The "pouch chest" (see Fig. 21) represents a variation of the membrane chest. A pouch replaces the membrane valve. Its principle of operation is identical to that of the membrane chest.

Electropneumatic Action

The electropneumatic action (see Fig. 22) replaces the pouch of the tubular-pneumatic action (see Figs. 17 and 18) by a "lever-

Fig. 22. An electromagnetic relay

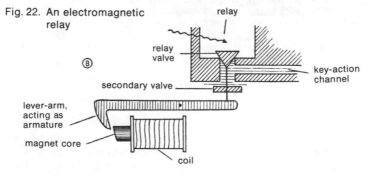

relay
relay valve
key-action channel
secondary valve
lever-arm, acting as armature
magnet core
coil

arm magnet." When the key is depressed, the circuit is closed. The lever arm, acting as an armature, is attracted by the magnet core, thereby opening the relay valve and simultaneously closing the secondary valve.

The real significance of the electropneumatic action lies in its application to the stop action and to the manual coupler system rather than to the key action, particularly in larger instruments. In electropneumatic stop actions the sliders are moved by strong electromagnets or by small electric motors. Motors function quietly but not always swiftly enough; magnets function swiftly but with considerable noise—an equally unpleasant alternative. In electro-magnetic coupling, the coupled divisions function electromag-netically: The pallets are fitted with electromagnets; when electri-cally charged, they open the pallet by means of their armatures whenever the division is played through the coupler. When the division is played from its own keyboard, the electromagnets remain inactive and the pallets function mechanically.

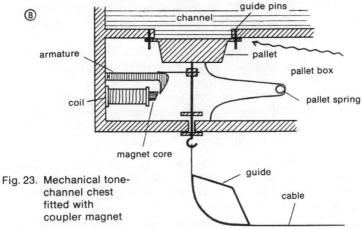

Fig. 23. Mechanical tone-channel chest fitted with coupler magnet

In Fig. 23 a cable replaces the former tracker, and a "guide" functions in lieu of the former square, two features favored by some present-day organ builders. The cables consist of nine steel strands twisted around a nylon core and saturated with nylon; the guides minimize wear through friction. Torsion-free light metal rather than wood for the rollers has recently been used with good results. The pallet shown in Fig. 23 is guided by two "guide pins" and a 3 mm. pull-down wire. Since the pallet moves vertically in a given plane rather than in an arc, it needs to open only a minimal amount in order to admit sufficient wind to the channel. This condition plus the relatively large pallet opening favor a light touch.

Evaluation of the Several Actions

The primary advantage of tracker action is its absolute precision. The speech of the pipes responds instantly and sensitively to the player's attack. This advantage will be gratefully acknowledged by the organist who knows from experience with electro-pneumatic or direct-electric consoles, how the rhythmic movement of polyphonic textures becomes paralyzed by the imprecision of electric action. How different with tracker action organs!

But tracker action is vastly superior to electric action not only with regard to articulation but also with regard to touch. In this respect, electric action effects absolutely nothing; the initial excitation of the speech is totally unaffected by the touch. Yet, it is precisely this inception of the tone which is essential for the overall character of the speech. The tracker action—and even the Barker lever—by contrast, faithfully transmit the touch to the speech of the pipe. Oscillograms of relevant tests furnish indubitable proof. The possibility of influencing the initial excitation is essential, if music rather than impersonal sound is to be produced. Naturally, no player can consciously cultivate every single tone by his touch, but he does convey, both consciously and subconsciously, a detailed personal expression to the structural elements of the total sound spectrum, which—by contrast to the tracker action—is obscured by electric action.

In depressing a key of a tracker-action keyboard, a definite point of resistance must be overcome. The organist can feel the sudden overcoming of resistance at the instant the pallet is engaged. Through his finger his mind perceives exactly the disposition of the initial excitation, thereby gaining a felicitous sense of security in the playing of complex polyphonic textures. A further convenience is the circumstance that far less effort is required to hold down the key than to depress it; that also contributes to clean and rhythmic playing.

Electric action, on the other hand, does permit placing the console a considerable distance from the pipes. Although this offers the advantage that the organist hears the organ in the same manner as the audience—enabling him to choose his registrations accordingly—it cannot compensate for the concomitant loss of the benefits derived from mechanical action. Good organ tone and a proper balance of stops within a given room must be the concerns of the architect, who has to create favorable conditions of reverberation and multiple reflection, and of the organ builder, who has to scale and voice the ranks accordingly. If need be, the organist can check his registrations by listening or by having someone listen to them from the nave. For the rhythm and meter of his playing, however, he bears sole responsibility; this requirement, again, reinforces the advantage of mechanical action. There is a further consideration: The farther the organist is removed from the pipes, the more remotely does he hear his own playing, a circumstance apt to irritate him considerably or at least absorb his powers of concentration to an overlarge extent. In any case, he is deprived of the impulse communicated to music under normal conditions by instantaneous response. A console placed close to the instrument is the best solution, and one that wholly meets the engineering requirements of the tracker action. Mechanical action, then, is the best, provided that it is constructed so as to be light and sensitive.

The stop action is another matter. This should be harnessed electrically, so as to permit the introduction of an effective combination action (see pp. 79ff.), which relieves the organist from overmuch mechanical manipulation allowing him to devote much greater attention to the art of playing, an aspect particularly important for the performance of recent organ literature.[8] Mechanical key action and electrical stop action can be combined within the same console without the slightest difficulty. Good examples for such combined actions can be found everywhere at the present time. (See Plate XII.)

The Pipes

Having examined the construction of the organ with regard to the key and stop actions, let us now direct our attention to the pipes. There are "labial" (or "flue") pipes and "lingual" (or "reed") pipes. In both types the tone is produced by vibrating air columns, but the vibrations are induced by different methods of excitation.

---

[8] At least one North American organ company has recently installed mechanical combinations that can be operated with relative ease. With further improvement, such mechanical combinations might well become an equivalent alternative to electric stop action. [*Translator*]

In the case of labial pipes, wind passes through the "flue" (or "windway"), is refracted at the edge of the upper "lip," and thereby excites the air column within the pipe "body" (or "corpus"). In the reed pipe the wind first excites an elastic metal blade, called a "reed" (or "tongue"). The reed communicates its vibrations to the air column within the body of the pipe, known as "resonator."

Labial Pipes

Let us first examine the labial pipes, as they constitute approximately 85 percent of all pipes in an organ. Figure 24 shows a labial

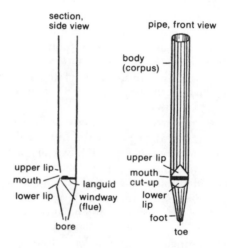

Fig. 24. A labial pipe

section, side view

pipe, front view

body (corpus)

upper lip
mouth
lower lip
languid
windway (flue)
bore

upper lip
mouth
cut-up
lower lip
foot
toe

pipe. The wind, admitted to the channel through the open pallet in the chest, passes through the bore and the windway in the form of a wind sheet toward the edge of the upper lip, which functions as a deflector. The wind sheet is deflected either toward the interior of the pipe or toward the exterior atmosphere. As a result of the wind sheet's deflection toward the interior of the pipe, the air column in the pipe body is compressed. Simultaneously the wind sheet is momentarily disturbed. The compression in the body in turn deflects the wind sheet toward the exterior atmosphere, causing a momentary decompression within the pipe with the attendant redeflection of the wind sheet toward the interior of the pipe. The cycle, once established, repeats continuously and sets the air column within the pipe body into vibration, thereby resonating the air column.

Requisite Pipe Lengths

If a pipe is short, the frequency of vibration will be great and the pitch of the resulting tone "high"; if a pipe is long, the frequency of vibration will be small, and the pitch of the resulting tone will be perceived as relatively "lower." If the upper end of the pipe is covered rather than open, the pipe will speak approximately one octave lower than it would if it were open. There are also conical pipes, that is, pipes that taper toward the top; these speak slightly lower than cylindrical pipes but higher than covered pipes of the same length. Of three pipes of identical pitch, the open cylindrical is the longest, the open conical the second longest, and the covered cylindrical the shortest. There are also covered conical pipes. These are shorter than open conical, but longer than covered cylindrical pipes of a corresponding pitch.

Relative Lengths of Labial Pipes

Pitch	C	c	c'
Length of open cylindrical pipe	ca. 8'	ca. 4'	ca. 2'
Length of open conical pipe	ca. 7' 5"	ca. 3' 7½"	ca. 1' 9½"
Length of covered conical pipe	ca. 5' 3½"	ca. 3'	ca. 1' 4"
Length of covered cylindrical pipe	ca. 4'	ca. 2'	ca. 1'

Ears and Beards

In order to steady the speech of a pipe, so-called "ears" or "box beards" are often attached to the mouth of the pipe. These promote promptness in the speech of a pipe under relatively strong wind without overblowing the same and obviate the necessity of a high cut-up (see below); concomitantly, the tone develops a rich harmonic spectrum ("string" sound). Since they also tend to lower the pitch, they are also used for purposes of tuning. Application of more sophisticated types of ears and beards such as "roller beards" and "harmonic bridges" (*freins harmoniques*) is undesirable.

Fig. 25. Ears of pipes

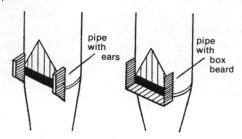

Scales of Labial Pipes, Tonal Characteristics

When excited by an equally dense wind, narrow-scaled pipes exhibit a richer harmonic spectrum but a more impoverished fundamental tone than wide-scaled pipes do; their tone is characterized as "string" tone. Wide-scaled pipes, excited by an equally dense wind, exhibit a less developed harmonic spectrum but a more extensive fundamental; their tone is more full-bodied and less intense than that of the narrow-scaled pipes and is characterized as "flute" tone. The term "flute" describes the round, soft, and flute-like quality of the recorder rather than the timbre of the transverse flute, which is relatively rich in its harmonic spectrum.

Width of Mouth

The width of the mouth is proportional to the circumference of the pipe. Mouths that are one-fourth or even two-sevenths as wide as the circumference of the pipe are considered "wide"; those which are one-fifth or even one-sixth of the circumference are considered "narrow." A pipe with a mouth width of one-fifth, sounds relatively softer than an otherwise identical pipe of the same tone color with a mouth width of one-fourth; at the same amplitude, the tone of the latter becomes more pronounced in harmonics, more aggressive and "stringy." If the circumference of this same pipe were to be increased to the point where its mouth would be as wide as that of the pipe with one-fourth mouth width, both pipes would match in sound color and volume, but the tone of the wider pipe would carry farther [i. e., it would become acoustically more extensive].

The Cut-Up

Much depends also on the distance between the upper and lower lips of the pipe. Depending on the actual disposition, one speaks of a high or low "cut-up." A pipe with a high cut-up sounds duller and fainter than one with a low cut-up. Pipes produce a beautiful tone only when the appropriate wind pressure and a commensurate cut-up are not exceeded. Nobility, beauty, and volume — and to a certain extent even timbre — of speech appropriate to a given room are achieved by "voicing" the pipes. To attain these qualities simultaneously we must create the condition of perfectly balanced proportions between the pipe's circumference, the width of its mouth, and the cut-up. These proportions,

Fig. 26. Pipe shapes, group I

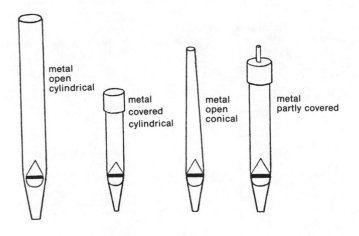

metal
open
cylindrical

metal
covered
cylindrical

metal
open
conical

metal
partly covered

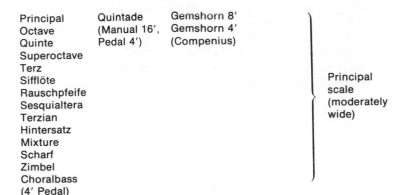

Principal	Quintade	Gemshorn 8'	
Octave	(Manual 16',	Gemshorn 4'	
Quinte	Pedal 4')	(Compenius)	
Superoctave			
Terz			
Sifflöte			Principal
Rauschpfeife			scale
Sesquialtera			(moderately
Terzian			wide)
Hintersatz			
Mixture			
Scharf			
Zimbel			
Choralbass			
(4' Pedal)			

(Fig. 26 cont.)

Offenflöte 8'	Untersatz 16'	Spitzflöte 8'	Rohrflöte 8'	⎫
Offenflöte 4'	Subbass 16'	Viola da	Hohlpfeife 8'	
Nasat 2²/₃'	Bourdon 16'	Gamba 8'	Rohrflöte 4'	
Waldflöte 2'	Gedackt 8'	(Silbermann)	Hohlflöte 4'	
Gemshorn 2'	Flöte 4'	Flöte 4'	Flöte 4'	
(Scherer)	Blockflöte 4'	Blockflöte 4'	Nasat 2²/₃'	wide
Nachthorn 2'	Nasat 2²/₃'	Spitzflöte 4'	Bauerflöte 1'	scale
(Pedal)	Bauerflöte 1'	Barpfeife 4'	(Pedal)	(flutes)
Terz 1³/₅'	(Pedal)	Nasat 2²/₃'		
Quintflöte 1¹/₃'		Waldflöte 2'		
Sifflöte 1'		Flachflöte 2'		
Nachthorn V		Terz 1³/₅'		
(Manual)		Quintflöte 1¹/₃'		
Kornett V				⎭

Viola	Quintade 8'	Viola	Hohlschelle	⎫ narrow
da Gamba	(Manual)	da Gamba	[Rohrquintade]	scale
Salicional	Schellpfeife		[Rohrpommer]	(strings)
Klingend	Barpfeife			⎭
Zimbel				

Fig. 27. Pipe shapes, group II

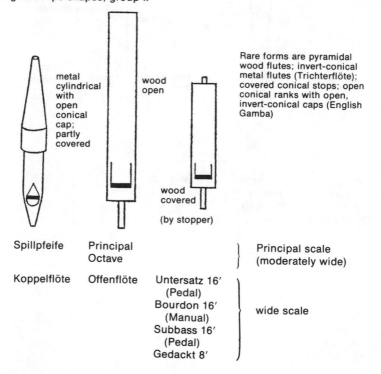

metal
cylindrical
with
open
conical
cap;
partly
covered

wood
open

wood
covered

(by stopper)

Rare forms are pyramidal
wood flutes; invert-conical
metal flutes (Trichterflöte);
covered conical stops; open
conical ranks with open,
invert-conical caps (English
Gamba)

Spillpfeife	Principal Octave		⎫ Principal scale ⎭ (moderately wide)
Koppelflöte	Offenflöte	Untersatz 16' (Pedal) Bourdon 16' (Manual) Subbass 16' (Pedal) Gedackt 8'	⎫ wide scale ⎭

known as the "scale" of a rank of pipes, must be carefully calculated and executed.

Shapes of Labial Pipes

Pipes are built in various shapes (see Figs. 26 and 27). Both metal (alloys of tin and lead, also copper) and wood (oak, spruce, Brazilian pine, mahogany, linden, ramie, etc.) are used as material for the pipe bodies. The alloys of tin and lead differ in their tin content; approximately 30% tin is used for wide covered ranks and for flutes; approximately 60% tin is used for stops of the Principal choir; approximately 75% tin is used for reed stops, string stops, Quintades and façade pipes. Alloys of approximately 51% tin are used as cast [i. e., unplaned] because of their intriguing casting patterns; they are known as "spotted metal." The lower the tin content, or the softer the wood, the heavier must be the wall of the pipe. The older terminology, *zwölflötig* (24 ounces), referred to a tin content of 75%; pure tin accordingly was called *sechzehnlötig* (32 ounces). The proportion of the alloy's components was formerly also given in pounds (e. g., 100 pounds of tin to 300 pounds of lead). Other materials, such as silver and ivory, are of rare occurrence.

Stop Nomenclature

The names of the stops are variegated. They may allude to the shape: Spitzflöte, Flachflöte, Spillpfeife, Spindelpfeife, Offenflöte, Gedackt, Rohrflöte; or to the pitch of a stop (see pp. 49ff.): Subbass, Principal, Octave, Superoctave, Quinte, Terz, Terzian, Sesquialtera; they may be descriptive in the sense of comparing the tone to that of a musical instrument, both obsolete and contemporary: Zimbel, Rauschpfeife, Kornett, Fugara (shepherd's whistle), Salicional (Latin *salix*—"willow," thus willow flute), Viola da Gamba, Nachthorn, Schweizerpfeife, Querflöte, Blockflöte, Gemshorn; a fourth group of appellations seeks to describe tonal characteristics: Quintade (narrow-scaled, covered pipes, which emphasize the third partial tone, a twelfth—*Quinte*), Scharf (composed of fairly high-pitched [and narrow-scaled] pipes), Nasat (French *nasarder*—"to speak in a nasal manner"); still other circumstances are indicated by certain stop names: Mixture (the stop is composed of several ranks, a "mixture" of pipes), Untersatz (because of the length of its pipes this rank was "set down" on a low chest), Hintersatz (denotes

47

placement of this rank "behind" the Principal pipes); the names Bauerflöte ("peasant's whistle") and probably also Waldflöte ("forest whistle") imply whistling with pursed lips; Bourdon likens the tall pipes of the bass range to long pilgrims' staffs ("burdones"). Prefixes often refer to tone color (Harfen-, Singend-, Geigend-, Lieblich-, Zart-, Sanft-, Still-); to pitch (Gross- or Grob-, Klein-); or to pipe material (Holz-, Metall-, Kupfer-). The adjectives "Singend" and "Geigend" usually [but not necessarily] imply 4' pitch. The particular method of construction does not influence the tone color of pipes as decisively as one might be inclined to suppose. Important is the classification to which a given stop belongs: the Principal family, the wide-scaled family, and the order of reeds. Important also is the pitch level of each stop (a factor presently to be discussed). These two factors outweigh the question of the particular shape of the pipe. Rohrflöte 8', Gedackt 8', and Koppelflöte 8' are so similar in tone color that perhaps only the experienced organ expert can aurally distinguish between them. Therefore one needs to be less concerned with the particular shapes within a uniform genus and pitch level — since they account for relatively negligible differences in tone color — than with selection of stops with the greatest possible variety in pitch level and stop genus; the result will be genuine richness of organ tone. The selection of pipe shapes usually is determined by externals: available space and financial resources. Both are compatible in the sense that anything that demands much physical space also demands much building material and will be proportionately more expensive. For example, a Gedackt 8' occupies the least space, hence it needs the least material of all stops of 8' pitch within the wide-scaled genus. The Rohrflöte is already wider scaled and has slightly longer pipes; it occupies more space and needs more material than the Gedackt 8', and the manufacture of the little chimneys represents an extra cost. The conical flute is even wider and longer than the Rohrflöte, and the Offenflöte is the widest and longest, hence also the most expensive and space-consuming. This explains why ranks of low pitch were — and still are — built as Gedackts and Rohrflötes, ranks of a medium pitch as Rohrflötes and open conical flutes; and only high-pitched ranks as open cylindrical flutes. Sometimes conical shapes were terraced: the 4' level was constructed in strongly conical forms for reasons of economy; the 2⅔' level in slightly conical forms; and the 2' level in open cylindrical forms.

Synthetic Derivation of Tone Colors

Stop names usually are given with a qualifying foot-designation, such as 8', 16', 2⅔', and so forth. For all practical purposes this implies that a stop labeled 8' sounds exactly as indicated by the notation and by the letter names of the keyboard: it sounds at normal pitch. A 4' stop sounds one octave, a 2' stop, two octaves higher; a 16' stop sounds one octave, a 32' stop, two octaves lower; a 2⅔' stop sounds a twelfth higher, and so forth. In order to explain the meaning behind such designations, it will be necessary to discuss the matter in greater detail.

It is a well-known fact that a musical tone, such as we perceive it, is not (strictly speaking) one single tone; rather it is a composite of several tones, perceived by the ear as a blended unity. Fig. 28 gives a few examples. The single tone that we perceive, the "resultant tone" from the blending of its "partial tones," has the same pitch as the lowest partial tone. It is called the

Fig. 28. Acoustic spectra

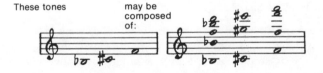

"fundamental tone"; the remaining partial tones are known as "harmonics," or "overtones." Such composite tones consist of partial tones derived from the harmonic series. Fig. 29 shows the first 16 partial tones of the harmonic series for the fundamental tone of F. This does not mean that every tone F we hear is composed

Fig. 29. Harmonic series on the fundamental tone F

of all of these partials; but all partial tones that constitute its acoustic profile are derived from its harmonic series. The acoustic profile of a given tone is determinant for one of its essential characteristics, its tone color. Particular combinations of partial tones produce particular tone colors.

This phenomenon is utilized in the art of organ building. A good organ contains, in addition to stops of fundamental pitch, a number of ranks that sound the pitch of certain partial tones in carefully balanced shades of tone color, capable of perfect blend; some of these ranks boast several pipes per key, thus sounding pitches of several partial tones simultaneously. If, for example, the key F is depressed with several such ranks in registration, one may sound f, another a', a third f', a fourth c'', a fifth c', the sixth may even contain the pipes c', f'', c''', f''', c'''' in correspondence with the sixth, eighth, twelfth, sixteenth, and twenty-fourth partial tones, and so forth. If such ranks are well built, a capable organist can realize countless permutations of tone color through imaginative registration.

Problems of Sound I

It is difficult to convey a comprehensible concept of the wealth of organ tone colors by verbal description; one cannot familiarize himself with sounds except by listening. Genuine organ tone cannot even be approached by an orchestra, regardless of how variegated its color palette may be; thus there is no legitimate basis of comparison for the nobility of sound produced by well-scaled Principals; the mysterious singing of the Rohrflöte; the delightfully retiring aloofness of the Quintade; the incredibly velvety gentleness of Nachthorns; the caressing, magic tone quality of the Blockflöte; the spellbinding effect of combinations with the Nasat; the exquisitely tinkling bell tones of the Zimbel; the infinite beauty of an overblown Querflöte; the multiple gradations and color formations of the Principal plenum with Mixtures of varying composition, whose resplendent brightness and solemn tonal expressiveness constitute the commanding ensemble tone of the classical organ. This listing merely suggests characteristic tone colors of certain labial stops. In the grand period of classical organ building all organs, large and small, were equipped with stops of such genuine organ tone colors. Needless to say, various types of carefully balanced upper-work stops constituted important ingredients of these instruments.

In subsequent periods, different ideals of sound prevailed. Strange as it may seem, a trend toward the imitation of orchestral instruments coupled with an abandonment of indigenous organ colors absorbed the interest of the day. Not content with the color pallette contributed by a rich diversity of organ pipes, some seriously believed that even more beautiful sounds could be achieved by extracting from the pipes, for example, the sounds of a violin solo. The result was the gradual loss of the splendid organ colors, while the orchestral "imitation" remained an imitation only; indeed, it often had the effect of caricature. The negative aspects of this development remained the more unnoticed as the interest in tone color per se gradually shifted to a preoccupation with volume and intensity of sound and with possibilities of multiple dynamic gradation: piano and forte no longer sufficed; pianissimo, fortissimo, and above all crescendo and diminuendo were explored. To be able to effect crescendo and diminuendo on the organ is very nice — but it is not the sole attraction of organ tone. Dynamically gradated sound without tonal beauty, variety, and character is of no great value.

Foot Designations and Pitch Levels of Stops

The reader may be curious about the custom of designating the fundamental pitch of a stop by units of linear measure, such as 8′, 4′, 1⅗′, etc. Originally the physical length of the lowest pipe body of a stop was used as the pitch designation for it. It was assumed that the stop was composed of open, not covered, pipes. The lowest note of a rank of open pipes of normal pitch sounds C and is 8′ long. The lowest of a rank of covered pipes is only half as long. Formerly such a rank was labeled 8′ pitch rather than merely 8′. This was to indicate that the stop sounded the same pitch as one consisting of open pipes (of which the lowest pipe measured 8′), even though its lowest pipe measured only 4′. Today this distinction has fallen into disuse. A stop is said to be 8′ when sounding as notated, 4′ when sounding one octave higher than notated, etc.; this applies to all stops, even to covered and conical ranks that in reality do not exhibit the implied measurements.

The tables illustrate the system of pitch designation.

Partial Tone	Pitch designation in feet	Actual Sound
1st partial tone (also fundamental tone)	8'	sounds as written (normal pitch)
2d partial tone	4'	sounds one octave higher
3d partial tone	$2\frac{2}{3}'$	sounds one octave and a perfect fifth higher
4th partial tone	2'	sounds two octaves higher
5th partial tone	$1\frac{3}{5}'$	sounds two octaves and a major third higher
6th partial tone	$1\frac{1}{3}'$	sounds two octaves and a perfect fifth higher
7th partial tone	$1\frac{1}{7}'$	sounds two octaves and a minor/major seventh higher
8th partial tone	1'	sounds three octaves higher
9th partial tone	$\frac{8}{9}'$	sounds three octaves and a major second higher
10th partial tone	$\frac{4}{5}'$	sounds three octaves and a major third higher
11th partial tone	$\frac{8}{11}'$	sounds three octaves and a perfect/augmented fourth higher
12th partial tone	$\frac{2}{3}'$	sounds three octaves and a perfect fifth higher
13th partial tone	$\frac{8}{13}'$	sounds three octaves and a major sixth higher
14th partial tone	$\frac{4}{7}'$	sounds three octaves and a minor seventh higher
15th partial tone	$\frac{8}{15}'$	sounds three octaves and a major seventh higher
16th partial tone	$\frac{1}{2}'$	sounds four octaves higher

overtones (bracketing 2d through 16th partial tones)

Naturally, one can also erect such a series over a 32', 16' and 4' basis:

52

Pitch Designation: 32', 16', 4' Bases

Partial Tone	32' basis		16' basis		4' basis	
	Pitch designation in feet	Actual sound	Pitch designation in feet	Actual sound	Pitch designation in feet	Actual sound
1st partial tone (also fundamental tone)	32'	sounds two octaves lower (than normal pitch)	16'	sounds one octave lower (than normal pitch)	4'	sounds one octave higher (than normal pitch)
2d partial tone	16'	sounds one octave lower	8'	sounds as written (normal pitch)	2'	sounds two octaves higher
3d partial tone	$10\frac{2}{3}'$	sounds a perfect fourth lower	$5\frac{1}{3}'$	sounds a perfect fifth above the 8' pitch	$1\frac{1}{3}'$	sounds a perfect fifth above the 2' pitch
4th partial tone	8'	sounds as written (normal pitch)	4'	sounds one octave higher than 8' pitch	1'	sounds three octaves higher than 8' pitch
5th partial tone	$6\frac{2}{5}'$	sounds a major third above the 8' pitch	$3\frac{1}{5}'$	sounds a major third above the 4' pitch	$\frac{4}{5}'$	sounds a major third above the 1' pitch
6th partial tone	$5\frac{1}{3}'$	sounds a perfect fifth above the 8' pitch	$2\frac{2}{3}'$	sounds a perfect fifth above the 4' pitch	$\frac{2}{3}'$	sounds a perfect fifth above the 1' pitch
7th partial tone	$4\frac{4}{7}'$	sounds a minor/major seventh above the 8' pitch,	$2\frac{2}{7}'$	sounds a minor/major seventh above the 4' pitch,	$\frac{4}{7}'$	sounds a minor/major seventh above the 1' pitch,
etc.	etc.	etc.	etc.	etc.	etc.	etc.

(Partial tones 2d through 7th are bracketed as "overtones.")

Labial stops of 32', 16', 8', and 4' pitches are called foundation stops; all other labial stops are known as mutation stops.

The Principal Choir

The Principal choir consists of a number of Principal stops whose fundamental pitches are organized according to the harmonic series; it constitutes the basic ensemble of the classical *organum plenum, plein jeu, ripieno, Volles Werk, lleno,* which we shall call the mixture plenum, and is usually confined to the 1st, 2d, 3d, 4th, 6th, 8th, etc. partial tones of the harmonic series, that is, to ranks of octaves [or unisons] and fifths; however, stops containing the tierce element are traceable [in the Principal choir] since about 1450.

The particular characteristics of the composition of the Principal choir are conditioned by the following circumstances: The human ear prefers low tones that exhibit an acoustical profile favoring relatively high partial tones (up to the 32d); others are perceived as being too "dull"; on the other hand, only such high tones that exhibit an acoustical profile favoring relatively low partial tones (up to the fourth, fifth, or sixth partial tones) seem to be pleasing to the ear; others appear to be too "shrill." This phenomenon is taken into consideration in the composition of the Principal choir. Some of its stops exhibit several pipes per key, three, five, eight each, or — more infrequently — even ten or twelve. The pitches of the individual pipes of such compound stops are terraced so as to be relatively higher in the grave region of the compass than in the acute region; this terraced arrangement is achieved by "repetition" or "breaks"; compound stops are said to "break back" by octaves to relatively lower pitches in the acute region, while the low keys produce the splendor achieved by high partial tones.

Mixtures

The design and construction of compound stops that exhibit regularly recurring breaks — collectively called "mixtures" [more properly, "crowns"] — is one of the great arts of organ building. Such masters as Hans Suisse of Cologne and his pupil, Hendrik Niehoff of 's Hertogenbosch were famous for their artfully contrived mixtures; decades after their deaths their art was still lauded. Builders such as Scherer, Compenius, Fritzsche, Schnitker, Languedeuil, Thierry, Clicquot, Lefèbvre, Silbermann, and Riepp were their worthy successors. It is the touchstone of organ building since about 1930 to have recognized as exemplary the mixture layout and design of these classical builders, to have studied them carefully, and to have realized them in the form of creative developments. The following table gives some examples of compound stops:

Tarragona

Plate III

Organ of the Cathedral in Tarragona, Spain; built by the canon Amigó of Tortosa in 1563. Over the Rückpositiv, reed pipes extend horizontally into the nave (in this instance a later addition), according to Spanish tradition (compare also p. 65 and Plate VIII).

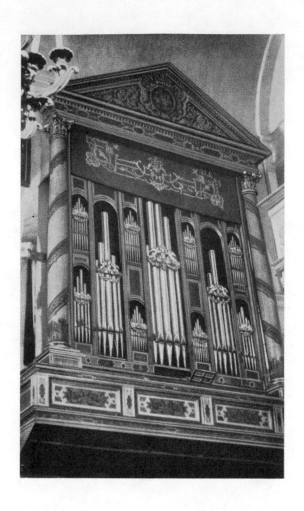

Plate IV

Organ of S. Guiseppe in Brescia, Italy; built by Graziadio Antegnati of Brescia in 1581 (one manual, 12 stops). The early Italian organs had, as a rule, only one manual. This instrument has been preserved. For its specification, see p. 156.

Typical Compositions of Compound Stops

Stop name	may exhibit such acute pitches in the grave bass region as:	may exhibit such grave pitches in the acute treble region as:
Sesquialtera II	$\frac{2}{3}'$ $\frac{2}{5}'$	$2\frac{2}{3}'$ $1\frac{3}{5}'$
Terzian II	$\frac{2}{5}'$ $\frac{1}{3}'$	$1\frac{3}{5}'$ $1\frac{1}{3}'$
Mixture III	$1'$ $\frac{2}{3}'$ $\frac{1}{2}'$	$4'$ $2\frac{2}{3}'$ $2'$
Zimbel IV	$\frac{1}{2}'$ $\frac{1}{3}'$ $\frac{1}{4}'$ $\frac{1}{6}'$	$4'$ $2\frac{2}{3}'$ $2'$ $1\frac{1}{3}'$
Hintersatz VI	$2'$ $1\frac{1}{3}'$ $1\frac{1}{3}'$ $1'$ $1'$ $\frac{2}{3}'$	$4'$ $4'$ $2\frac{2}{3}'$ $2\frac{2}{3}'$ $2'$ $2'$
Scharf VIII	$1\frac{1}{3}'$ $1'$ $\frac{2}{3}'$ $\frac{1}{2}'$ $\frac{1}{2}'$ $\frac{1}{3}'$ $\frac{1}{3}'$ $\frac{1}{4}'$	$4'$ $4'$ $2\frac{2}{3}'$ $2\frac{2}{3}'$ $2'$ $2'$ $1\frac{1}{3}'$ $1\frac{1}{3}'$

These are, of course, examples applicable to specific cases only; but they do convey a concept of the composition of compound stops. The breaks are, obviously, organized by sophisticated stages leading eventually up to the composition given for the acute treble. The fact that some pitch levels appear doubled or tripled at various stages contributes essentially to the beauty, extensity, and splendor of the stop. Formerly, mixture breaks exhibited octave skips (for example: $F-e$ $1'$ $\frac{2}{3}'$ $\frac{1}{2}'$, $f-e'$ $2'$ $1\frac{1}{3}'$ $1'$, and $f'-f''$ $4'$ $2\frac{2}{3}'$ $2'$; so-called octave breaks); but already about 1450 examples of half-octave breaks—universally employed in modern organ building—can be observed (applied to the same example, this means: $F-B$ $1'$ $\frac{2}{3}'$ $\frac{1}{2}'$, $c-e$ $1\frac{1}{3}'$ $1'$ $\frac{2}{3}'$, $f-b$ $2'$ $1\frac{1}{3}'$ $1'$, etc.). In addition to the keys c and f, the keys g were also used as points for breaks; modern organ builders no longer adhere to regular breaks, preferring to design compound stops to achieve a maximum effectiveness. The following examples demonstrate this principle:

Mixture IV	$4'$	$2\frac{2}{3}'$	$2'$	$1\frac{1}{3}'$	$1'$	$\frac{2}{3}'$
C–c-sharp		x	x	x	x	
d–g'	x	x	x	x		
g'-sharp–c'''-sharp	x	x	x	x		
d'''–a'''	x	x	xx			

Scharf V	4'	2⅔'	2'	1⅓'	1'	⅔'	½'	⅓'	¼'
C−F					x	x	x	x	x
F-sharp−c				x	x	x	x	x	
c-sharp−g-sharp			x	x	x	x	x		
a−c''		x	x	x	x	x			
c''-sharp−g''-sharp	x	x	x	x	x				
a''−d'''-sharp	x	x	xx	x					
e'''−a'''	x	xx	xx						

Zimbel II	2'	1⅓'	1'	⅔'	½'	⅓'
C−B					x	x
c−a				x	x	
b-flat−d''			x	x		
d''-sharp−c'''		x	x			
c'''-sharp−a'''	x	x				

Ranks of fifths at 5⅓' pitch level or of thirds at 3⅕' pitch level do not belong in compound stops [associated with an 8' basis]; furthermore, every organ−excepting quite small instruments− should have among its compound stops one Scharf or Zimbel without ranks of the fifth at 2⅔' pitch level nor of the third at 1⅗'; such a stop is needed for a mixture plenum predicated upon a 4' basis. Here are some examples for Principal choirs:

Principal 8'
Octave 4'
Sesquialtera II
Superoctave 2'
Quinte 1⅓'
Mixture V
Scharf III

Principal 16'
Octave 8'
Superoctave 4'
Rauschpfeife II
Terzian II
Mixture VII

Principal 4'
Octave 2'
Quinte 1⅓'
Zimbel II

The Rauschpfeife is composed of 2⅔' and 2' ranks and does not break. Registrations with Principal choirs are particularly appropriate for polyphonic textures (toccatas, preludes, and fugues). In the classical *organum plenum* the Bourdon 16' and / or the Gedackt 8' could be added to the Principal stops.

Wide-Scaled Choir; Labial Solo Components; Farbenzimbel

The Gedackt serves also as basis for the wide-scaled choir, which forms a contrast to the Principal choir. The oldest known wide-scaled choir is still preserved; it is found in the organ of St. Laurentius in Alkmaar, Netherlands (completed in 1511 by

Hans Franckens of Coblenz) and consists of a Hohlpfeife 8' (built as a Rohrflöte), an open conical Barpfeife 4', and an open cylindrical Gemshorn 2'. It is evident that the builder consciously designed these three stops as a choir in contrast to the Principal choir, since the Principal choir is mounted on the lower chest, while the wide-scaled choir is mounted on the upper. The channels of the two chests are connected by air ducts, making both chests playable from one manual—originally probably the only manual.

Stop combinations with wide-scaled labial ranks of a high pitch level (from 2$\frac{2}{3}$' on up) find excellent use in solo registrations; for this reason such solo stops as the narrow-scaled, quite high-pitched Klingend Zimbel and the Carillon, which may exhibit Principal scale as well as wide scale, are listed together with the wide-scaled choir in the examples below. By contrast with the Principal choir, the wide-scaled choir can very well absorb such stops as the Terz 3$\frac{1}{5}$', in spite of the fact that this represents a partial belonging to a 16' foundation. Wide-scaled ranks at 8', 4', 2$\frac{2}{3}$', 2' and 1$\frac{3}{5}$'—found also in the form of mixed voices (Nachthorn V or Kornett V)—together with Trumpets 8' and 4', Krummhorn 8', and Principal 4' constitute the classical "Grand Jeu," which we shall call "reed plenum." Developed in the 16th century by the 's Hertogenbosch group of organ builders, it was introduced for the first time (however, without the rank of a third) in 1539 in the **organ of the Oude Kerk in Amsterdam, Netherlands. Some exam**ples for wide-scaled choirs with additional solo components follow:

Bleigedackt 8'	Holzgedackt 8'	Rohrflöte 8'
Rohrflöte 4'	Holzflöte 4'	Spitzflöte 4'
Terz 3$\frac{1}{5}$'	Nasat 2$\frac{2}{3}$'	Waldflöte 2'
Nachthorn III	Carillon II	Hörnlein II
(wide-scaled)	1$\frac{3}{5}$'+$\frac{8}{9}$'	(wide-scaled)
2$\frac{2}{3}$'+2'+1$\frac{3}{5}$'	(wide-scaled third,	2$\frac{2}{3}$'+1$\frac{3}{5}$'
Quintflöte 1$\frac{1}{3}$'	narrow ninth)	Sifflöte 1'
(wide-scaled bass,	Repetierend Septime $\frac{2}{7}$'	(wide-scaled bass,
narrow-scaled treble)	(narrow-scaled)	narrow-scaled
		treble)

Spitzflöte 8'	Spillflöte 8'
Koppelflöte 4'	Blockflöte 4'
Terz 1$\frac{3}{5}$'	Kornett V (wide-scaled)
Glasglockenspiel	8'+4'+2$\frac{2}{3}$'+2'+1$\frac{3}{5}$'
II, treble range	Farbenzimbel IV (narrow-scaled)
2'+$\frac{3}{4}$' (wide-scaled octave,	
narrow-scaled fourth)	

The Glasglockenspiel was inspired by a registration suggested by Gottfried Silbermann: Nasat $2\frac{2}{3}'$ plus Sifflöte $1'$; its $\frac{3}{4}'$ rank sounds the "nonharmonic" partial of a perfect fourth. The Terz $3\frac{1}{5}'$, the Repetierend Septime (with segments at $\frac{4}{7}'$, $1\frac{1}{7}'$, $2\frac{2}{7}'$, and $4\frac{4}{7}'$), and the Farbenzimbel introduce partials which properly belong to the $16'$ and $32'$ bases into ensembles of an $8'$ basis. The term Farbenzimbel is an arbitrary appellation and may be exchanged for another; it refers to stops containing ranks that sound the pitches of upper partial tones (such as the 7th, 9th, 11th, 13th) in a high pitch range, with irregular disposition and intermittent segments. Here follow two examples from the numerous options for such layouts:

Farbenzimbel III

	$1\frac{1}{7}'$	$\frac{8}{9}'$	$\frac{8}{11}'$	$\frac{4}{7}'$	$\frac{4}{9}'$	$\frac{4}{11}'$	$\frac{2}{7}'$	$\frac{2}{9}'$	$\frac{2}{11}'$	$\frac{1}{7}'$	$\frac{1}{9}'$
C−D-sharp							x		x		x
E−G-sharp						x		x		x	
A−c					x		x		x		
c-sharp−f				x		x		x			
f-sharp−a			x		x		x				
b-flat−d'		x		x		x					
d'-sharp−f'-sharp	x		x		x						

	$4\frac{4}{7}'$	$3\frac{5}{9}'$	$2\frac{10}{11}'$	$2\frac{2}{7}'$	$1\frac{7}{9}'$	$1\frac{5}{11}'$	$1\frac{1}{7}'$	$\frac{8}{9}'$	$\frac{8}{11}'$	$\frac{4}{7}'$
g'−b'						x		x		x
c''−d''-sharp					x		x		x	
e''−g''-sharp				x		x		x		
a''−c'''			x		x		x			
c'''-sharp−f'''-sharp		x		x		x				
f'''-sharp−a'''	x		x		x					

Farbenzimbel IV

	$1\frac{1}{3}'$	$1\frac{3}{13}'$	$1'$	$\frac{4}{5}'$	$\frac{2}{3}'$	$\frac{8}{13}'$	$\frac{1}{2}'$	$\frac{2}{5}'$	$\frac{1}{3}'$	$\frac{4}{13}'$	$\frac{1}{4}'$	$\frac{1}{5}'$	$\frac{1}{6}'$	$\frac{2}{13}'$	$\frac{1}{8}'$	$\frac{1}{10}'$
C−D									x	x		x	x			
D-sharp−F								x	x		x	x				
F-sharp−A							x	x		x	x					
B-flat−c						x	x		x	x						
c-sharp−e					x	x		x	x							
f−g				x	x		x	x								
g-sharp−b			x	x		x	x									
c'−d'		x	x		x	x										
d'-sharp−f'-sharp	x	x		x	x											

	$5\frac{1}{3}'$	$4\frac{12}{13}'$	$4'$	$3\frac{1}{5}'$	$2\frac{2}{3}'$	$2\frac{6}{13}'$	$2'$	$1\frac{3}{5}'$	$1\frac{1}{3}'$	$1\frac{3}{13}'$	$1'$	$\frac{4}{5}'$	$\frac{2}{3}'$	$\frac{8}{13}'$	$\frac{1}{2}'$
g'−a'								x	x		x	x			
b'-flat−c''-sharp							x	x		x	x				
d''−e''						x	x		x	x					
f''−g''-sharp					x	x		x	x						
a''−b''				x	x		x	x							
c'''−d'''-sharp			x	x		x	x								
e'''−f'''-sharp		x	x		x	x									
g'''−a'''	x	x		x	x										

The disposition of these stops is considered irregular, because the pitch levels of the various ranks are so designed as to omit one or two adjacent partial tones (for example, $2/9'$, $1/7'$, and $4/13'$, $1/5'$, $1/6'$, $1/8'$ in each of the first ranks of the quoted examples); the segments are called intermittent because the individual pitch levels change from segment to segment, only to continue with the third or fourth segment (for example, the $2/7'$ rank of the first example falls out from E to G-sharp and from c-sharp to f; the $1/4'$ rank of the second example falls out from D-sharp to A and from c-sharp to e.

Special Group

Some labial stops can be classified neither with the Principal choir nor with the labial solo components. These include, for example, the narrow-scaled stops Quintade, Viola da Gamba, and Salicional; as early as about 1500 the Quintade was known under the name of Hölzern Glechter ("wooden laughter"), while the Salicional went by the name of Schwegel. Occasionally, the Quintade may serve as a fundamental stop for mutation [9] registrations; the Viola da Gamba and Salicional are especially useful for accompanying left-hand cantus firmi in the soprano range. The Nachthorn 2', a very wide-scaled pedal stop (its scale is proportionately wider by 12 semitones than that of normally scaled 2' ranks) with a very narrow mouth width (one-sixth) adds gratifying clarity to the pedal foundation stops; (it must be very delicately voiced in its high range). Undulating stops have been known since the 16th century (Voci umane, Unda maris, Voix céleste); unfortunately, they have often been misused. Overblown stops, such as the Querflöte, Flûte harmonique, and Flûte octaviante can be used for polyphonic textures as well as for solo registrations. A word of explanation regarding the phenomenon of overblowing is now in order.

Overblown Pipes

Boring a small hole at three-seventh of the speaking length into the body of a pipe with a low cut-up causes the air column — provided it is amply winded — to vibrate in two halves rather than as a whole; the pipe will consequently speak one octave higher:

---

[9] Mutations are wide-scaled stops above 4' pitch. [*Translator*]

it is said to overblow. Causing a covered pipe to overblow results in its air column vibrating in three rather than in two portions: the pipe will consequently speak a twelfth higher. Thus, an overblown pipe sounding at 4′ pitch needs to be 8′ long if it is an open pipe, or 6′ long if it is a covered pipe.

Fig. 30. A lingual pipe

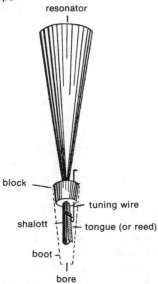

resonator

block

tuning wire

shalott

tongue (or reed)

boot

bore

Lingual Pipes

When a lingual pipe is excited, a thin brass blade called a "tongue," or "reed" is set into vibration, which, in turn, excites the air column within the pipe body, or "resonator." The "tuning wire" presses the upper part of the reed against the "shalott." Moving the tuning wire upward results in a lowering of the pitch, as the free, lower part of the reed becomes longer and vibrates more slowly. Moving the tuning wire downward produces the opposite effect.

Scales of Lingual Pipes; Tonal Characteristics

A thin reed produces a tone richer in harmonics than does a relatively thick reed. However, reed stops do not offer the same degree of variability in this respect as do labial stops; all reed stops are quite rich in harmonics. The shape of the resonator exerts a great influence: wide-scaled resonators produce a stronger tone than do narrow-scaled ones; cylindrical resonators produce a more transparent sound than do conical resonators. The air column within the resonator has its own frequency of vibration; when these are faster than those of the reed, the pipe sounds brighter and richer in harmonics than it would sound with air column vibrations slower than those of the reed. Correctly proportioned cylindrical resonators approximate the speaking length of covered labial pipes of identical pitch; conical resonators approximate the speaking length of open conical labial pipes of identical pitch:

Relative Lengths of Resonators

Pitch	C	c	c'
Conical resonators	7' 2½"	3' 8"	1 ' 10½"
Cylindrical resonators	3' 11¼"	2'	1'

The vibrations of the air column within the resonator — and with them the tone color of the pipe — can be adjusted at the regulating slot near the top of the resonator or by similar adjusting devices. The tuning of reed pipes must be accomplished by moving the tuning wire rather than by handling these regulating devices.

Shapes of Resonators

Cylindrical resonators produce only the odd partials 1, 3, 5, 7, 9, etc. of the harmonic series. The frequency of vibration within the resonators of such types of stops as shown in Fig. 31 corresponds to that of their needs.

Absence of normal-length resonators favors the development of harmonics but reduces the extensity of the tone. Certain tone colors of excellent quality, however, can only be attained by using such short resonators. The most beautiful stops of this kind I know are the Rankett 16', the Sordun 16', the Geigendregal 4', and the Jungfrauregal 4' of the organ in the castle at Hilleröd, Denmark, built by Esaias Compenius about 1610. The most valuable and useful reed stops are the Trompete/Posaune and Krummhorn, or Dulzian. Figuratively speaking, they are the "Principals" of the reed family.

Fig. 31. Pipe shapes, group III

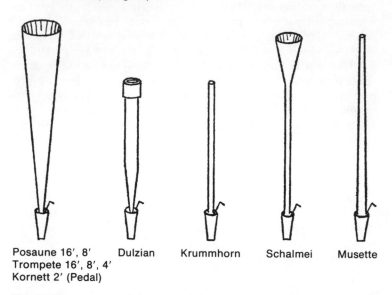

Posaune 16', 8'	Dulzian	Krummhorn	Schalmei	Musette
Trompete 16', 8', 4'				
Kornett 2' (Pedal)				

Fig. 32 shows stops of the Regal family with resonators of fractional length.

Fig. 32. Pipe shapes, group IV

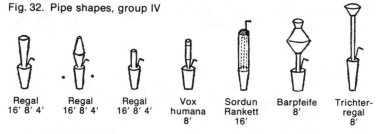

| Regal 16' 8' 4' | Regal 16' 8' 4' | Regal 16' 8' 4' | Vox humana 8' | Sordun Rankett 16' | Barpfeife 8' | Trichter-regal 8' |

Reed stops are preferably built at 16', 8', and 4' pitch levels. The same has already been said for the string stops of the labial groups. Both groups, strings and reeds, have in common the quality of rich overtone structures. In the pedal, the Kornett 2' (Arp Schnitger called it Trompete 2') is frequently found.[10] There are also

---

[10] The relative sizes of the pipes of a 2' pedal rank correspond to those of a Trompete 4' in a manual division between c and g''; thus reed pipes of 2' pedal stops are not as diminutive in measurements as one might think. [*Translator*]

reed stops with double- or quadruple-length resonators. In such resonators, the air columns vibrate not only in one unit but in two and four portions respectively. Thus the double- and quadruple-length resonators of lingual ranks correspond to overblown labial stops. However, double-length stops are not usually extended all the way through the bass range, except in some instances the trumpet species. Overlength Dulzian stops require triple length resonators as they correspond acoustically to covered labial pipes; that is, their air columns vibrate either as a whole or in three portions, five portions, etc., rather than in two or four. However, they are rarely built. Lingual stops with overlength resonators excel in nobility of tone and in carrying power but are, of course, very expensive.

Spanish Trumpets (trompettes en chamade)

Entire series of lingual stops mounted horizontally in the façade are frequently encountered in Spanish organs (see Plates III and VIII). In recent years this practice has been much imitated, often without comprehension of the intrinsic principle of design that should govern their incorporation: one or the other of the chorus reed stops of an organ are mounted horizontally in the façade rather than in their logical place within the case. Such a disposition upsets the artistic balance between the ranks mounted in the façade and those mounted within the case; the reeds within the case are as incomplete as those ranks arbitrarily mounted in the façade. The design of the classical Spanish organs is, in this respect, fundamentally different, as *en chamade* installations in the Hauptwerk occur only where the Hauptwerk reed chorus is already complete in itself; the same is true for the Oberwerk or the Rückpositiv. The ensemble of stops within the case forms an organic entity, complete with lingual ranks. As complete divisions *(Werke)* they hold their own against the *en chamade* divisions; both are independent of one another; that is, their tonal design is noncomplementary. For example, a Hauptwerk designed with a Trompete 8' and a Trompete 4' must not be altered by simply mounting one or both of these ranks in the façade; instead they should remain within the case and an additional set of lingual stops, complete in itself, should be mounted horizontally in the façade if Spanish trumpets are desired, for example, three trumpet ranks (8', 4', 2') and a Krummhorn 8' for the bass range, and another three trumpet ranks (16', 8', 4') and a Krummhorn 8' for the treble range. These reed stops form an independent division of the organ and had best be given their own keyboard. Good examples may be found in the Propsteikirche in Bochum, Germany, and in the Cathedral in Hildesheim, Germany (see Plate VIII). Incidentally, the division between bass and discant at c′ and c′-sharp (rather than the usual division at b and c′) in the case of classical Spanish trumpets was carefully observed by composers, as is evident from the Spanish organ literature.

Problems of Sound II

It is theoretically possible for the organist to combine any stops, not only those of a certain stop family, but virtually all stops of the various families and genera. Thus he has at his disposal practically limitless combinations. One precondition, however, has to be met: the stops have to be mutually balanced in the finest possible proportion. Unfortunately this is often not the case; many organs have one grave fault in this respect: although they boast of high-pitched stops of various kinds as well as reed stops, these are either too loud or too soft in intonation. It is quite understandable that such instruments soon become tiresome to player and listener alike.

Very enlightening in this respect are the comparative experiments in sound conducted by Werner Lottermoser [11] on various organs. According to these experiments, good organs — dating from the Baroque period — show the following average values:

Sound Pressure in Microbars (μb)

Division	C	c	c′	c″	c‴
Manual	1.0	0.9	0.8	0.6	0.5
Pedal	1.6	1.3	0.9		

The plenum may reach as high as 1.6 μ b in the manuals and 2.0 μ b in the pedal. Instruments of lesser quality — dating from later periods — show, for example, 2.0−1.5−1.9−1.9−0.7 μ b, in the manual plenum 2−4 μ b and in the pedal plenum 4−6 μ b, i. e., quite considerably higher sound pressures. Sound pressure analyses have yielded the further evidence (see Fig. 33) that each

---

[11] In Fritz Winckel, *Klangstruktur der Musik* (see Bibliography, p. 212).

partial tone column shows two points of maximal intensity which, from the bass to the treble range of the keyboard, gradually approach the fundamental tone in such a way that their curves gain steadily in absolute pitch levels or possibly remain on the same pitch level but never drop. To state it more simply: in the bass range the partial tones are stronger, in the treble range the fundamental tone is stronger.

The sound spectra of classical organs meet two important and seemingly contradictory conditions: on the one hand, the sounds increase in overtone richness toward the bass and decrease toward the treble range; on the other hand, the bass range, in spite of this, sounds darker and the treble range brighter. These conditions favor beauty of sound in individual tones as well as clarity of sound in polyphonic textures. The zones of maximal intensity may differ in various organs; they should differ within the single divisions of an organ. Since the zones of maximal intensity extend through the zones of vowel formants (see Fig. 33, phonetic symbols are given in parentheses), the plenum character of organs and their divisions may aptly be described by indications such as "from O (ō) to E (ā)," "from A (ä) to E (ā)," "from A (ä) to I (ē)," "constantly I (ē)," and so on. The nasal zone should be avoided.

It is an immensely rewarding task for our present-day master builders to reintroduce good voicing and intonation of mixtures and lingual stops in order to restore to the organ its classical richness of sound.

Up to this point our discussion has covered the main parts of an organ: wind chests with ranks of pipes (stops); pallets and mechanisms of registration; the blowplant; keyboards with stop knobs (or tablets); the important connection between the blower and the chest, the wind trunk; the connection between the keyboard and the chest, the harness; the connection between the stop knobs (or tablets) and the chest, the stop action.

Werke (Corpora, Divisions)

It was mentioned earlier that an organ generally has more than one keyboard and more than one chest; that each keyboard usually has its own chest, occasionally even two. A keyboard together with its chest(s) is called a *Werk*, corpus, or division; thus an organ has several corpora, or divisions, in order to augment its usefulness and flexibility. It was mentioned earlier that

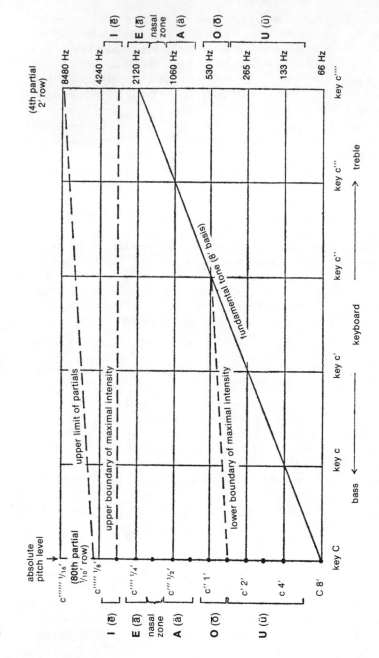

Fig. 33. Zones of partial tone columns and of formants

the most variegated tone colors can be created by judicious combinations of the various stops. For example, the opening bars of Bach's "Kommst du nun, Jesu, vom Himmel herunter" (see

Fig. 34. A Duo

Fig. 34) may be played with a great number of registrations: Gedackt 8', Rohrflöte 4'; Principal 8', Nasat $2^2/_3$'; Schalmei 8', Octave 4', Terz $1^3/_5$'; and similar possibilities. However, if we want to play the upper part with a registration different from that of the lower part, we must have two keyboards with separate registrations, for example:

right hand: Quintade 8', Blockflöte 2'
left hand: Dulzian 16', Rohrflöte 8'
or
right hand: Krummhorn 8', Sifflöte 1 1/3'
left hand: Quintade 16', Spitzflöte 4'

In this context, a further aspect must be discussed: "Kommst du nun, Jesu, vom Himmel herunter" has three rather than two voices. After a few initial measures in two-part texture, a third voice enters carrying the hymn melody. (See Fig. 35)

The composer's directions call for this voice to be realized in yet another, distinctly different tone color, that is, with a registration contrasting to that of the two other voices. In accordance with the composer's intention, this part is assigned to a 4' pedal stop. By playing it one octave lower than notated, we gain the desired pitch level within the confines of the pedal compass.

69

I have treated this example in such detail because this custom of playing the cantus firmus (abbreviated c. f.) of a high range in the pedal was widely used in Germany up to Bach's time. It has great advantages. Usually it is the task of the pedal to carry the bass part. However, florid bass lines are not easily realized in the pedal. Therefore, if the pedal is assigned a calmly moving inner or upper part (to be registered with 4', 2', or 1' stops), the left hand may take over the animated bass line, which is thus more comfortably playable. With this method in mind, bass parts may

Fig. 35. A Trio

be composed which would otherwise hardly be playable in the pedal. The main task of the pedal, however, is to sound the foundation for polyphonic textures (the bass part) in a distinct tone color. Stops of 16' pitch *may* and *should* be designed for the manual; they *must*, however, be represented in the pedal without question. The 16' pitch in the pedal does not suggest the "normal" pitch level — 8' basis as normal pitch applies to the pedal as well as to the manual — but it doubles it in the lower octave (similar to the double bass doubling the cello in the orchestra). This is why the largest pipes of an organ are regularly found mounted on the pedal chests.

The bass range will project most effectively when the wind chest is symmetrically divided into C and C-sharp chests. The pipe arrangement on such chests is as follows:

G F D-sharp C-sharp   C D E F-sharp

or

G D-sharp C-sharp F A   G-sharp E C D F-sharp

The C and C-sharp chests are located in front, at either side of the gallery. As these parts of the organ do not have many pipes and are, therefore, not very wide but — owing to the very large pipes — of considerable height, they are often referred to as "pedal towers" (see Plate VI). Of course, not only the pedal chests, but also the manual chests can be divided, symmetrically or otherwise. A disjunct rather than a chromatically conjunct arrangement has the distinct advantage of producing a greater clarity of tone, both in homophonic and polyphonic textures; this, of course, is particularly important in large halls. It is advisable not to place the windchests in the organ case directly next to or behind one another. The great German organ builders of the classical period (17th century) placed the main chest, the Hauptwerk, into the high center, below it the Brustwerk; the Rückpositiv was mounted at the gallery's parapet, protruding into the nave, and the aforementioned pedal towers were placed in front, to either side of the organ (see Plates II, III, V — X). This free spatial arrangement of the various chests favors the emergence and unhindered propagation of sound incomparably better than the practice of placing all or the greater part of the chests next to or behind one another, and screened with one large façade.

Problems of Sound III

It is, of course, acoustically essential that all divisions of an organ project their sound equally well. This applies particularly to the Hauptwerk, the large Positiv, and the Pedal. Full exploitation of the wealth of colors of an organ is contingent upon this condition. The diversified realization of many two- and three-part textures in the manner described above is impossible to achieve on instruments where one corpus is too strong, another too weak. In this respect, organ builders have committed many an offense by building instruments whose divisions lacked the desirable mutual balance. The dynamic element, the question of "loud" versus "soft," had been overemphasized to the point of a nearly complete disregard for tone color and variety of registration. It had become fashionable so to graduate the dynamic level of organ voices that the loudest stops were assigned to Manual I, the softest, to the top keyboard. Organ builders and organists of that period considered this a very sensible arrangement; they failed to realize that one of the greatest assets of the organ, the multiplicity of color combinations, would be entirely lost in this way.

The concept of dynamics in the classical organs consisted in mutual dynamic equality of the Hauptwerk and of the large Positiv (Rückpositiv, Oberpositiv), while the small Positiv (Brustwerk) was of a considerably lower dynamic level. Gottfried Silbermann aptly formulated this concept by describing the Hauptwerk as "grand and grave" (*gross und gravitätisch*), the Oberpositiv as "sharp and penetrating" (*scharf und penetrant*), and the Brustwerk as "delicate and sweet" (*delikat und lieblich*). The concept of dynamic levels in the contemporary organ will be discussed later.

Expression

In order to facilitate fine dynamic gradation, one of the chests may be "enclosed" by being placed in a box, whose front wall contains a row of "shutters" (see Fig. 36). Opening or closing the shutters clears or obstructs the path of sound: The listener perceives dynamic increase or decrease. Of late, folding-type shutters

Fig. 36. A swell box with vertical shutters

swell box

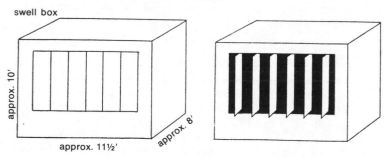

approx. 10'

approx. 11½'

approx. 8'

are also being built (see Fig. 37 and Plate VIII). These have the distinct advantage that the interior of the box is completely uncovered when the shutters are open; this is not possible with the older type of louvres. Not only is the scope of dynamic variety increased, but the enclosed division functions simultaneously as a fully effective Positiv. A folding type of shutter could also be mounted horizontally for greater evenness of crescendo and diminuendo. (See Fig. 37.)

An "expression pedal" (or "shoe") is installed directly above the pedal board; it is connected with the shutters (either type) of the swell box. By moving this pedal, the organist can open or close the shutters, thereby increasing or decreasing the volume of sound emanating from within the swell box (see Plate XII). Horizontal folding shutters can also be opened and closed by means of a cylinder (*Walze*) rather than by a pedal.

The expression affects particularly the acute and delicate sounds. A Gedackt 8′ is less affected than are mixtures and lingual ranks. For this reason the enclosed divisions of the Spanish Baroque organs include mostly stops of the latter type. During the period of the *Empfindsamkeit* (Preclassicism, *stylo galante*) it was customary in Southern Germany to place only weak and thin sounding stops under expression. This was a manifestly gross mistake, which, unfortunately, enjoyed considerable imitation. The intention was to express certain effects by way of dynamic shadings of "rustling," thin sounds. Meanwhile we have realized that such effects have no place in an organ. Only beauty and wealth of sound, not cheap artificialities, are in order. The expression mechanism of an organ should be utilized either as a means of musico-architectural formation on a grand scale or not at all. Contemporary Northern and Central European organ builders not infrequently place the Brustwerk under expression. The advantage of this practice is that this division does include lingual ranks and mixtures among other stops, rather than thin-sounding, rustling stops. However, it is not an ideal solution. Although it seems to be derived from architectural principles of the Baroque organ, it does not conform to the

Fig. 37. A swell box with horizontal folding type shutters

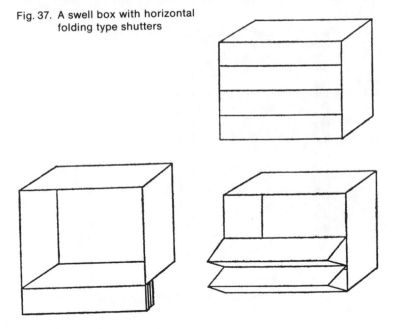

code according to which the large, "sharp and penetrating" Positiv—which is dynamically on a par with the Hauptwerk—should be placed under expression rather than the small, "delicate and sweet" Positiv; only by following this code can the dynamic proportions of the entire organ achieve overall balance: The closed swell box serves as a measured step to the small Positiv; a similar step leads from the small Positiv over the open, large Positiv to the combination of all three corpora, to which the Pedal is finally added.

Case and Façade

The various chests of an organ, including the necessary structural framework, are mounted in the "case." Such pipes as are visibly mounted in the front of the case are called "façade" pipes, or "Prestants." These pipes are almost always Principals, usually belonging to the largest Principal stop of the chest right behind the façade. They are not mounted directly on the top board; rather, they are connected with it by metal tubes,[12] called conductors, which supply wind from the chest. For reasons of visual design, some façade pipes must be longer than their pitch requires. Such pipes receive incisions in the back so as to compensate for their overlength and the attendant pitch alteration (see Fig. 38).

Fig. 38. Pipe, showing incision in back

Fig. 39. Mitered pipes

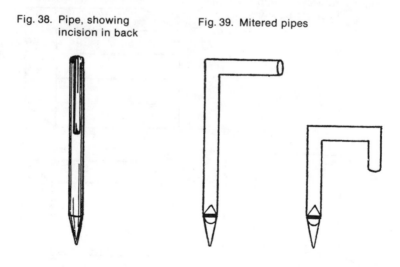

---

[12] American organ builders have successfully used nylon tubing. [*Translator*]

Incidentally, the opposite situation is often encountered in the interior of the organ: some pipes may be too long for the ceiling height. In such cases the organ builder resorts to "mitering" the pipes. (See Fig. 39.)

The Console (Key Desk)

Manuals, pedal, expression shoe, stop knobs (or tablets), push buttons, toe studs, couplers, and pistons are located in the "console" or "key desk" (see Plate XII). Favorable console measurements are important for the player. The pedal should have a total width of 112 cm. with 30 keys (C−f')[13]; each key should be 22 mm. wide, with its edges and corners appropriately beveled. Although it may look more symmetrical if the keys d-sharp of manual and pedal are lined up, it is more advantageous for the player if the pedal c is lined up with the manual c'. Total width for 21 adjacent white manual keys[14] (C−b') should be 48 cm. (the modern grand piano exhibits a width of 49.6 cm. for the same number of keys, which is less advantageous for polyphonic textures). The black keys should be narrow. Measured in the center, the bottom keyboard should be mounted 75 cm. above the pedal; the white manual keys should be 12.5 cm. long; the keyboards should be mounted 6.0 cm. above one another with a 2.5 cm. recession successively from lower to upper keyboards. The pedal keys c-sharp and d-sharp should be approximately 13.5 cm. long, the key d should be 60 cm. long (playing surface, i. e., total length minus the length of the black keys). The height of the white pedal keys should measure a minimum of 3.5 cm., as should the difference in height between black and white pedal keys. The pedal board should be concave and radiating (the outer black keys should be longer). Measured perpendicularly, the front edges of the pedal keys c-sharp and d-sharp should be 20 cm. behind the front edge of the bottom manual. In a good tracker organ, the manual keys require approximately between 150 and 200 g., the pedal keys approximately between 2 and 2.5 kg. of weight of [i. e., resistance to the] touch. The key

---

[13] The reader is reminded that a 32-note pedal compass is the accepted American standard. For exact data applying to the American scene, he is referred to the *Revised A. G. O. Report on Standardization of the Console, 1961,* repr. in William H. Barnes, *The Contempory American Organ.* Glen Rock, N. J.: J. Fischer and Bro., 1964, p. 198, whose recommendations are generally accepted. [*Translator*]

[14] The term *white* refers to the long (c, d, e, f, g, a, b), the term "black" to the short (c-sharp, d-sharp, f-sharp, g-sharp, b-flat) keys. [*Translator*]

resistance is the sum of the wind pressing against the pallet, of the tension of the pallet spring, and of the inertia of the various parts of the harness. The relation of these components to one another is considered good if a key can be held down with half the force required to depress it initially. Generally speaking, manual keys should depress with about 10–11 mm. depth of touch, pedal keys about 18–20 mm. Incidentally it should be stated that we should change to the English, radiating type of pedal board,[15] which encourages a better pedal technique than the straight pedal. I do not refer to the antiquated, impractical measurements, according to which the so-called English pedal is manufactured in Germany, but to the modern Durham specifications.

Couplers

One of a number of "accessories" is the "coupler." A few examples will quickly illustrate its function. When one draws the "manual coupler" II–I, Manual II will automatically play along, when the keys of Manual I are depressed. Correspondingly, Manual II will play along with the pedal, when the "pedal coupler" II–Pedal is drawn; Manual III with Manual II, when III–II is drawn, etc. The manuals are counted upward from the bottom, the lowest being I, the next higher II, etc. It is better, however, to use the names of the divisions for designation, for example "Schwellwerk to Hauptwerk," "Positiv to Pedal," etc. Incidentally, the coupling action functions one way only. If Manual III is coupled to Manual I, both manuals will sound only when the playing is done on Manual I; Manual III alone will sound when the playing is done on it, and Manual I will remain silent. This one-way action is far more practical than two-way coupling would be.

Formerly the Hauptwerk was often coupled permanently to the pedal; this was called a pull-down pedal. Figures 40–42 illustrate some coupling mechanisms.

Fig. 40. Cleat coupler (mechanical)

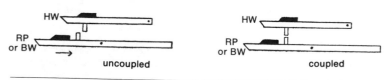

[15] The majority of German organ builders still use straight pedal boards. [Translator]

The Cleat Coupler

When the keyboard of the Rückpositiv is moved back length-wise by approximately 1"−1¼", the cleats fall into registration. When the Hauptwerk is played, the keys of the Rückpositiv are depressed also.

Fig. 41. Fork coupler (mechanical)

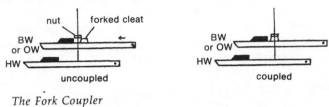

uncoupled　　　　　　　　　coupled

The Fork Coupler

The keys of the Brustwerk have longitudinal incisions; the trackers of the Hauptwerk are threaded through these incisions. When the keyboard of the Brustwerk is pulled out by approximately 1"−1¼", the tracker nut touches the forked cleat. When depressed, the Hauptwerk keys pull down the corresponding Brustwerk keys, but not vice versa.

Fig. 42. Lever-arm coupler in "off" position

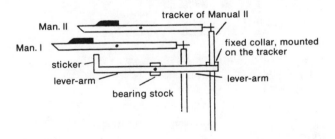

The Lever-Arm Coupler

When the gang of levers are lifted a little, the stickers touch the underside of the keys of Manual I. When Manual I is played, its keys move the stickers; the stickers, in turn, rotate the lever arms, which push up the trackers of Manual II by means of the fixed collars. (See also Fig. 67.)

77

The Ventil Coupler

In tone-channel chests, pedal couplers were often built as ventil couplers. For the lower octaves a second pallet box was attached to the chest of the division to be coupled, containing a separate row of pallets, which were connected with the trackers of the pedal board. This connection could be engaged or disengaged by the coupler draw knobs. The mechanism was usually the same as that described for the lever-arm coupler.

Electric Couplers

Essentially, there are two types of couplers in electric action; they are illustrated in Figures 43 and 44.

Fig. 43. Electric coupler (roller contact system)

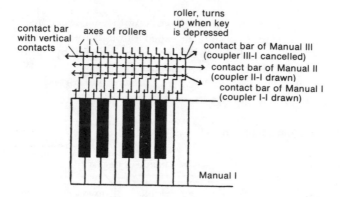

In the "roller contact" (or "eccentric") system a contact bar is moved when the coupler is drawn, whereby the contact pins of Manual I (or of Manuals II or III) are placed in close proximity of the contact roller. When keys are depressed, the roller turns, making contact with the pins of the drawn bar. When all couplers are drawn, contact is made with the pins of all bars upon depression of the keys: Manuals II and III are coupled to Manual I. In Fig. 43, only the contact bars of Manuals I and II are drawn, the contact bar of Manual III is in the "off" position. When the keys are depressed, only the circuits for Manuals I and II are closed: Only Manual II is coupled to I.

In the "contact block" system (see Fig. 44) a spring-blade contact completes the circuits for all leads when a key is depressed.

The positive terminals are connected to a common lead for each manual to be played or coupled; the negative terminals lead to the chest. Drawing or canceling the coupler closes or breaks the circuits.

Fig. 44. Electric coupler (spring-blade contacts, contact block system)

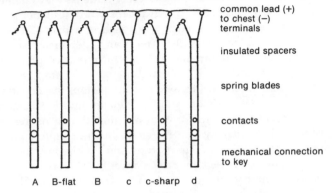

common lead (+)
to chest (−)
terminals

insulated spacers

spring blades

contacts

mechanical connection
to key

A   B-flat   B   c   c-sharp   d

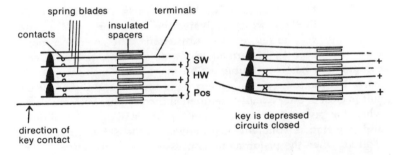

spring blades   terminals

contacts   insulated
                  spacers

SW
HW
Pos

direction of
key contact

key is depressed
circuits closed

There are also "octave couplers," which couple keys whose pitches are one octave higher or lower. Their value is seemingly great, but in reality they are of little worth.

Fixed and Free Combinations (pistons); setter system

In organ playing, it is often necessary to change registration quickly, within a very limited span of time. The "combinations," or "pistons" facilitate such rapid changes of registration. Fixed combinations bring on the same, fixed selection of stops whenever they are engaged. They cannot seriously be considered, as they represent an artistic "straitjacket."

Now and then automatic pedal switches are encountered which change the pedal registration whenever the organist touches Manuals II or III. This device is impractical. A better solution would be a separate toe stud, which the organist could use to bring on fixed, lighter pedal registrations whenever necessary. Free combinations, on the other hand, are of great value, as they enable the organist to select, and set up in advance, stop combinations of his own choice that will come on at the touch of a piston. The best type of free combination is the American setter piston, because it eliminates the need for the countless, diminutive preparation knobs of the older types of free combinations; the stop knobs are visibly affected when, at the touch of the piston, the registration changes to the desired stop combination. In addition to general pistons, individual pistons for each division should be available. A piston in the setter system is set up in the simplest possible manner: One draws the desired stops and—while holding down the setter button—presses the piston once.[16] This at the same time erases the combination previously set up. The "cancel button" (annullateur, Nullknopf) is an essential aid, as it moves to the "off" position all stop knobs that may have been drawn.

The setter system (see Fig. 45) utilizes two circuits: a registration circuit (RC), which activates the lever arms, and a setter circuit (SC) for the setting of combinations. The lever-arm movement is induced by the armature of a double-action magnet; each combination has one double-action magnet for each stop. At the setter button, the registration circuit is broken and the setter circuit is closed. Both circuits are open at the pistons; both are closed when the piston is pressed. When the setter button is held down and a piston is simultaneously engaged, the setter circuit is in motion; when the piston alone is pressed, the registration current is activated. Diodes ensure the desired direction of the current and eliminate the need for expensive, though often undependable circuit-breaker mechanisms.

The double action armature of each magnet (see Fig. 46) moves a contact tongue, which directs the current in one of two possible directions. During the setting cycle the setter current is directed

---

[16] Some builders eliminate the setter button; the piston is held down while the stops are being drawn. [*Translator*]

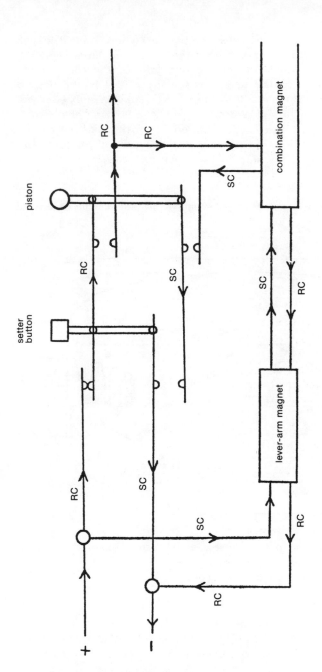

Fig. 45. Circuit diagram (setter system)

81

onto the housing of the lever-arm magnet, whose contact tongue corresponds with the position of the lever arm. From there the setter current enters one of the two coils of the combination magnet, whose contact tongue is thereby placed in the desired position. The stop is set. When the piston is subsequently engaged, the registration current is directed on to the housing of the combination magnet and—depending on the position of the contact tongue—into one or the other of the two coils of the lever-arm magnet, causing the stop to be drawn or canceled, as the case may be.

Fig. 46. Lever-arm magnet and combination magnet of setter piston

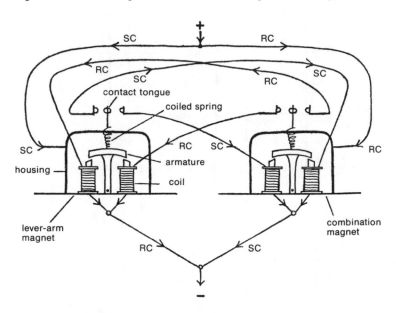

Distribution in the console and functioning of the coupler knobs should conform to that of the stop knobs. Reversible toe studs for couplers are advantageous.

Tremulant

Tremulants effect a more or less intense vibrato in the speech of the pipes by influencing the wind on its way to a given chest. Well-made tremulants, properly but rarely used, can produce very beautiful effects. The functioning of a tremulant is illustrated in Fig. 47. Wind from the trunk inflates the pneumatic, the sticker opens the rising pneumatic's valve, causing the wind to escape:

Fig. 47. A tremulant

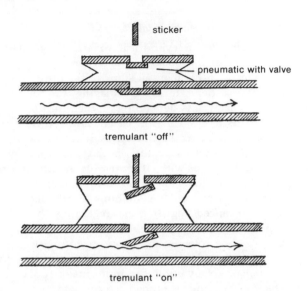

the pneumatic collapses, whereby the valve is closed, allowing the pneumatic to inflate again, and so forth. In a good tremulant, this process is repeated approximately 120 times per minute. The alternate rising and collapsing of the pneumatic with the attendant escape of wind through the valve produces air pressures and vacuums in fast succession which affect the wind heading for the chest; the result is the tonal vibrato. Under no circumstance must a tremulant affect the entire organ, but always only one chest.

Undulating Stops

Tonal effects similar to that produced by tremulants are derived from "undulating stops." A stop equipped with two pipes per key, of which one is tuned slightly sharp, yields a gently beating tone. In 16th-century Italy, an undulating Principal built in this manner was called Voci umane ("human voice"); Silbermann, having become acquainted with this stop through Fritzsche, built it under the name Unda maris; French builders of the 19th century called their undulating Viola da Gamba "Voix céleste" ("celestial voice"). This Voix céleste was soon imitated in Germany.[17]

Rollschweller (Crescendo Pedal) [18]

The *Rollschweller*, a cylindrical roller, is mounted directly above the center of the pedal board. When the organist slowly turns this roller with his foot, all stops of the organ are gradually engaged. If this is done during the playing, the sound increases or decreases dynamically, depending on the direction of the turning motion. This device can still be encountered here and there in new organs despite its worthlessness. It cannot be used for the rendition of good organ literature, because it is unartistic in its basic concept. To begin with, it represents an artistic straitjacket to an even higher degree than the fixed combination, as it consists of an entire series of fixed registrations. Furthermore, there are problems of balanced registrations regarding the relationship between pedal and manuals and between the individual manuals; of appropriate tone color in any given, fixed registration for any given, specific musical texture; of tolerable transitions. All these conditions remain totally unfulfilled in the majority of cases. Lastly, any mechanical crescendo designed according to the concept of the *Rollschweller* cannot realize a regular and even gradation on an organ that exhibits truly characteristic voices. Corrective measures such as the "pedal moderator" and a *Rollschweller* that permits the organist to choose stop combinations constitute a concession to the concept of clean, independent registration, which is ultimately

---

[17] The organist must not attempt with unsolicited zeal to "tune" the undulating stops in his organ; they would, of course, lose their effect. I mention this because it actually happened that an organist tuned "pure" the Voix céleste and Unda maris, only to be utterly surprised at the loss of the beating effect.

[18] In American (and many European) organs, a Crescendo *shoe* rather than a *roller* is used. The description, otherwise, applies to the Crescendo pedal as well as to the *Rollschweller* with the exception of placement within the console: The Crescendo shoe is mounted to the right of the expression shoes, the *Rollschweller* to the left in center. [*Translator*]

the best solution, particularly also for artistic realizations of crescendo and diminuendo, a feature to be discussed later. Incidentally, the contention that the *Rollschweller* is indispensable for the performance of Max Reger's organ works is quite incorrect; the opposite is true. Such an unartistic means as the *Rollschweller* cannot be used for the interpretation of the creations of this greatest German master after Bach. Reger's organ music, like all genuine organ music, requires a well-designed instrument with slider chests, mechanical key action, and electric stop action.

Miscellaneous Accessories

Other accessories include the "Calcant" *(Kalkantenruf)*, which signals to the person in charge of treadling or cocking the bellows; the "Exhaust" *(Windablasser, Evakuant)*, which exhausts the bellows when the organist has finished playing; the starter button for the blower; the "Zimbelstern"; the "Cuckoo's call" *(Kuckucksruf)*; the "Nightingale" *(Nachtigallenruf)* and others. The Zimbelstern sets into rotation a star-shaped disc attached to the central façade pipe; little bells suspended from the corners of this star are caused to tinkle by the rotating motion. The Cuckoo's call excites two pipes (f'' and d'') in regular repetition. The imitation of the nightingale is achieved through a contrivance in which one or more pipes are mounted upside down, their lower, open ends being immersed in a water container. The last-named stops have rarely been built since about 1750.

Duplexing (Transmission)

"Duplexing" makes possible the independent playing of one rank of pipes from two keyboards. It also facilitates use of one rank of pipes on various pitch levels, for example Gedackt 8', Gedackt 4', or Oktavbass 8', Oktavbass 4'. Both stops are independently playable and may belong to the same keyboard. In a certain way, one gains the advantage of an additional stop at reduced cost. In spite of this advantage, duplexing is a dubious practice, not to speak of "unification" (see pp. 118f.) which consists in the indiscriminate exploitation of duplexing. Another method of gaining new stops without new pipes is to feed a stop with wind from two sides at different pressures. This works best with the Subbass 16'; the lower wind pressure yields a Gedacktbass 16' or a Stillbourdon 16' or whatever else the "new stop" might be called; it is not by any means an unalloyed pleasure.

Organ Design

The art of selecting registers and accessories and of distributing them to the various windchests and keyboards of an organ in a sound and practical manner is known as organ design. In the framework of this book, only some of the basic aspects of organ design can be outlined.

Basic Principles of Specification

The two most important rules of specification may be formulated as follows:

1. Rather than assigning the same pitch level to all stops, specify the greatest possible number of pitch levels.
2. Rather than choosing all registers from the same stop family, consider all families and genera.

These rules may give the impression of banal truisms, yet they have often been bypassed. By way of elaboration, let us consider the first rule: Each of the two corpora specified below has one keyboard with six stops.

Corpus A	Corpus B
Spitzflöte 8'	Principal 8 '
Principal 4'	Querflöte 8'
Nasat 2⅔'	Salicional 8'
Blockflöte 2'	Quintade 8'
Mixture	Spitzflöte 8'
Dulzian 16'	Gedackt 8'

Corpus A has six stops of different pitch levels, Corpus B has six stops of identical pitch. Corpus A resembles a specification according to the classical method of design, which offers no financial, but very many artistic advantages. A trial by playing either instrument would leave no doubt as to which organ is the better with regard to beauty and character of sound as well as resources of tone color; Corpus A is infinitely superior to Corpus B.

The second rule can be understood as easily as the first: Limiting the specification of the following small organ to 12 stops, we should strive for representation of all stop families, rather than choose all 12 stops from only one of the three main classifications — Principals, wide-scaled labial ranks and lingual ranks:

Principal Choir	Wide-Scaled Choir	Reed Chorus
Principal 8'	Rohrflöte 8'	Trompete 16'
Octave 4'	Koppelflöte 4'	Dulzian 8'
Rauschpfeife	Nasat 2⅔'	Schalmei 4'
Mixture	Gemshorn 2 '	
Zimbel		

With the given 12-stop maximum it is already possible to design three choruses. With a 6-stop maximum, one could, of course, easily design one single chorus, such as the following wide-scaled choir:

> Querflöte 8'
> Rohrflöte 4'
> Nasat 2⅔'
> Gemshorn 2 '
> Terzflöte 1⅗'
> Sifflöte 1'

However, a chorus composed of several stop families is much to be preferred:

> Rohrflöte 8' (wide-scaled choir)
> Principal 4' (Principal choir)
> Rohrnasat 2⅔' (wide-scaled choir)
> Waldflöte 2' (wide-scaled choir)
> Mixture (Principal choir)
> Trompete 16' (reed chorus)

Thus we have arrived at a specification quite similar to that of Corpus A.

The Question of Dynamics

As stated earlier, the characteristic tonal palette of an organ is contingent upon the beauty, balance, and multiple usefulness of its mutations and reed stops. Mutations such as the Quinte, Terz, Nasat, Sesquialtera, Rauschpfeife, Terzian, Mixture, Scharf, and Zimbel, as well as reeds such as the Trompete, Posaune, Dulzian, Krummhorn, Barpfeife, Zink, and Sordun, must blend well with all other stops. They must not sound so obtrusive as to be unusable in chamber music. If they are built as "fortissimo formants," they become useless for the genuine art of registration.

We established earlier that the Hauptwerk and the large Positiv must be dynamically well balanced, so as to be on a par; only then can the tonal resources of an organ be realized to the fullest. That does not mean, of course, that these two corpora should be composed of identical stops; rather, they should be made up of stops of equal dynamic strength but of different tone color: contrast of color but equality of dynamic level. The registration of preludes and fugues presupposes a quite different sound of the mixture plenum of the Hauptwerk versus that of the Positiv; when coupled, the two plena must produce yet a third new quality of sound. Contrast in dynamic level traditionally is furnished by the small Positiv, the Brustwerk.

As we have seen previously, only the large Positiv is the logical division to be enclosed; such an arrangement is the only basis for a healthy dynamic conception, and only in this way does the organist have at his disposal artistically useful dynamic steps consisting of the three basic "forte" categories — mixture plenum (*les pleins jeux*), reed plenum (*les grands jeux*), and foundation stop ensemble (*les grands fonds*). The dynamic proportions of the individual divisions must be so designed that the Hauptwerk and the Schwellwerk (enclosed division) with open shutters are equal; the small Positiv must rank dynamically a measured step above the closed Schwellwerk in the three aforementioned categories (but still below the Hauptwerk), but for chamber music of solo and ensemble nature, it must be on the same level with the Hauptwerk for the purpose of well-balanced duo and trio registrations. With such a design the organist is furnished the means for chamber music as well as symphonic playing; he has at his disposal simultaneously contrasting and characteristic tone colors as well as flexible dynamics.

More Rules for Specifications

The following rules apply to specific aspects of specification: Each of the three corpora — Hauptwerk, Schwellwerk, and Positiv — should contain the three aforementioned registrational categories — mixture plenum, reed plenum, and foundation stop ensemble; in addition, each must furnish solo possibilities for cantus firmus, duo, and trio registrations as well as accompanimental stops; the Pedal needs, in addition to the simple bass ranks, cantus firmus stops and a mixture for pedal solos. All of this can be achieved with a minimum of 25 stops, providing that correct scaling and voicing prevail; the example below illustrates this. (See also Fig. 67.)

Hauptwerk

Principal 8'	Bourdon 16'	Trompete 8'
Octave 4'	Gedackt 8'	
Mixture IV 2'	Flöte 4'	
	Nachthorn III	
	Farbenzimbel II	

Schwellwerk

Principal 4'	Offenflöte 8'	Dulzian 16'
Scharf VI 1⅓'		Trompete 8'
		Viola da Gamba 8'

Positiv

Principal 2'	Gedackt 8'	Krummhorn 8 '
Zimbel III 1'	Flöte 4'	(French)

Pedal

Offenbass 8 '	Subbass 16'	Posaune 8'
Choralbass 4'		
Rauschpfeife IV 2⅔'		

The qualifying word "French" for the Krummhorn denotes the form of construction with full, cylindrical resonator of 4' length, as built by the old masters of the Netherlands. The mixture plenum of the Hauptwerk consists of the Principal, Octave, and Mixture with or without Bourdon and Gedackt; that of the Schwellwerk consists of the Offenflöte, Principal, and Scharf; that of the Positiv consists of the Gedackt, Flöte, Principal, and Zimbel; the reed plena include in the Hauptwerk Trompete, Gedackt, Octave, and Nachthorn with or without the Bourdon; in the Schwellwerk, the Dulzian, Trompete, Offenflöte, and Principal; and in the Positiv, the Krummhorn, Gedackt, and Flöte. With coupled keyboards, the crescendo unfolds from the Schwellwerk (shutters closed) over the Positiv and the gradually opened Schwellwerk to the Hauptwerk with appropriately balanced pedal registrations.

It will be noticed that our specification assigns considerably more stops to the Hauptwerk than to the other divisions. This is explained by the fact that those Positiv stops which constitute the mixture plenum are also usable for solo purposes, a feature not achievable by the corresponding Hauptwerk stops; thus the Hauptwerk needs additional stops to be used for solo purposes. Hauptwerk and Positiv are the most important divisions for solo registrations, as the two lower keyboards lend themselves best to the difficult technique of trio playing. It is important that the solo stops are distributed on Hauptwerk and Positiv in reasonably equal proportions. For a proper relationship of mixture and reed plena, trumpets and mixtures must be dynamically equivalent. Furthermore, the Krummhorn in combination with the Gedackt and Flöte must yield a good accompanimental level for the Hauptwerk reed plenum; in turn, the Hauptwerk Principal must serve as accompanimental stop for the Krummhorn of the Positiv. The Subbass, Offenbass, and Choralbass of the Pedal should adequately support the mixture and reed plena of the coupled manual divisions; at the same time, however, the Offenbass, alone or in combination with the Subbass, should furnish a good bass level for a trio registration. Incidentally, in this respect the pedal coupler of the unused manual division offers additional possibilities. The Choralbass should serve as a solid cantus firmus voice in trio textures; the Posaune 8' must sustain a cantus firmus against the mixture plena of the coupled manual divisions.

The Schwellwerk is assigned to the top keyboard, the Hauptwerk to the middle keyboard, and the Positiv to the bottom keyboard; this arrangement facilitates the performance of Bach's works, because the organ builders in Bach's Saxony assigned the Oberpositiv to the top keyboard and the Brustwerk to the bottom keyboard. This, incidentally, corresponds to an extent with the contemporary English practice of assigning the Swell to the top, the Great to the middle and the Choir to the bottom keyboard. The voicing of the individual stops must be precisely interrelated: The Gedackt must well sustain any other stop; c'' of the Bourdon and c of the Flöte must correspond to c' of the Gedackt; c''' of the Bourdon must correspond to the c'' of the Gedackt, and so forth; likewise, the c of the Octave must correspond to the c' of the Principal, and so forth. In a similar manner, c' of the Nachthorn (Kornett) must be related to the pipes g'', c''', and e''' of the Gedackt, the C of the Mixture with the pipes c, g, c', g' of the Octave, and so forth.

Regarding the number of stops and pipes, the following distribution is recommended: the total number of stops should be compounded of 45% foundation (labial) stops, 35% labial stops

Plate V

Organ of the Cathedral St. Johannis Evangelistae in's Hertogenbosch,
Netherlands; built successively by Florentius Hocque, Hans Goldfuss,
and Galtus Germersz van Hagerbeer, 1618—34. Brabant design; in fore-
ground below, the Rückpositiv; above it, the Hauptwerk with its two
large bass towers on either side; top center, the Oberwerk. Façade
pipes belong to the Principals of each division. The case has been
preserved.

Lübeck : Ægidienkirche.

Plate VI

Organ of St. Ägidien in Lübeck, Germany; built by Hans Scherer the Younger, of Hamburg, 1624—25. Front center, the Rückpositiv; to either side, the pedal towers; top center, the Hauptwerk divided over two manuals, Hauptwerk proper and surmounted Oberwerk (this physical division is not discernible in this picture). The façade pipes belong to Principals of the Hauptwerk, Rückpositiv, and Pedal.

of pitch levels above 4′, and 20% lingual stops. Half of the total number of stops should belong to the family of Principals.

Scales

The normally used Principal scales are in most cases satisfactory; the scales of open pedal stops and of wide-scaled manual stops, however, are frequently far too narrow. The table on p. 94, which gives circumferences in mm., may serve as a point of reference:

Fig. 48. Scale diagram of various types of stops. Octave ratio of basic scale: 7:11. Circumference at c′=161 mm.

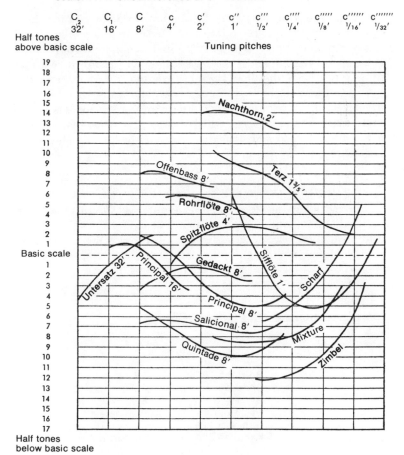

Key	CC	C	c	c'	c''	c'''	c''''	c'''''	c''''''
Pedal open 16'	750	430	250						
Pedal open 8'		600	350	200					
Pedal open 4'			320	190	120				
Manual Rohrflöte 4'			320	200	125	70	40		
Manual Offenflöte 2'				210	135	85	50	30	15

The proportions of scales may best be illustrated by relating them to a basic scale of an octave ratio of 7:11. The diagram in Figure 48 is based on such a basic scale; for c' a pipe circumference of 161 mm. is assumed. The curves of the scales are given according to actual (tuning) pitches rather than keys. For example, c' of the Nachthorn is 14 half-tones above the basic scale, which means it corresponds in width to the B-flat of the basic scale; c' of the Salicional is 7 half-tones below the basic scale, which means it corresponds in width to the g' of the basic scale. The diagram roughly illustrates favorable scale curves for typical stops.

Representative Specifications

In the following listings of representative specifications, the Principal choir appears in the column at left, the solo group including the wide-scaled choir in the center, and the reed chorus in the column at right; stops belonging to the special group are listed a double space below the reed stops in the third column.

CHRISTUSKIRCHE, AACHEN (built in 1937—38)

Hauptwerk

Principal 8' I—II (façade)	Bourdon 16'	Trompete 16'
Octave 4' I—III	Spitzflöte 8'	1. Trompete 8'
Rauschpfeife II—VI	Blockflöte 4'	2. Trompete 8'
Mixture V	Nasat 2⅔'	Trompete 4'
	Gemshorn 2'	
	Klingend Zimbel III	Salicional 8'
		Querflöte 8'

Positiv

Principal 4' I–III	Gedackt 8'	Dulzian 8'
Octave 2' I–IV	Rohrflöte 4'	Barpfeife 8'
Sesquialtera II	Sifflöte 1⅓'	
Scharf III		Quintade 8'
		Flötenschwebung 8'

Schwellwerk

Violprincipal 8'	Quintade 16'	Dulzian 16'
Gross Octave 4' I–III	Stillgedackt 8'	Trompete 8'
Klein Octave 2' I–IV	Metallflöte 4'	Hautbois 8'
Superoctave 1'	Quinte 2⅔'	Vox humana 8'
Mixture V	Terz 1⅗'	Trompete 4'
		Geigenschwebung 8' I–II

Pedal

Principal 16'	Subbass 16'	Kontraposaune 32'
Octave 8'		Posaune 16'
Superoctave 4'		Trompete 8'
Hintersatz VII		Trompete 4'
		Quintade 16'
		Violflöte 8'

An essential feature in this specification is the multiple-ranked Principal choir. The Principal choir is the oldest and most essential tonal element of the organ. Formerly the larger portion of Principal pipes was assigned to the mixtures, which often included 20, 30, 40, or even more ranks. In the specifications quoted above, the principle of assigning several ranks to almost every Principal, Octave, etc., has been carried out to a great extent. Thus the advantage of multiple-ranked chorus sound is found not only in the mixtures but individually in the Principal and in the Octave. The multiple-ranked specification has almost no influence on the dynamic level, but it does affect favorably the nobility of the tone; the sound becomes richer and more lively and gains in extensity. However, the tuning of such stops offers difficulties; therefore it is more correct to specify several independent Principals 8', etc., as is the English custom. The French manner of building a double-ranked Trompete has persisted into the present. 95

Hauptwerk C−a′′′

Principal 8′ (façade)	Holzpommer 16′	Trompete 8′
Octave 4′	Rohrflöte 8′	Trichterregal 8′
Mixture IV 2′	Spitzflöte 4′	
Scharfzimbel IV ½′	Nasat 2⅔′	
	Waldflöte 2′	
	Terz 1⅗′	
	Sifflöte 1′ / ⁸/₉′	
	(wide scale in bass, narrow scale in treble)	

Rückpositiv

Principal 4′ (façade)	Gedackt 8′	Krummhorn 8′
Octave 2′	Rohrflöte 4′	(French)
Scharf III ⅔′	Gross Terz 3⅕′	
	Quintflöte 1⅓′	
	Repetierend Septime ²/₇′	Quintade 8′
	(narrow scale)	

Schwellwerk

Principal 4′	Lieblich Gedackt 8′	Dulzian 16′
Octave 2′	Rohrtraverse 4′	Trompete 8′
Hintersatz V 1′	(overblown)	Rankett 8′
	Rauschzimbel IV ⁴/₇′	
	(narrow scale)	Salicional 8′

Pedal C−f′

Offenbass 8′ (wide scale) (façade)	Untersatz 16′	Posaune 16′
Choralbass 4′	Kammerbass 8′	Trompete 8′
Rauschpfeife IV 2⅔′	Nasat 5⅓′	Kornett 4′
	Nachthorn 2′	

The Gross Terz in the Rückpositiv does not require a 16′ foundation; it is meant for combinations with an 8′ foundation. The segments in the Rauschzimbel are intermittent, beginning with:

C−E	⁴/₇′	²/₅′	⅓′	²/₉′
F−A	⅔′	⁴/₉′	²/₅′	²/₇′
B-flat−d	⁴/₅′	⁴/₇′	⁴/₉′	⅓′

The Mixture breaks at d, e', and f''-sharp; the Scharfzimbel at G-sharp, g, d'-sharp, d'', b''-flat, and f'''; the Hintersatz at B, a, g'-sharp, f'', and f'''; and the Scharf at F, c-sharp, g-sharp, b'-flat, and c'''.

CHURCH OF THE CARTHUSIANS, COLOGNE (built in 1956−60)

Hauptwerk C−a'''

Principal 8'	Rohrflöte 8'	Bass Schalmei 16'
Octave 4'	Kleingedackt 4'	Trompete 8'
Superoctave 2'	Nasat 2⅔'	
Mixture IV 2'	Terz 1⅗'	Viola da Gamba 8'
Zimbel IV ⅔'	Sifflöte 1'	Glockenspiel

Schwellwerk C−a'''

Principal 8'	Stillgedackt 16'	Trompete 8'
Octave 4'	Metallgedackt 8'	Vox humana 8'
Mixture IV 1⅓'	Nachthorn 4'	Schalmei 4'
	Spillfeife 2'	
	Rauschzimbel III ⅓'	

Rückpositiv C−a'''

Principal 4'	Holzgedackt 8'	Krummhorn 8'
Octave 2'	Rohrflöte 4'	(French)
Scharf IV 1'	Waldflöte 2'	
Zimbel II ¼'	Quintflöte 1⅓'	Quintade 8'
	None ⁸/₉'	

Pedal C−g'

Principal 16'	Subbass 16'	Posaune 16'
Octave 8'	Violflöte 8'	Trompete 8'
Choralbass 4'	Nachthorn 2'	Clairon 4'
Rauschpfeife IV 2⅔'		
		Xylophon

EVANGELISCHE KIRCHE, OPLADEN-ALTSTADT (built in 1965)

Hauptwerk C−a'''

Principal 8' (façade)	Barem 16'	Trompete 8'
Octave 4'	Holzgedackt 8'	Rankett 8'

Mixture IV 2′

Metallflöte 4′
Nachthorn III 2²/₃′
Nonencarillon III
   (wide scale in bass,
   narrow scale in treble)

Schwellwerk

Principal 4′
Hintersatz VI 1¹/₃′

Offenflöte 8′

Trichterdulzian 16′
Holzschalmei 8′

Viola da Gamba 8′

Positiv

Principal 2′ (façade)
Scharf III ²/₃′

Bleigedackt 8′
Rohrflöte 4′

Krummhorn 8′
(French)

Pedal C−f′

Offenbass 8′
   (façade, **wide scale**)
Choralbass 4′
Rauschpfeife IV 2²/₃′

Subbass 16′

Posaune 8′

The Nachthorn is composed of 2²/₃′, 2′, 1³/₅′, and the Nonencarillon of 4′, 1³/₅′, ⁸/₉′; they are best mounted on elevated top boards.

EVANGELISCHE KIRCHE, REMSCHEID-SIEPEN (built in 1965)

Hauptwerk C−a‴

Principal 8′ (façade)
Octave 4′
Mixture IV 2′

Holzpommer 16′
Holzgedackt 8′
Metallflöte 2′
Repetierend Sesquialtera III
   (narrow scale)

Trompete 8′

Schwellwerk

Principal 2′
Scharf III ²/₃′

Rohrflöte 8′
Koppelflöte 4′

Krummhorn 8′
(French)

Pedal C−f'

Offenbass 8'	Untersatz 16'	Posaune 8'
(façade, wide scale)		
Choralbass 4'		
Hintersatz III 2²/₃'		

The Mixture breaks at d, f', and g''; the Scharf breaks at c, b, b', and b''-flat. The Sesquialtera has intermittent segments of the following scheme:

C−D-sharp	²/₅'	¹/₄'	¹/₆'
E−G-sharp	¹/₂'	¹/₃'	¹/₅'
A−c-sharp	²/₃'	²/₅'	¹/₄'

In drawing up specifications for small organs, it is best to compile a stop list first before assigning the stops to the single divisions. Even the great masters of the classical period of organ building employed this method. For example, Schnitker's designs of organs with a 4' Principal foundation proceed from a preliminary Hauptwerk stop list, which is then distributed on the two manuals in such a way that one manual contains Rohrflöte 8', Principal 4', Octave 2', and Sesquialtera, and the other Gedackt 8', Rohrflöte 4', Waldflöte 2', Mixture, and Trompete 8'. In the following examples, the Roman numerals in front of the stop names indicate first or second manual.

CLARENBACHKIRCHE, COLOGNE (built in 1952)

Manuals

I Offenflöte 8'	II Gedackt 8'	I Dulzian 8'
I Principal 4'	II Rohrflöte 4'	
II Octave 2'	I Waldflöte 2'	
I Mixture IV	I Sifflöte 1' (narrow scale)	
II Zimbel III	II Hörnlein II	
	2²/₃'+1³/₅' (wide scale)	

Pedal

Offenbass 8'	Subbass 16'	Posaune 8'
(metal, wide scale)		
Choralbass 4'		Nachthorn 2' 99

Manuals

I Principal 4'	I Rohrflöte 8'
II Octave 2'	II Holzgedackt 8'
I Mixture IV	II Rorhflöte 4'
	II Sesquialtera II (narrow scale)

Pedal

Offenbass 8'	Untersatz 16'
(wood, wide scale)	
Choralbass 4'	

The design of Positivs—small one-manual organs without pedal or with a pull-down pedal only—should adhere to the classical concept of a basic core of voices: Gedackt 8', Flöte 4', Principal 2', Zimbel II or III. Treble and bass ranges should be divided at the keys c' and c'-sharp rather than b and c', as the only type of organ literature specifically written for divided keyboard ranges—the Spanish organ music—assumes the former. Also in Spanish style, bass stops in excess of the aforementioned basic core of voices should be built on higher pitch levels than the added treble stops; the imagination of the designer is challenged by many interesting possibilities even in such small designs.

Summary

At the conclusion of this chapter on organ building and design, let us glance at the compendious Fig. 67, which represents a section of an organ with 25 stops, distributed over three manuals and pedal. The top keyboard and the pedal board are lined up perpendicularly; in many organs, the pedal board extends too far out, which affects the posture of the player adversely: In order to reach the upper manuals, he has to stretch his arms forward, tensing the deltoid and trapezius muscles to the detriment of relaxed hand and finger motion. The six couplers employ lever-arm mechanisms; the trackers are replaced by strings, which—steered by guides—connect the keys with the horizontally moving pallets; the pallet grooves are relatively deep. The Positiv is designed as a Rückpositiv, the Pedal resembles the classical placement in two "Hamburg towers" (see also Plate VI) to each side of the Hauptwerk, the Schwellwerk being located behind the latter. Façade ranks are the Holzgedackt 8′ in the Rückpositiv, the Principal 8′ in the Hauptwerk, and the Offenbass 8′ in the Pedal. The Krummhorn 8′ of the Rückpositiv is mitered; the 8′ ranks of the Schwellwerk extend as open pipes all the way to C, because of their usefulness—when coupled to the Pedal—for trio textures involving Hauptwerk, Rückpositiv, and Pedal. The wind supply is regulated by Schwimmers. The pipework corresponds roughly with the specification quoted on p. 89; it serves to show that the largest portion of organ literature from Schlick to the present can be realized with relatively small means.

CHAPTER 2

What the Church Architect Must Know About Organs

Architectural Orientation

The question whether the organ should be placed in the front of the church, in the south or north transept,[19] in the nave, or on the gallery can be answered only in one way: The organ must be placed in the spatially largest of these locations, from where it can fill all parts of the room. This is the first principle of organ placement; the second follows from the acoustical observation that sound travels not only horizontally forward, but sideways and upward as well. Thus we must make provisions for the sound to travel forward, sideways, and upward without obstruction if the instrument is to realize its full potential. These two principles are illustrated in the figures below:

Fig. 49. Poor placement. Only a fraction of the organ sound has unobstructed passage to the nave.

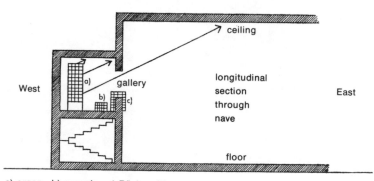

a) organ   b) console   c) Rückpositiv

Both Romanesque and Gothic churches usually offer poor locations for an organ. Nowadays the best choices within such churches seem to be the west galleries, even though they were

---

[19] This discussion is based on the church architectural convention according to which the front of the church (altar) faces east, the back of the church (main portal and façade) faces west. [*Translator*]

originally not conceived as choir or organ galleries, but rather as typical St. Michael's chapels. Therefore, a satisfactory placement can be gained in most of these instances only by extending the gallery forward into the nave and placing the organ on it.

Fig. 50. Good spatial conditions. Here, the organ sound can unfold unhindered.

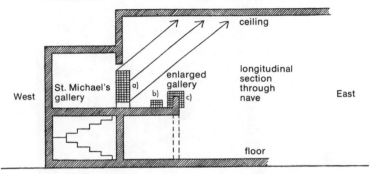

a) organ, b) console, c) Rückpositiv

Fig. 51. Good organ placement

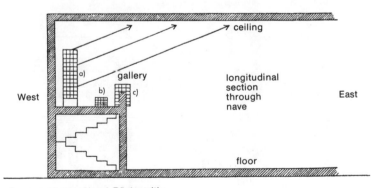

a) organ, b) console, c) Rückpositiv

In Figs. 50 and 51, forward propagation of the sound is illustrated; Figs. 52 and 53 are concerned with sideways propagation.

Great difficulties attended the choice of an auspicious organ location in the Church of St. Liudgerus in Norden, Germany (Ostfriesland). The chancel with the high altar constituted by far the largest single space within the church; the nave proper was even smaller than either the south or the north transepts. Also, the

Fig. 52. Poor organ placement. Only fractions of the sound reach the nave.

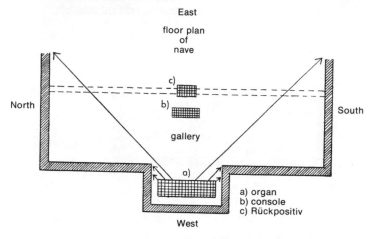

Fig. 53. Good organ placement. Organ sound is permitted to develop to the fullest.

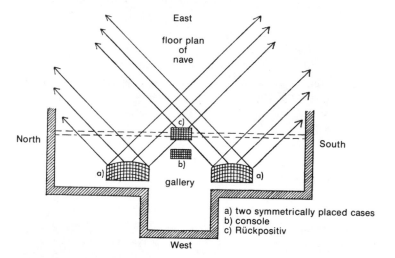

customary placement on the west gallery was out of the question. The organ builder, Arp Schnitker, decided on a spacial disposition as shown in Fig. 54.

Fig. 54. Good organ placement. The organ is located forward in the chancel on a gallery-like structure, from where it commands completely the 4000-seat church.

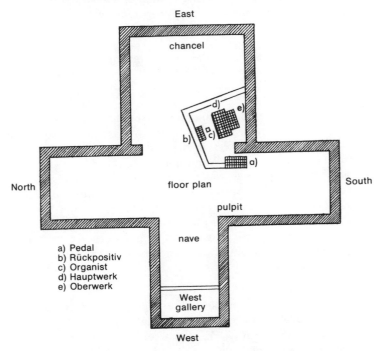

a) Pedal
b) Rückpositiv
c) Organist
d) Hauptwerk
e) Oberwerk

As a matter of principle, then, the sound of the organ must be given the opportunity to unfold in the largest space of the church. Its movement forward, sideways, and upward must not be obstructed.[20]

---

[20] Placement of the organ in the attic is, of course, impossible. (I am not referring to the so-called "Echo organ.") Even through the largest tone openings in the ceiling only a small portion of the sound reaches the interior of the church. Besides, the organ is constantly going out of tune. Contact between the choir and the organist and between the organist and the organ cannot be established. I would not mention this contingency if such mistakes were not made time and time again. Echo organs are, of course, equally undesirable.

Location of Blower

It is essential that the blower collects air that is neither colder nor warmer than the air within the church interior; otherwise the organ will too easily sound impure and out of tune. Furthermore, no dust should be blown into the chest. Thus it is best to have the blower collect air from the church interior. Blower rooms should be affected by the heating system of the church interior.[21] The air duct from the blower to the chest requires openings in the wall of the following approximate dimensions:

14"×18" for small organs
22"×28" for medium-sized organs
32"×40" for large organs

Windows and Doors

Placement of windows and doors should be planned with the proposed organ location in mind. Placement of an organ in front of window surfaces is detrimental to its mechanism as well as to its sound; cold, humidity, heat, and dryness have all too easy access and may cause failures by their adverse effects on wooden and leather parts of the instrument. Furthermore, since the sound of the organ is literally permitted to go "out the windows," it will appear weak as heard from the nave. Doors at the wrong place may cause unnecessary difficulties for the organ builder and will be a nuisance to the organist. (See Figs. 55, 56.)

Space Requirements for an Organ

Usually an organ consists of a Hauptwerk, Positiv, Schwellwerk, and Pedal. The Positiv may be placed as a Brustpositiv directly under the Hauptwerk, or it may be designed as a Rückpositiv; its placement as a Kronpositiv[22] is less advantageous because of the difference in temperatures, which adversely affects the tuning. The Pedal is best arranged in two towers (see pp. 70f., 143, and Plate VI); these towers may be placed to either side of the

---

[21] In American churches equipped with forced air or similar heating systems, it is often necessary to protect the wooden chest mechanism by installing automatic humidifiers (or, in humid climates, dehumidifiers). Also, the installation of an air filter in front of the intake is a simple and inexpensive precaution against dust. [Translator]

[22] The Kronpositiv (crown Positiv) is mounted high, often visually linking the façades of two larger divisions. [Translator]

Fig. 55. Poor placement of windows and door. Although organ and console are placed in the best possible locations, the windows will cause eventual damage to the mechanism, and the door will be a source of irritation to the organist.

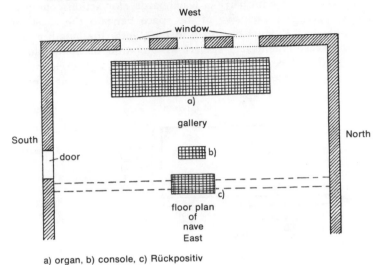

a) organ, b) console, c) Rückpositiv

Fig. 56. Good placement of window and door

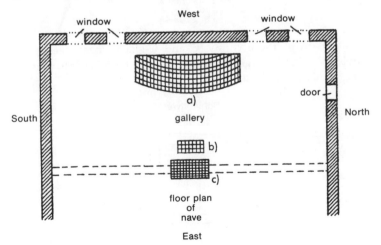

a) organ, b) console, c) Rückpositiv

Hauptwerk, or also forward in line with the Rückpositiv.

The following floor plans indicate schematically the approximate space requirements for the individual divisions. The given measurements are inclusive of walkboards, stop actions, and pipe-chest space, but exclusive of the space beneath the chest. For a façade ½'−1' must be added to the depth; the length and/or depth measurements are subject to alteration of up to plus or minus 10%, depending on the choice of scales. The Hauptwerk may also be arranged in two symmetrical and separately placed

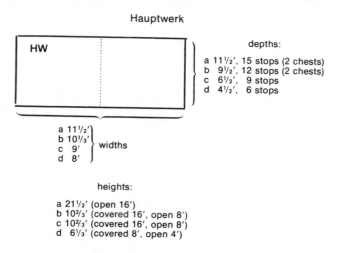

Hauptwerk

HW

depths:

a 11½', 15 stops (2 chests)
b 9½', 12 stops (2 chests)
c 6½', 9 stops
d 4½', 6 stops

a 11½'
b 10⅓'
c 9'
d 8'
widths

heights:

a 21½' (open 16')
b 10⅔' (covered 16', open 8')
c 10⅔' (covered 16', open 8')
d 6⅓' (covered 8', open 4')

chests. Each of these chests (C and C-sharp chest, see pp. 70f.) would be slightly larger than one half of the total floor plan (see dotted line) of the Hauptwerk.

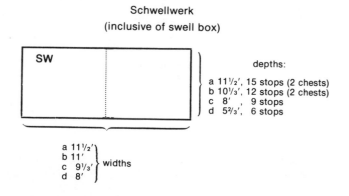

Schwellwerk

(inclusive of swell box)

SW

depths:

a 11½', 15 stops (2 chests)
b 10⅓', 12 stops (2 chests)
c 8' , 9 stops
d 5⅔', 6 stops

a 11½'
b 11'
c 9⅓'
d 8'
widths

Heights of the swell box:

a, b, and c: 11⅓' (covered 16' or open 8')
d: 7'   (covered 8' or open 4')

Pedal

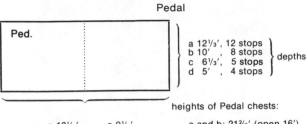

a 12⅓', 12 stops
b 10' , 8 stops
c 6⅓', 5 stops   } depths
d 5' , 4 stops

heights of Pedal chests:

widths { a 13⅓'   c 9⅓'   a and b: 21⅔' (open 16')
         b 12⅓'   d 8⅓'   c and d: 11⅓' (covered 16')

Like the Hauptwerk chest, the Pedal chest may be divided; indeed, especially the Pedal is the logical division for such an arrangement. Because of the great height, separate placement to either side of the organ is particularly suitable; for this purpose, the two chests are usually divided symmetrically.

Positiv

If the Positiv is designed as a Brustwerk or a Rückpositiv, the walkboard is unnecessary.

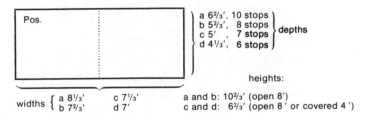

a 6⅔', 10 stops
b 5⅔', 8 stops
c 5' , 7 stops   } depths
d 4⅓', 6 stops

heights:

widths { a 8⅓'   c 7⅓'   a and b: 10⅔' (open 8')
         b 7⅔'   d 7'   c and d: 6⅔' (open 8' or covered 4')

The distance of the chests from the floor must amount to a minimum of 2⅔'. Additional floor space of 5⅓'×5⅓' must be figured for a free-standing, two- or three-manual console, inclusive of pedal board and bench, while a key desk — also inclusive of pedal board and bench — protrudes a mere 3⅔' out of the case.

A Positiv organ of four stops (Gedackt 8', Rohrflöte 4', Principal 2', and Zimbel II 1') with a pull-down pedal is 7⅔' high, 5' wide, and 2⅔' deep; its total depth — inclusive of pedal board

109

Plate VII

Organ in the church of the Franciscans in Vienna, Austria (two manuals,
20 stops); built in 1642 by Johannes Woeckerl, organist of St. Stephan's
Cathedral, Vienna, and organ builder. Bottom center, the console; above
it, the Rückpositiv mounted as a cantilevered Brustwerk. The façade
pipes are Principals of the Hauptwerk and Positiv respectively; the Pedal
division is not visible. The instrument has been preserved.

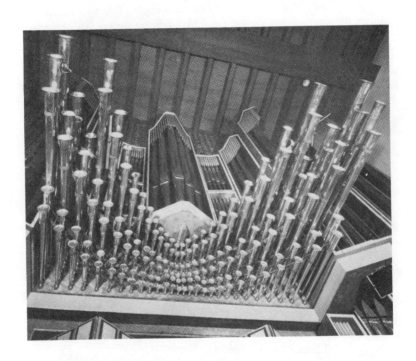

Plate VIII

Organ of the Cathedral in Hildesheim, built in 1960 (four manuals, 52 stops). Top center, the Hauptwerk with its Principal 16' in the façade; below it, a chorus of Spanish Trumpets at 16', 8', and 4' (90% tin, Spanish scale); at the bottom can be seen the top of the Swell with its folding-type shutters. The Pedal is mounted on either side of the Hauptwerk (Principal 16'); the Rückpositiv is not visible.

and bench — is $5^2/_3'$. A smaller Positiv organ without the Zimbel and without pedal is $2^1/_3'$ deep. Total depth is $5^1/_3'$.

It is advisable to place the organ approximately 3′ away from the rear wall, rather than right up against it. Such a placement is not only extraordinarily beneficial to the development of the sound, but it also protects the organ from direct effects of weather conditions.

Organ, Choral Director, and Choir

Frequently the organist is also the choir director. Since the choral literature often calls for organ accompaniment, the organist must play and conduct at the same time, which makes it necessary for him to see his choir and to be seen by them. Notwithstanding this requirement, he ought to be seated directly in front of his instrument. (See Fig. 57.)

Fig. 57. Good placement of organ and console

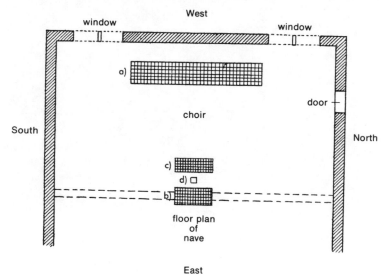

a) organ case   b) Rückpositiv   c) console   d) organist

As to the question of organ placement in relation to the choir, one basic condition must be fulfilled: it should always be behind the choir; it is desirable but not absolutely necessary that a few stops

(Rückpositiv) be mounted in front of the choir. The reasons for such placement are as follows: Accompanimental playing must be clearly audible to the choir if it is to fulfill its function of support; it must be relatively strong in order to be heard by the singing choir. To the listener in the nave, however, the organ accompaniment must not appear to obtrude on the choral singing. These two conditions can only be met by an arrangement which assigns to the choir the part of the gallery directly in front of the organ. Alternate arrangements usually cause the organ to offer ineffectual support for the choir and, concomitantly, to overshadow the same in the ears of the listeners in the nave.

Wherever such an ideal arrangement (see Fig. 57) cannot be realized, at least a small Positiv of two or three stops playable from the console of the main organ, should be placed behind the choir. Such a choir-Positiv will also have to be provided in cases where the organ, even though in back of the choir, has to be mounted in an elevated position.

Fig. 58. Good position of organ, Positiv, organist, and choir

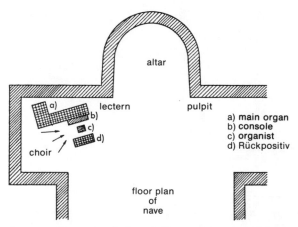

In a medium-sized church [23] enough room for approximately 120 singers and instrumentalists should be provided. Without exception, all performers must have visual communication with the conductor and among themselves. Gerhard Langmaak has solved the problem of relative placement of the main organ, the

---

[23] For European conditions, such a church would seat between 1500 and 3000. [*Translator*]

Positiv, the organist-conductor, and the choir in the form of a chancel installation in the Christuskirche in Wolfsburg, Germany, as illustrated in Figure 58.

Case and Façade

The shape of the façade surface is of decisive importance with regard to sound projection: Convex shapes, curved out, improve the projection of sound; concave façade surfaces, curved in, hinder it. (See Fig. 59.)

The Rückpositiv and Pedal towers in front should be mounted slightly lower than the Hauptwerk; such divisions as are placed behind the Hauptwerk (e. g., Schwellwerk or Pedal) should be mounted slightly higher. Modern heating systems work fast, but

Fig. 59. Good façade shape   Poor façade shape

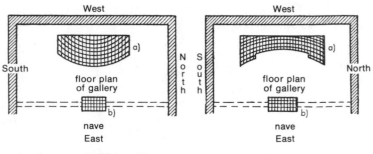

a) **main organ**   b) Rückpositiv

Fig. 60. Good relative position of chests

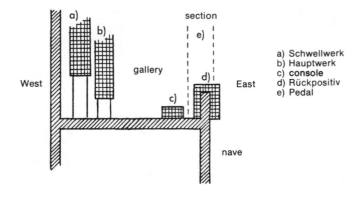

a) Schwellwerk
b) Hauptwerk
c) **console**
d) Rückpositiv
e) Pedal

unevenly, often considerably affecting the tuning; the suggested directives for placement of the chests may ameliorate or correct this condition. (See Fig. 60.)

Special advantages may be gained by placing one or the other chest to run lengthwise from front to back rather than transversely (here, too, the disjunct pipe arrangement is preferable to the chromatically conjunct) or by placing two completely independent divisions on one common chest. In the latter contingency, each division has, of course, its own separate pipes, top boards, sliders, channels, wind chest, and action. The following two examples illustrate some of the numerous possibilities of double chest arrangements:

Double chest	Schwellwerk	Positiv	Schwellwerk	Double chest
Hauptwerk/Pedal	C side		C-sharp side	Pedal/Hauptwerk
C side/C-sharp side				C side/C-sharp side

| Pedal | Schwellwerk | Double chest | Schwellwerk | Pedal |
| C side | C-sharp side | Hauptwerk/Positiv | C side | C-sharp side |

Each division should be placed in a case of 2½' to 4' (maximum) to insure compactness and better projection of sound (the cases for Pedal towers may be slightly deeper); the large pipes should be mounted along both side walls of the cases. Even in instances where one division is mounted behind another, each should be placed in a separate case. The division in back must be mounted slightly higher, and the walkboard must run between the front and the back divisions (see Fig. 60). Each of two adjacent divisions must have its own side walls to guarantee better resonance. Reeds and mixtures should be mounted in front or at the back wall of the case. The walkboard must be mounted behind the back wall, i. e., outside rather than inside the case. The doors in the back wall should be divided into upper and lower halves so that the reed stops will have the benefit of resonant walls even while being tuned. The pipework exposed in the façade should offer a visual sample of the symphony of sound within the cases. Thus it is fitting to mount in the façade large and small, wide-scaled and narrow-scaled, metal, wood, labial, and lingual pipes. (See Schnitker's organ in Norden, Mosengel's in the Cathedral in Königsberg [present-day Kaliningrad], Fritsche's organs in Dresden and Bayreuth, and the Compenius organ in Hilleröd.)

Acoustical Properties

Reverberation is not the only determining factor for good acoustical conditions (2.5 seconds of reverberation are favorable for organ sound); equally important are the surface profiles of walls, ceiling, and pillars, which shape the total sound perception by multiple reflection of the sound waves as they emanate from the source. It is recommended that reverberation conditions be created which are independent of the variable size of congregations or audiences by installing sound-absorbent materials in seat or pew cushions.

CHAPTER 3

What the Pastor and Congregation Should Know in Planning for a New Organ[24]

Basic Considerations

It is better to buy an organ built of the best materials with the best of workmanship and containing beautiful stops than one built of mediocre materials with average workmanship and containing stops of less beautiful tonal qualities. It is better to economize in the total number of stops — if sufficient financial means do not seem to be available — than to economize in quality and artistic beauty of the instrument. Slider chests and tracker action are two items that under no circumstance should be sacrificed to considerations of economy. Do you prefer an instrument of 25 stops that has a genuinely beautiful, solemn tone, is dependable and serviceable and of high quality? Or do you prefer an instrument of 40 stops, that has only mediocre tonal qualities and develops unforeseen mechanical difficulties?[25] The choice is obvious; the inexperienced person knows that a good organ has a richer tone color palette and greater variety of sound than a mediocre instrument with a larger number of stops. This simple insight is in strange contrast with the fact that almost all planning committees are inclined to consider bids purely on the basis of quantity and cost. Usually the primitive procedure of dividing the total cost by the number of stops is adopted as a measure of comparing the relative values of submitted bids.

---

[24] In this chapter I merely mention some points of special importance. Many specifics pertaining to use, maintenance, contracting for and testing of the instrument — and especially evaluation of bids — must go unmentioned. These points are discussed in detail in "Geschäftsanweisung für die Wahrnehmung der Orgelpflege," *Musik und Kirche,* VI, 1934. Compare also pp. 86ff. and 105.

On the American scene, a number of worthwhile publications are available, e. g., William P. Stroud's *Prelude to the Purchase of a Church Organ* (Philadelphia: Fortress Press, 1965). [*Translator*]

[25] Detailed instructions for obtaining contractual guarantees with regard to defect-free workmanship are given in this same "Geschäftsanweisung."

The following considerations will show how absurd such a procedure is: Any five organ stops may bear identical names and yet be of very different qualities. The difference in quality may be traced to the type and durability of building materials; to scaling; to precision workmanship; and, not least, to voicing. The finest stop will sound fair at best if it has been carelessly and hurriedly voiced; conversely, the most diligent voicing will be ineffective, if the material is of mediocre quality. Again, the best material and the most expert voicing avail nothing unless the scales are carefully and conscientiously calculated on the basis of long experience and study. All these considerations concern the pipe work only, which represents a mere one-fourth of the total expenditure of man hours and materials needed for building an organ. The defects, faults, shortcomings, and embarrassments caused by mediocre workmanship and by the use of not quite fault-free materials are so numerous that within a period of 10 years the inferior organ will have cost more than an instrument of the same number of stops but of a high quality and of a higher initial purchase price. The difference in cost between an inferior and a superior instrument accrues at least a 10 percent dividend, in the form of beauty of tone and mechanical dependability.

The best proof is furnished by such venerable instruments as the organs in St. Mary's Cathedral in Freiberg, Saxony; in the Abbey in Ottobeuren, Bavaria; in the Chapel of the Royal Castle in Hilleröd, Denmark, and in St. Sulpice in Paris, France: — outer appearance, action, and beauty of tone in these instruments are so well preserved as to render them as new as they were on the day of their solemn dedication! What has been possible in these cases should be possible in all cases.

The Unit Organ

The practice of unification represents an attempt to gain the greatest possible number of "stops" by deriving them from the smallest possible number of ranks. It is based on the principle of duplexing. Throughout the centuries, organ builders — even masters of the highest reputation such as Compenius and Fritzsche — have been intrigued by the seeming advantages of this principle, only to find out time and time again that it is unworkable. This false principle of duplexing, however, is exploited so irresponsibly in the unit organ that up to 20 or 30 stops, duplexed from two or three basic ranks, are distributed on various pitch levels over the several keyboards. Such an arrangement yields profit to the builder and appeals to the purchaser as inexpensive; but it must be emphatically rejected, because a unit organ always sounds inferior to a normal instrument with genuine stops. Further examination will illustrate this statement:

1. The *organum plenum* of the unit instrument—though it deceptively lists a greater number of stops—sounds considerably fewer pipes than the *organum plenum* of a good instrument of identical cost.

2. The various stops of a unit organ are different by name only; in reality, 78 percent of the pipes of one unified stop serve in another unified stop also. Usually the Pedal of a unified organ has only 12 pipes of its own as against a minimum of 30 in very small organs of a straight specification but more frequently 60 or 90 Pedal pipes.[26] In effect, a unified organ has only two or three stops in the sense in which the term applies to good organs of straight (nonduplexed) design.

3. The bass range of a unified instrument, by dint of circumstance, is too weak in comparison with the middle and treble range; the treble range tends to be too loud ("screaming").

4. The principle of unification eliminates the possibility of artistic voicing, because each single pipe has to serve three to five different functions; obviously a pipe can either be voiced to suit one function only or it will have to be voiced neutrally, that is, without specific character.

5. Unified fifths and thirds, as derived from one or another of the basic ranks are impure. Furthermore, genuine and characteristically organistic terracing of mixtures cannot be approximated even faintly by unification. Yet, just such good and correctly designed mixtures are essential for the festive splendor of an organ, for the measured balance of its tonal characteristics, and for the clarity of its sound.

6. Experimentation in search of systems which would offer the low-cost advantage of unification but at the same time

---

[26] The figures 30, 60, and 90 are based on the German pedal compass C—f'. The corresponding figures for the usual pedal compass in American organs are 32, 64, and 96. [*Translator*]

avoid the disadvantages here listed yielded only the simple recognition of the incompatibility of these two propositions.

7. Calculations with the objective of singling out truly useful registrations from the unified organ proceed from the following premises: Perhaps certain aspects of the registrations of a unified organ might not be wholly impracticable; or perhaps the number of them might be large enough to justify the principle of unification from a financial point of view. However, even though the ever-present difference in quality between the straight and unified organ was not taken into account, these calculations corroborated the fact that the unified instrument consistently offers fewer worthwhile registrations than a good, straight organ of identical cost.

The foregoing discussion has clarified the issues involved. It is unwise to purchase a unified organ. The smallest organ of straight specification is more beautiful and altogether better.

Appropriate Size of an Organ

The organ has to perform certain functions within the worship service for which it must be equipped with various kinds of appropriate stops. If an instrument is to satisfy ideally the requirements imposed on it from this point of view, it should furnish the organist with the tonal resources necessary for:

festive preludes and postludes to
   the service;
introductions to congregational
   singing;
leading congregational singing;
choral accompaniments;
playing during the Offertory, Communion, Wedding, and Baptism.

in various gradations suitable to the character of a service; to the liturgical season; to the size of the congregation; to the size and volume of the choir.

An organ that can successfully perform these five functions is a priori capable of reproducing independent organ literature of any kind. A certain minimum of stops, however, is needed to meet this qualification. Such a minimal specification has been discussed on pp. 88ff. Unfortunately it has become customary to build organs with no more than 20 stops as a matter of course. This is insufficient. Since a three-manual organ of 25 stops (see example on pp. 97ff. and Fig. 67) represents an absolute minimum design capable of rendering the largest portion of classical and contemporary literature in a sufficiently authentic manner, churches that desire a little more than the bare accompaniment of congregational singing should adopt this figure as a minimal standard. The small amounts saved represent a relatively great loss, for a considerable portion of literature becomes inaccessible. On the other hand, small margins of additional cost yield enormous profit in terms of an instrument's versatility; the additional, single stops are far less costly than the single stops comprising the minimal core of a specification, when measured in terms of the greater versatility and usefulness of the instrument. Incidentally, after 10 years of service, the initial cost of an organ will be a matter of interest to no one — provided it is a good instrument.

CHAPTER 4

Maintenance and Care

An organ must be kept in good condition. Then it will be dependable and sound its best. It should not be forgotten that the organist's playing is judged to a large extent by the beautiful or ugly sound of the instrument. Regular care and maintenance not only keep the instrument in good working condition but insure considerable, long-range savings.

On Planning for a New Church Building and Organ

The church architect should provide a good location for the organ: It must not be placed near window surfaces; rather too much than too little space for the organ should be provided — the interior of the instrument has to be spacious for easy accessibility. The church must have adequate provisions for ventilation in order to control the humidity, which is detrimental to an organ in various ways.

In installing the organ, the organ builder must have in mind the instrument's subsequent maintenance and care: The organ interior — as has already been stated — must be spacious and easily accessible, especially the lingual ranks; further, the organist or the organ technician in charge of maintenance must be able to gain access easily and comfortably from the keyboards to the corresponding pallets, and from the stop knobs to the chests.

Nowadays, with electricity obtainable anywhere, the practice of fumbling inside the organ case by candlelight or similar insufficient sources of illumination must not be tolerated. A permanent mode of lighting belongs inside the case of any organ; the switch should be located near the entrance to the case and should control the entire inside lighting. In addition, a drop cord with attachable fixture and a number of hangers inside the case are desirable.

Protection from Dust, Humidity, Excessive Dryness, etc.

Dust is more damaging to an organ than one would imagine. Therefore, it is advisable to keep the interior of the organ clean. Cleanliness as well as easy accessibility facilitate touch-up tuning. An organist will think twice before entering an organ case whose floors, walks, rafters, and boards are covered with thick layers of dust; rather than soiling his clothes and appearing in disarray for a formal musical function, he will forego a quick dash into the case for a necessary touch-up tuning. Likewise even a conscientious and thorough organ technician in charge of maintenance will subconsciously tend to his job with less than his customary thoroughness. Obviously the real burden is borne by those who have to listen to an organ that is dusty and thus out of tune, one that often ciphers or fails mechanically otherwise, and they will also have to pay for an eventual "thorough overhauling."

Dust settles in the windway of the pipes, especially of small pipes, thus impairing the quality of their speech; to a large extent dust is the cause of ciphers and other mechanical failures. Therefore the church should be cleaned only when the windows have been opened. The organ gallery must never be swept; rather it should be damp-mopped, possibly with the aid of moist sand or sawdust. Once every eight years, a conscientious organ technician should thoroughly clean all pipes and vacuum-clean the chests, floors, walks, and structural parts of the case.

Humidity and dryness alike can damage leather and wooden parts of an organ; wind leakage in the forms of ciphers and runs, valve failures, and similar defects are commonly caused by such conditions. Moisture will also result in the rusting of metal parts. Churches with a high humidity content must often be thoroughly aired (on dry, not too cold days) especially after the floors have been washed or damp-mopped. Excessive dryness is often caused by the heating system. Modern, fast acting heaters dry out the air; the logical solution is to install humidifiers that can maintain a relative humidity of no less than 40 percent at a temperature of 68—70 degrees Fahrenheit, a ratio beneficial to the organ (as well as to the congregation). Under direct exposure to sun rays wooden parts of the organ will warp or even crack. Heavy window drapes are the answer to this problem.

The organ must also be protected from the hands of uninformed persons by keeping it locked; this includes securing the console, the motor switch, and all doors (to the blower room, the interior of the case, and the console). It is of particular advantage to have a competent organ technician tune the organ regularly and check it for existing or developing defects. It is wise to negotiate a service contract with the organ builder which covers regular tuning and maintenance. Such contracts enable him to offer financially reasonable conditions, which he will honor conscientiously because of his interest in the continued tonal beauty and mechanical dependability of one of his instruments.

Tips for Touch-Up Tuning and Small Repairs

It is always advisable to keep some of the following spare parts in stock: pallet springs; leather washers for the tracker joints; wire (for joining of trackers); pins, and screws. Furthermore, the following tools should be kept handy: screwdrivers; tuning knives for reed stops; round nose pliers; tuning cones and rods for labial pipes; a mallet for covered wooden pipes; some soft, rather thick paper to steady caps and stoppers of covered pipes; midget precision pliers; a soft dust cloth, and soft and coarse hairbrushes.[27] The small cost of these items should not be shunned. The pipes should positively never be handled with bare hands. Your organ technician will be pleased to help you choose these tools and materials.

The organ's propensity to go out of tune in hot or cold weather is explained by the following circumstances: Essentially, an organ consists of two types of ranks — labial and lingual. In labial pipes air columns vibrate, in lingual pipes, metal reeds. The frequency of vibrations of the air column within a labial pipe is far more drastically affected by heat or cold than that of the metal reed. Two pipes that sound exactly in tune at a temperature of 50 degrees Fahrenheit will differ considerably in pitch at a temperature of 65 degrees; the labial pipes will sound higher than the lingual pipe. At a temperature of 35 degrees, the lingual pipe will sound higher than the labial pipe, which by now has dropped in pitch. Since it is impossible to engage an organ tuner in the wake of every change of weather, the organist must be able to touch up the tuning of his instrument whenever necessary. In such cases the reeds are touched up, although the labial pipes have actually gone out of tune. However, it is easier to adjust the tuning of three lingual stops than it is to adjust the tuning of 15 labial stops. For tuning a reed stop, one draws the Octave 4' (or the Principal 4') along with it. If there is no Octave 4' on the same manual, a coupler must be

---

[27] Most American organ builders equip labial pipes with tuning slides (with the possible exception of façade ranks), thus largely eliminating the need for tuning cones. Felt or leather are also good materials for steadying caps or stoppers. [*Translator*]

employed. The organist should take care not to knock, bend, or crush any pipes on his way to the reed stop which he wants to tune. The custodian or any volunteer should remain at the console to hold down the keys as needed. If the temperature is expected to drop, the reed should be tuned slightly flat and vice versa. The tuning wire *only* should be moved up or down by gentle, lightly repeated taps with the tuning knife. Great caution should be exercised, as the tuning wire's position needs to be altered by mere fractions of millimeters only. Tapping the tuning wire upward lengthens the free end of the reed, thus lowering the pitch, and vice versa. (See Figs. 61, 62.)

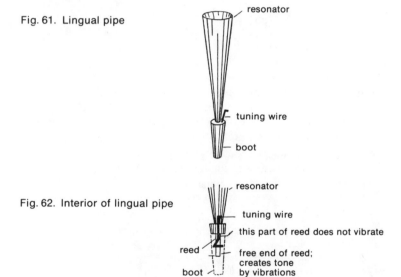

Fig. 61. Lingual pipe

resonator

tuning wire

boot

Fig. 62. Interior of lingual pipe

resonator

tuning wire

this part of reed does not vibrate

reed

free end of reed; creates tone by vibrations

boot

The organist should not attempt to tune the lingual pipe by tampering with the slots in the resonator or by turning the caps: These should be used for regulating the tone color but not for tuning. Beats will be audible as long as the two pipes (the lingual pipe and the corresponding pipe of the Octave 4′) are not exactly in tune. The faster these beats are, the farther the pipes are from matching. With correct tuning technique, the beats grow successively slower and will finally cease altogether. High reed pipes must be tuned with the lightest possible touch, as movements of the tuning wire by as little as $1/30$ of a millimeter are decisive.

Covered pipes now and then go out of tune by slippage of the caps or stoppers. To correct this, take off the cap or stopper and attach a new layer of packing material; then adjust the cap or stopper by gentle taps of the mallet. Care must be taken not to dent the pipe. The more the cap or stopper is lowered, the higher the pitch becomes, and vice versa. Stopped pipes are also to be tuned

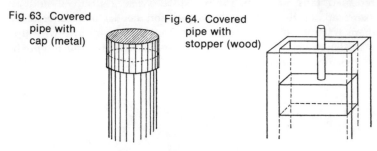

Fig. 63. Covered pipe with cap (metal)

Fig. 64. Covered pipe with stopper (wood)

with the Octave 4'. Open pipes without tuning slots or similar devices are tuned with the tuning cone. Application of the point (coning out) dilates slightly the edge of the top end of the pipe, so that the pitch becomes higher, and vice versa (see Fig. 65).

Fig. 65. Tuning methods for open labial pipes
(not shown: pipes with tuning slides)

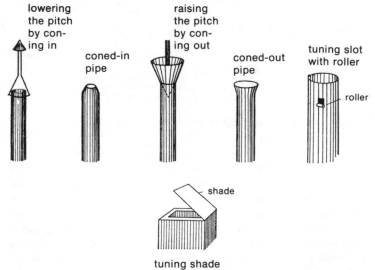

lowering the pitch by con-ing in

coned-in pipe

raising the pitch by con-ing out

coned-out pipe

tuning slot with roller

roller

shade

tuning shade

Other open pipes are tuned by manipulation of either the tuning slide or the metal roll at the bottom of the tuning slot; the tuning rod should be used for the former, pliers for the latter method. Moving the tuning roll down results in raising the pitch, and vice versa. Open wood pipes are tuned by lowering or raising the tuning shade. Before tuning an open pipe, slowly move your hand toward its top; if the beats grow slower, the pitch must be lowered, and vice versa.

If one or another pipe of an organ is out of tune, the organist himself should tune it, but always by using appropriate tools rather than the bare hands, lest the pipes be damaged. Furthermore, the touch of the hands warms the pipe; thus it cannot be tuned correctly, and the organist would be quite disappointed when upon his return to the console he would find the pipes "tuned" in this manner sounding slightly flat, for they would have cooled off again.

In organs with slider chests, not all lingual ranks are tuned with the Octave 4' alone; instead, the following tuning combinations are used:

Trompete 8'	with the Octave 4'				
Trompete 4'	''	''	''	and with the Trompete 8'	
Regal 8'	''	''	''	and with the Gedackt 8'	
Regal 4'	''	''	''	and with the Regal 8'	
Krummhorn 8'	''	''	''		
Dulzian 8'	''	''	''		
Trompete 8' Pedal	''	''	Trompete 8' Manual		
Trompete 4'	''	''	''	8' Pedal	
Trompete 16' Manual	''	''	''	8' Manual	
Posaune 16' Pedal	''	''	''	8' Pedal	
Dulzian 16'	''	Dulzian or Krummhorn 8'			
Rankett 16'	''	Regal 8'			

The 12 lowest pipes are tuned last, in octaves with the pipes of the next higher octave.

When ciphers occur, one should first try repeated tapping of the key; if this is of no avail, the failure may be remedied by one of the following measures:

In slider chests with tracker action: loosen the key-tracker nut; if the cipher persists, the tracker may have become entangled with an adjacent tracker and needs to be bent in line; the pull-down through the pallet box may be jamming and needs cleaning or replacement of its leather sheath; if none of these measures are effective, the pallet box must be opened; some foreign body between the pallet and the chest may have to be removed; the pallet may be slightly dislodged and needs to be repositioned; the pallet spring may have slipped out of position and needs stretching to regain proper resilience; the pallet spring may be broken and must be replaced.

In stop-channel chests: First one must find out if the key ciphers with all stops or with one only. In the first contingency the fault must be sought within the console or in the relay; one must check the key spring; the key chest; the relay valve (for dust particles, stiff valve action, or hardened pneumatic); the key contact (for jamming). In the latter contingency—when the key ciphers in one stop only—the pipe valve in the bottom of the chest must be checked for stiff action, for particles of dust, plaster, or sand; the pneumatic may be inert, frozen, or dried up. All of these faults are quickly traced and easily corrected.

The opposite of a cipher is a dead note. It is traceable to a number of causes: The key-tracker nut may be too loose and must be tightened; the tracker may be unhooked or broken and must be reconnected; valves or pneumatics may be worn out and must be replaced; the pipe may be dusty and must be cleaned with a coarse hairbrush; the position of the pipes in the rack and of the lead tubes must be checked; possibly a stopper may have slid down the inside of a pipe and must be steadied by fastening a layer of new packing material around its edges; the tuning wire may have slipped and must be carefully bent back into a firm position.

Should a pipe be found damaged by insects, it will have to be replaced; the organ builder must be consulted immediately for further measures. In testing for wind leakage, do not check the bellows and chests with an open flame. The fire hazard is too great. Instead, a fine hairbrush, dipped in flower and moved along the bellows seams and chest joints will signal the smallest leakage. After finding the leak, you may best stop it with a piece of sheep skin. Placing a piece of appropriate size on a smooth surface of hard wood or marble, rough side up, scrape the edges clean with a sharp knife or a razor blade, then apply hot glue (the more transparent the glue, the better), and put it in place to stop the leak. A towel, folded four times, dipped in hot water, and wrung out, should be pressed against the glued piece of sheep skin until it adheres without wrinkles. Then the excess glue, water, and spots are wiped off with the towel.

The Electric Blower

Like the pipe work, the electric blower needs the organist's attention. Good insulation of the wires, especially in the vicinity of the starter, must be provided.[28] The motor must be checked for lubrication every six or eight weeks. Motors driven by direct current require intermittent sandpapering of the commutator. Commutator and brushes should not give off sparks; when worn down, the brushes must be replaced. A blower, carefully maintained, remains virtually indestructible.

---

[28] Some of the electro-motors found in European churches are quite dated; starter boxes are unwieldy metal cases with elaborate instructions on them calling for slow motion and the use of various stages of the starter arm, lest fuses be blown, etc. [*Translator*]

CHAPTER 5

Service Playing

The Organ in the Liturgy

From Dunstable or Dufay [29] to Bach and more recent masters we have inherited genuine treasures of service music for the organ; this literature—discounting for the moment the art of improvisation as practiced by gifted organists—ought to be played in the service. In reality, however (that is to say, in the majority of present-day churches), the organ is confined to accompanying congregational singing (which is appropriate) or to accompanying the choir (which is frequently less desirable), to which are added "fitting," usually artlessly extemporized introductions and interludes.

The exalted liturgical—and appropriately artistic—significance of organ playing remains unrealized to a great extent in present-day usage; in many instances the organ is only "tolerated" in the sanctuary. In a few isolated instances the royal instrument rises to its true greatness at least at the end of the service (although by rights this should have been happening during the liturgy), when it sings the praise of the Almighty in an appropriate work, such as a fantasia by Bach or a chorale-fugue by Reger.

By its very origin and character the organ is the obvious musical instrument of the church and of the liturgy. Classical antiquity knew of an "organ," which had pipes, wind chests, a system of bellows, and valves and keys similar in principle to those of our organs. In the most essential aspect, however, the sound, it differed greatly from our instrument. When this ancient type of organ was first introduced into the services of the church, it was given an entirely new dimension consistent with its new and exalted office. Its tonal options were multiplied, greatly enriched, and developed to a state of economical, but at the same time universal, perfection and completeness. Purely instrumental

---

[29] Music of the Gothic period was not scored for specific instruments in every case; rather, it invited a number of appropriate performance possibilities, one of which—and frequently a preferred one—was performance on the organ: It was literature simultaneously useful for organ as well as for choral groups *(Kapellen)*. The organists of that day transcribed the individual parts into an organ score ("tablature") by way of letter notation.

music is a fundamental necessity for the Christian worship service. God's command to "subdue" and to "have dominion over" the earth must be obeyed not only with respect to bodily existence but also in spiritual growth that serves "to the honor of God and for the recreation of the mind."

The church assigned tasks to its liturgical instrument which from their very inception were as important as those fulfilled by the liturgical singers. The first and most important task — the rendition of the prescribed chants — was carried out by assigning certain parts of the vocal music to the organ and leaving the remaining portions to the singers. Organ and singers did not perform together, but in alternation *(alternatim)*. Whereas the singers were positioned near the altar, in the "choir" (chancel), the organ was usually located in the nave (later on the St. Michael's gallery in the west end of the nave). The singers most often performed in unison *(choraliter)*, but organ music developed the art of playing polyphonically *(figuraliter)*.[30] For example, the organ performed the first, third, fifth, seventh, and ninth of the nine *Kyrie* invocations, and the *schola* sang the second, fourth, sixth, and eighth; or the organ played (figuratively speaking, "sang") the odd-numbered verses and the *Amen* of the hymns [31], and the choir sang the even-numbered verses; as a rule, the *Sanctus* was organized as follows:

Sanctus:	organ
Sanctus:	choir
Sanctus Dominus Deus Sabaoth:	organ
Pleni sunt caeli et terra gloria tua;	
Osanna in excelsis:	choir
Benedictus qui venit in nomine Domini;	
Osanna in excelsis:	organ

---

[30] "Thus it was through the organs that our *figuralis musica* was invented," says Michael Praetorius (*Syntagma musicum*, II, 90). Accordingly, the polyphony of the first centuries was organ music, while polyphonic singing came later.

[31] The term "hymn" here applies to a Latin chant of non-Scriptural text, rendered by choir (and organ), but not sung by the congregation. [*Translator*]

The antiphon *Salve Regina* was organized thus:

Prelude (intonation):	organ
Salve:	officiant
Regina . . . :	organ
Vita . . . :	choir
Ad te clamamus . . . :	organ
Ad te suspiramus . . . :	choir
Eia ergo . . . :	organ
Et Jesum . . . :	choir
O clemens:	organ
O pia:	choir
O dulcis . . . :	organ

Throughout the centuries, the organ served the church in such an independent liturgical function.[32] The liturgical function of the organ was especially evident on feast days, particularly in Matins, Lauds, Mass, and Vespers, the ordinary parts of which were treated primarily *alternatim (Te Deum; Benedictus Dominus; Kyrie, Gloria, Sanctus,* and *Agnus; Magnificat).* But the organ also shared in the rendition of some proper parts *(Responsorium; Antiphon* and *Hymn; Introit; Antiphon* and *Hymn)* as well as in the Marian Antiphon at the conclusion of Matins or Vespers, and generally in the German songs.

Words and Music in the Liturgy

An important point must here be discussed. The choral music included words, whereas the cantus firmus and the counterpoints as rendered by the organ lacked the words of the vocal text.[33] The absence of words in the organistic rendition of liturgical portions is no longer universally accepted; today there is a tendency to interpret the rationally intelligible *word* of the texts as essential, and the *melody* as accessory and incidental; this tendency is accompanied by a corresponding value judgment. In this respect, the Middle Ages obviously differed. Apparently people then were favorably disposed both to the Biblical tradition, which both in

---

[32] Details concerning such genuinely liturgical organ playing are officially prescribed in the *Caeremoniale Episcoporum.*

[33] In the Catholic Church the text of an organistically rendered portion must be simultaneously recited according to a specific prescription by Pope Pius X in the *Motu proprio* of Nov. 22, 1903.

the Old and New Testaments does indeed accept textless, purely instrumental music, and to the musical practice of the early church, which in the melismatic Alleluia tropes also permitted liturgical music without a text. Particularly the tropes illustrate that the melody, the musical *Gestalt,* is an integral part of the visual, or rather, audible central point of the *sacrificium laudis;* the text ("Alleluia") serves the apparent function of interpreting the meaning of the music.[34] If the musical *Gestalt* is considered an integral part of the sacrifice of praise, it becomes increasingly clear why the liturgy of the medieval church and even of the following centuries included organistic solo rendition of basically vocal portions.

Other Liturgical Functions of the Organ

To the most important task of the organ—to take over certain portions of liturgical chants—two further assignments were soon added: intonations to the chants and musical accompaniment of certain actions and prayers. Themes and motives for such organ music were either derived from the individual chants or created especially for the particular liturgical context.

Musical accompaniment for liturgical actions always has been a liturgical requirement; the chants to the Introit, the Offertory, and the Communion served this purpose. Music for such liturgical actions as the Processional, the Reception of the Offering, etc., has its deep significance. Prayers and Lessons cease at such junctures within the service; an acoustical vacuum is created, dominated by the unorganized noises of footsteps; meaningful order is replaced by lack of order. Disorder and chaos, however, always represent an inlet for the non-good, the evil. Liturgical form strives to bestow order and harmony to such intervals of acoustical vacuum by consecration through liturgical choral or organ music, just as the liturgical room is marked by visual symbols of the divine will to save.

It would be rewarding to study the entire organ literature from the point of view of specifically intended liturgical usage of individual works. Such a study would find that almost the entire organ literature of the Gothic, Renaissance, and Baroque periods is liturgical in character; this applies not only to the various types of

---

[34] Compare the apostle's injunction, calling for comprehensible interpretation of the liturgical speaking in tongues, a mode of expression which also was not rationally intelligible (1 Cor. 12:10, 30; 14:5, 27, and context).

contrapuntal and fugal chorale and hymn elaborations, variations, and fantasias but also to such forms as the *praeambulum, ricercare, toccata, fantasia, canzona, passacaglia, praeludium, fugue, sonata,* and *concerto.*

Organ Accompaniment

The large organ was assigned the function of accompanying congregational singing rather late — at approximately the middle of the 17th century [35]; for choral accompaniment in the instance of *figuraliter* rather than *choraliter* singing, a Positiv organ was used, which was placed in the chancel, close to the choir. Genuine liturgical organ playing is practiced in but few present-day churches. In some churches new approaches are being tested. A true renewal can take place only in conjunction with a liturgical renewal of the church on the basis of a re-created theology of music.

---

[35] Samuel Scheidt's *Görlitzer Tabulaturbuch,* dating from 1650, may have been intended for congregational accompaniment.

CHAPTER 6

From the History of Organ Building

The "Large" Church Organ

Beside our church organs there are also small house organs called "Positivs." In the Middle Ages, such small organs were about as popular a home instrument as the piano is today. Performances of polyphonic church music in the Middle Ages invariably included a small organ among the orchestral instruments. Choir and orchestra were positioned in the chancel near the altar.

The "large" organs were placed not in the chancel but in the nave or in the west gallery. Their task was to alternate with the choral and orchestral groups in the chancel in performing the liturgical music, that is, verse by verse to take turns with the chancel musicians in presenting the prescribed chants. The large organs were the descendants of the Positivs; they came into vogue only after a prolonged period of gradual transition.

Some Data on the History of Organ Building

The table on pp. 138 and 139 offers a survey of the history of the organ. It shows that the important inventions with respect to organization and implementation of the instrument's tonal potential date back to the 15th and 16th centuries, whereas recent history—the 19th and 20th centuries—has produced technical inventions and devices aimed almost exclusively at simplifying the manipulation of keyboards and of the console.

Meanwhile it developed that some of these recent inventions did not satisfy initial expectations; organs became technically better, but less satisfying in their quality of tone. Therefore contemporary German [36] organ builders are striving to exercise selective judgment in utilizing the mechanical devices originated during the past hundred years and to attain beauty and variety of tone colors again as a primary objective. A number of problems of sound have already been discussed on pp. 50f., 66f., and 71f.; likewise, the art of organ design, which is of inestimable importance for the

---

[36]This is also true of Scandinavian, Swiss, Dutch, French, and a growing number of American organ builders. [*Translator*]

sound of the organ, has been mentioned on pp. 86ff. It is precisely this art which occupies a special place in the history of the organ. Its history and development commands our interest because it yields a wealth of information for the critical evaluation of contemporary problems in organ building. The pyramidal structure (Principal choir, wide-scaled choir) of organ design by way of mutations has been mentioned earlier; it is historically interesting, however, to observe that these mutations came into use only after the admission of the organ to the Christian service. Thus the organ has developed into a special instrument — the church organ. This church organ is an entity not only far superior to, but also essentially different from, the circus and theater instrument of classical antiquity, from which it has descended; the church organ is an instrument of unique qualities; it is, specifically, the musical instrument of the Christian worship service.

Representative Specifications of Classical Organs

(Unless indicated otherwise, the organs listed in
this section are located in Germany. [Translator])

As early as 1400, the large organs boasted a Principal choir of more or less complete design and, in most instances, playable from one single manual and a pedal.

CATHEDRAL, HALBERSTADT
(built by Father Nikolaus, the carpenter, 1361)

Hauptwerk

BB — a; 22 keys; pipework arranged in center; two keyboards — one for the Principal, the other for the Principal and Mixture combined; double chest

Principal 16'
Mixture XXXII — LVI

Pedal

BB — B-flat; 12 keys; flanking towers; two keyboards — one for the Principal, the other for the Principal and Mixture combined; double chest

Principal 32'
Mixture XVI — XXIV

Tuning: minor third higher; source: Praetorius, *Syntagma musicum*, II, p. 98

During the course of the 15th century, the three individual instruments — *grosse Orgel* (great organ), Positiv, and Regal — were combined within one instrument, the result of which was the large organ with several keyboards. Simultaneously, new stops were invented (Zimbel, reeds, and wide-scaled labial ranks).

AUGUSTINIAN MONASTERY, LANGENSALZA
(built by Johannes von Bergen, 1494) [40]

Hauptwerk

three chests and two keyboards

Principal 16' [37]	Zink 8' [39]
Octave 8' [37]	
Mixture [38]	
Zimbel [37]	

Rückpositiv

Zimbel	Gross Flöte 8'
	Klein Flöte 4'

Pedal

Principal 16'
  (duplexed)

Octave 8'
  (duplexed)

Zimbel
  (duplexed)

Here the Principal chorus is already further developed, and the beginnings of an ensemble design of wide-scaled and lingual ranks are evident. The physical arrangement may have been similar to that shown on Plate II. Duplexing of Hauptwerk stops in the Pedal was later practiced particularly in central Germany (Com-

---

[37] Main chest and main keyboard.

[38] Mixture chest, main keyboard.

[39] Small chest *(Brustlade)* and second keyboard.

[40] Source: contract, as reproduced in Hans Joachim Moser, *Paul Hofhaimer*, Stuttgart (1929), p. 92.

Time	Bellows	Windchests	Action	Stops
1300	multiple fold bellows	box chests	mechanical	undivided Principalwerk, later called Blockwerk
1400		double chest		Principal and Hintersatz; Position; Location (Mixture)
1500	*Spanbalg*	slider chest spring chest		Gedackt 8', Octaves; Rauschquinte II, Quinte, Zimbel or Scharf, Salicional 8', Flöte 4', Gemshorn 2', Sifflöte 1', Hornwerk/Nachthorn (multiple-rank Kornett), Klingend Zimbel III, Trompete 8' (Pedal), Krummhorn 8', Rankett, Zink 8' (treble), Quintade 8', Rohrflöte 8' and 4', Nasat 2⅔', Bauerpfeife 1' (Pedal), Subbass 16', Nachthorn 2' (Pedal), Quintflöte 1⅓', Trompete 8' (Manual), Quintade 16', Offenbass 8', Querflöte 8' and 4', Spillflöte, Posaune 16', Dulzian 16' and 8', Kornett 2' (Pedal), Gemshorn 8', Viola da Gamba 8', Tolkaan/Trichterflöte, Fiffaro or Schwebung 8', Choralbass 4', Quintade 4' (Pedal), Trompete 4', Terz 1⅗', Posaune 32', Trompete 16', Trichterregal 8', Bourdon 16', Terzian II, Vox humana 8', Septime, Carillon, Musette
1600				
1700				
1800	box bellows reservoir and feeder bellows	cone-valve chests; membrane chests pouch chests	Barker lever tubular-pneumatic action	
1900	electric blower with Schwimmers in the pallet box	tone-channel chests of modern construction	electro-pneumatic action; modern tracker constructions	various less important stops new partials in independent and compound stops (Ninth, Eleventh, Thirteenth, minor Second, minor Third)

N. B. The old organs were usually tuned a half tone higher *(Chorton)* in Germany than the present-day instruments *(Kammerton;* formerly the *Kammerton* was a half tone lower than the present-day *Kammerton).* On these organs c d e approximated

Accessories	Schwellwerk	Manual Compass	Pedal Compass	Divisions	Time
		c − d′		Manual	1300
		B − a′	B − b-flat	Pedal	
					1400
manual coupler		B − f′′			
				Rück-positiv	1500
Zimbelstern		FGA − g′′ a′′, (sometimes also FFGGAA − g′′ a′′)	FGA − b-flat	Brustwerk	
				Oberwerk	
tremulant	Regal-schwellwerk				
pedal coupler		C D E F G A − c′′′ (short octave)	C D E F G A − d′ (short octave)	Récit	1600
				Echo	
	reed and mixture Schwellwerk (Spain)	CDE − c′′′ or CD − c′′′ (broken octave)	CDE − d′ or CD − d′ (broken octave)	en chamade reeds (Spain) Bombardes or solo (France)	1700
coupler pedals, wind trunk ventil pedals (French pistons)	string Schwellwerk (Germany)	C − f′′′	C − d′		1800
Vorberei-tungsknöpfe (German combinations) setter pistons (American combinations)	fully equipped Swell divisions (France, England, Germany)	C − a′′′	C − f′		1900
		C − c′′′′′	C − g′		

today's c-sharp d-sharp f or d e f-sharp. The problem of pitch in these organs appears further complicated by the circumstance that many instruments sounded the pitch f on the key c, hence the pitches g, a, b-flat, c etc., on the keys d, e, f, g, etc. On such organs, f rather then c would correspond to the present-day pitches c-sharp or d respectively (Schlick tuning).

139

penius, Fritzsche). The practice of placing lingual stops in the Brustwerk became universal because of its easy access (directly above the key desk) for the necessarily frequent tunings.

The early 16th century witnesses the beginnings of the special group and the further development of the wide-scaled and reed choirs.

CATHEDRAL, TRIER

(built by Peter Breissiger von Saffych of Coblenz, 1537—38)

Hauptwerk
FF GG AA−g'' a'', 50 keys

Principal 8'	Rohrflöte 8'	Zink 8'
(façade)	FF−b-flat	b−a''
Octave 4'	Nachthorn VI	
Mixture	b−a''	
Zimbel		

Rück- or Oberpositiv
F A G−g'' a'', 38 keys

Principal 4'	Rohrflöte 4'	Schalmei 4'
Octave 1'	Flöte 2'	
Scharfzimbel		Quintade 8'
		Querflöte 4'

Pedal
F G A−b-flat, 16 keys

Principal 16'	Posaune 8'
(duplexed)	
Octave 8'	
(duplexed)	Flötenbass 2'

Schlick tuning, i. e., a fourth lower than was then customary (F sounds C-sharp); Trommel; source: original contract in the Staatsarchiv, Coblenz

Since the organ was tuned according to the Schlick tuning, and since the Hauptwerk extended to FF, its Principal 8' was a 16' stop in actual sound by virtue of the pipes' length.

The Brabant organ builders of that period exercised special influence on the development of organ building; they introduced new reed and wide-scaled ranks, and by preference built the

140

Trumpets and Krummhorns with full-length resonators; they built spring chests because of their tonal superiority and arranged the Hauptwerk in Principalwerk and Oberwerk with two chests and two keyboards. This all meant improvement of wind supply, better and more practical utilization of available space, a more complete and unhindered tone projection of individual ranks (as compared with the former Brustwerk arrangement), and a greater potential of tone color for the organist. The most important of the Brabant group of organ builders was Hendrik Niehoff, pupil of Hans Franckens of Coblenz and Amsterdam, of Hans Suisse of Cologne, and of Peter Breissiger of Coblenz.

ST. JOHANNIS, LÜNEBURG
(built by Hendrik Niehoff, his son Niclaes, and his partner Jasper Janszoon [son of Hans Suisse] of 's Hertogenbosch, 1551—53)

Hauptwerk
two chests and two keyboards

Prestant 8' [41]	Rohrflöte 8' [42]	Trompete 8' [42]
Prestant 8' [42]	Flöte 4' [42]	Zink 8' [42]
Octave II 4'+2' [41]	Nasat 2²/₃' [42]	
	Gemshorn 2' [42]	
Mixture [41]	Klingend Zimbel III [42]	
Scharf [41]		

Rückpositiv
F G A−g'' a'', 38 keys, bottom manual

Prestant 8'	Rohrflöte 4'	Regal 8'
Octave 4'	Sifflöte 1⅓'	Krummhorn 8'
Mixture		Barpfeife 8'
Scharf		Schalmei 4'
		Quintade 8'

Pedal
F G A−c', 18 keys, pull-down

Trompete 8'

Nachthorn 2'
Bauerflöte 1'

---

[41] Principalwerk chest and keyboard, FF, GG, AA−g'' a'', 50 keys.
[42] Oberwerk chest and keyboard, C D E−g'' a'', 41 keys.

The three Prestants are mounted in the façade; spring chests, tremulants, wind-trunk ventils, couplers. Sources: Praetorius, *Syntagma musicum*, II, 170, and the organ files on St. Johannis in the Stadtarchiv, Lüneburg. Eleven stops have been preserved, as was the beautiful façade, which is similar in basic design to that of the organ in 's Hertogenbosch (see Plate VI). The Prestant of the Principalwerk had pipes of 12' speaking length.

The Hamburg organ builder family of Scherer adopted and expanded this North Brabantine organ type by introducing 16' stops in the Principal choir, the wide-scaled labial choir, and the reed chorus. The octave CC—BB could thus be omitted; the compass extended to C in the bass. The Pedal became an independent division, and the Principalwerk received wide-scaled ranks of its own.

ST. ÄGIDIEN, LÜBECK

(built by Hans Scherer, the Younger, of Hamburg, 1624—25)

Hauptwerk

two chests and two keyboards

Principal 16' [43]	Quintade 16' [43]	Trompete 8' [44]
(façade)	Gedackt 8' [43]	Zink 8' [44]
Principal 8' [44]	Rohrflöte 8' [44]	treble
Octave 8' [43]	Flöte 4' [43]	
Superoctave 4' [43]	Flöte 4' [44]	
Rauschpfeife III [43]	Nasat 2²/₃' [44]	
	Waldflöte 2' [44]	
Mixture VI—X [43]	Klingend Zimbel III	

(probable composition 4' 2²/₃' 2' 1¹/₃' 1' ²/₃')
Scharf IV—VI [43]
(probable composition ¹/₂' ¹/₃' ¹/₄' ¹/₆')

Rückpositiv

bottom manual

Principal 8'	Gedackt 8'	Krummhorn 8'
(façade)	Rohrflöte 4'	Regal 8'
Octave 4'	Sifflöte 1¹/₃'	
Mixture IV—VII		
(2' 1¹/₃' 1' ²/₃')		
Scharf III (¹/₂' ¹/₃' ¹/₄')		Quintade 8'

Pedal

Principal 16'	Untersatz 16'	Posaune 16'
(façade)	Gedackt 8'	Trompete 8'
Octave 8'		Kornett 2'
Rauschpfeife		
		Nachthorn 2'

The beautiful case of the organ is preserved; it is reproduced on Plate VI. Source: Wilhelm Stahl, *Geschichte der Kirchenmusik in Lübeck*, Kassel, 1931.

---

[43] Principalwerk chest and keyboard.
[44] Oberwerk chest and keyboard.

The organ builder families of Compenius and Fritzsche, roughly contemporary with the Brabant masters, were not solely preoccupied with an organically stratified sound structure but also with construction *per se* and with imposing organ cases. For this reason their organs are technically among the most interesting examples from this period. Invariably they specified one large, duplexed chest, of which some stops were playable from the main keyboard (Manual II) as well as from the pedal; other chests were also combined with this keyboard and with the pedal: the *Brustwerk zum Manual* (or simply Brustwerk) was combined with Manual II. Connected with the pedal were: a chest mounted behind the Oberwerk (*Bässe oben in der Orgel*—"basses up in the organ"); the chests in the towers; and the chests in the *Brust zum Pedal* (or simply Brustpedal). Fig. 66 illustrates such an arrangement; in the early Baroque period, this arrangement of wind chests was very popular in central Germany.

Fig. 66. Arrangement of wind chests, characteristic of Compenius and Fritzsche [the sketch reproduces the layout in elevation rather than in plan — — *Translator*]

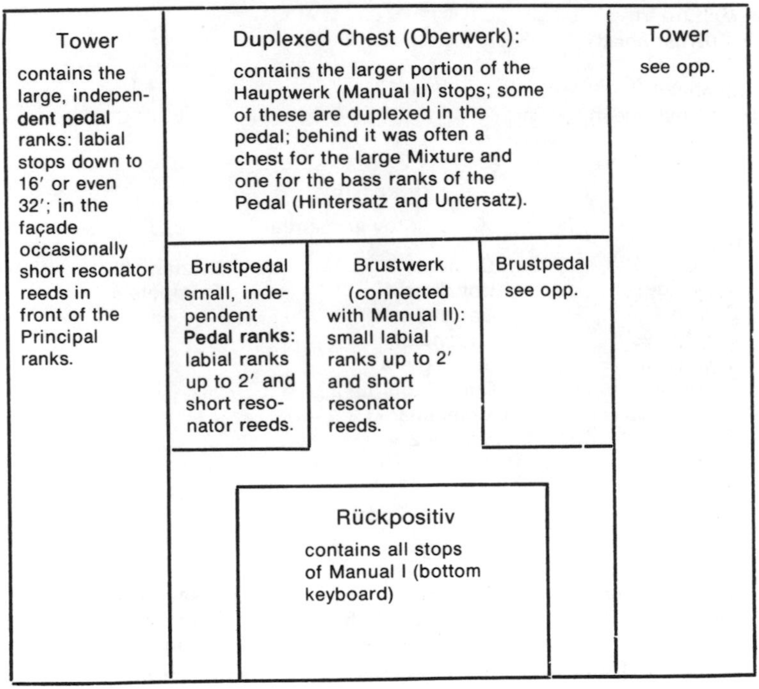

Tower	Duplexed Chest (Oberwerk):		Tower
contains the large, independent pedal ranks: labial stops down to 16′ or even 32′; in the façade occasionally short resonator reeds in front of the Principal ranks.	contains the larger portion of the Hauptwerk (Manual II) stops; some of these are duplexed in the pedal; behind it was often a chest for the large Mixture and one for the bass ranks of the Pedal (Hintersatz and Untersatz).		see opp.
	Brustpedal small, independent **Pedal ranks:** labial ranks up to 2′ and short resonator reeds.	**Brustwerk** (connected with Manual II): small labial ranks up to 2′ and short resonator reeds.	Brustpedal see opp.
	Rückpositiv contains all stops of Manual I (bottom keyboard)		

Since the systematic tonal organization typical of the Brabant and Hamburg organ builders is absent in the specifications of the following organs, we shall distinguish merely between Principal choir stops, other labial ranks, and lingual stops.

CATHEDRAL, MAGDEBURG
(built by Heinrich Compenius, the Younger, of Halle, 1604−05)

Hauptwerk

C−c'''; three chests, upper manual

Principal 16'
  (façade)
Gross Octave 8'
Quinte 5⅓'
Klein Octave 4'
Klein Quinte 2⅔'
Octave 2'
  (Brust chest)
Mixture IX−XVI
  (Mixture chest)
Mixture VI
  (Brust chest)
Zimbel III
Zimbel II
  (Brust chest)

Quintade
  Untersatz 16'
Grobgedackt 8'
Kleingedackt 4'
Nachthorn
  sehr lieblich 4'
Flachflöte 4'
  (Brust chest)
Gedacktnasat 2⅔'

Grob Messingregal 8'
  (Brust chest)
Messingregal
  singend 4'
  (Brust chest)

Rückpositiv

C−c'''; lower manual

Principal 8'
  (façade)
Octave 4'
Quinte 2⅔'
Mixture III
Zimbel II

Quintade 8'
Rohrflöte 4'
Gemshorn 4'
  (conical)
Schwegel 4'
Gedacktquinte 2⅔'
Kleingedackt 2'
Sifflöte 2'

Dulzian 16'
Trompete 8'

Pedal

C−d'; four chests

Gross Principal-
  untersatz 32'
  begins at F;
  (chest in front)

Gedackt
  Unterbass 16'
  (chest in rear)

Posaune 16'
  (Brust chest)
Klein Posaune 8'
  (Brust chest)

Principal 16'	Quintade 16'	Schalmei or
(duplexed)	(duplexed)	Kornett 4'
Octave 8'	Gross Gemshorn 8'	(Brust chest)
(duplexed)	(chest in rear)	Singend Kornett 2'
Zimbel III	Nachthorn 4'	(brass; Brust chest)
(Brust chest)	(Brust chest)	
	Bauerflöte 1'	
	as Rohrflöte;	
	(Brust chest)	

Vogelsang; Trommel; two tremulants; five wind-trunk ventils; Zimbelstern; couplers. Source: Praetorius, *Syntagma musicum*, II, 172, and Adlung, *Musica mechanica*, I, 253. Some single stops of this instrument can today be found in the organ of St. Martini in Crappenstedt; a completely preserved organ by Esaias Compenius can be found in the Chapel of the Royal Castle in Hilleröd, Denmark.

Of equal interest, though a little smaller is the organ in the

STADTKIRCHE, BAYREUTH
(built by Gottfried Fritzsche of Meissen, 1618—19; original design)

Hauptwerk
C D E − d''' or f'''; upper manual; two chests

Principal 8'	Gedackt Subbass	Rankett
(tin; façade)	lieblich 16'	or
Octave 4'	Holz Principal 8'	Sordun 16'
(tin; façade)	(narrow scale,	Posaune 8 '
Quinte 2⅔'	like recorders)	(wood, gilded;
(sharp)	Quintade 8'	2' long; façade)
Superoctave 2'	Nachthorn 4'	Geigenregal 4'
(sharp;	(open, wide scale)	(wood, gilded;
Brust chest)	Gemshorn still or	½' long,
Klein	Kleingedackt 4'	Brust chest; façade)
Quintadez 1⅓' [sic]	(tin; façade;	
Schwiegel 1'	Brust chest)	
(tin; façade;	Spitzflöte lieblich 4'	
Brust chest)	Blockflöte 2'	
Mixture VI	(Brust chest)	
Zimbel II		

Rückpositiv
C D E − d''' or f'''; lower manual

Principal 4'	Gross Koppel or	Rankett or
(tin; façade)	lieblich Flöte 8'	Barpfeife 8'
	Querflöte 4'	Krummhorn 8'
	Klein Quintade 4'	Klein Trompete
	Gemshorn or	(wood; gilded
	gedackt Flötlein 2'	blanks; façade;
		1' long)

Superoctave 2'
(gentle as a
Querpfeife; tin;
façade; 2' long)
Nasatquinte
lieblich 1⅓'
Zimbel I

Pedal

C D E—d'; two chests; pull-down

Grob Principalbass 16'	Gedackt Subbass	Gross
(tin; façade)	lieblich 16'	Posaunebass 16'
	(duplexed)	(façade; 4' long)
	Stark Subbass 16'	Kornettbässlein 2'
	(tin; covered;	(Brust chest)
	façade; 8' long)	

Couplers: Rückpositiv to Hauptwerk, Rückpositiv to Pedal; Vogelsang through entire Pedal; Zimbelstern; Kuckuck; Nachtigall; Hauptwerk tremulant; Rückpositiv tremulant; wind trunk ventils for all chests. Source: Praetorius, *Syntagma musicum*, II, 200. Preserved Fritzsche ranks can be found in the organs of St. Katharinen, Braunschweig, and of St. Marien, Wolfenbüttel.

These two organs have respectively eight and five wind chests and, in addition to the Principal choir and lingual ranks, a group of labial ranks of widely differing construction: covered ranks; narrow-scaled wooden labials, conical ranks, Quintades and others. Of special interest are the exceptionally complete Principal choir of the Magdeburg organ and the façades of the Bayreuth organ, which expose in the Hauptwerk Principal 8', in front of it the Octave 4', and in front of this a reed stop of 2' length with gilded, wooden resonators; in the Rückpositiv Principal 4', Flöte 2' and nonspeaking, ornamental trumpets of 1' length—nonspeaking because of the inaccessibility for tuning purposes of the Rückpositiv façade. The Brustwerk and Pedal façades are executed in a similar manner. The shortcomings of these organs are related to their tonal qualities: to begin with, all the reeds have short resonators; therefore, they sound more or less like Regals and too much alike; secondly, in spite of some interesting individual pipe constructions, the labial group lacks characteristic tone colors, owing particularly to the circumstance that none of the divisions has a complete wide-scaled ensemble. Furthermore, the Principal choirs of the Rückpositivs are too weak by comparison with those

146

of the Hauptwerks. All these weaknesses are aggravated by the tonal dependence of the Pedal.

The tradition of such organ builders as Breissiger, Niehoff, and Scherer was continued by the masters of the Hanseatic cities in northern Germany. These builders extended the bases of the Principal choir, of the wide-scaled labial, and of the lingual ensembles down to 32' pitch levels and enriched the Principal choir with mixtures containing thirds (which had already been universally known in the German-speaking South since the 16th century). Finally, they made the Brustwerk, or Oberwerk, tonally independent by giving it its own Principal choir. Arp Schnitker's tonal designs are similarly as matured and evenly weighted as those of Gottfried Silbermann, Dom Bédos, and Karl Joseph Riepp.

ST. JOHANNIS, MAGDEBURG
(built by Arp Schnitker of Hamburg, 1690 – 94)

Hauptwerk
C – c''', middle manual

Principal 16'	Rohrflöte 16'	Trompete 16'
(C – E covered,	Spitzflöte 8'	Dulzian 8'
beginning at	Quinte 5⅓'	
F; façade)	Rohrflöte 4'	
Octave 8'	Flachflöte 2'	
Octave 4'	Sesquialtera II	
Super-	(narrow scale)	Quintade 16'
octave 2'		
Rausch-		
pfeife III		Gedackt 8'
Mixture VI		(for accompaniment)
Zimbel III		

Oberpositiv
C – c''', upper manual

Principal 8'	Bourdon 16'	Vox humana 8'
(façade)	Rohrflöte 8'	Trichterregal 8'
Octave 4'	Spitzflöte 4'	Schalmei 4'
Scharf V – VII	Waldflöte 2'	
	Quintflöte 1⅓'	Quintade 8'
	Sifflöte 1'	Viola da Gamba 8'
	Sesquialtera II	or Salicional 8'
	(narrow scale)	Grobgedackt sehr
		lieblich 8'
		(for accompaniment)

147

Brustwerk
C−c''', lower manual

Principal 8'	Holzflöte 8'	Dulzian 16'
(façade)	Blockflöte 4'	Trompete 8'
Octave 4'	(wood)	Trompete 4'
Octave 2'	Nasat 2⅔'	
Scharf IV−VI	Gemshorn 2'	
	Terzian II	
	(narrow scale)	
	Klingend Zimbel III	
	(narrow scale)	

Pedal

Principal 16'	Subbass 32'	Posaune 32'
(façade)	(wood)	Posaune 16'
Octave 8'	Untersatz 16'	Dulzian 16'
Octave 4'	Gemshorn 8'	Trompete 8'
Rausch-	Flöte 4'	Trompete 4'
pfeife III		Kornett 2'
Mixture VI−VIII		Nachthorn 2'

Twelve bellows; two tremulants; two Zimbelsterns; Pauken (timpani); wind-trunk ventils; tuning: half tone higher; source: original contract.

Of the other German organ builders around and after 1700 we should mention: Casparini, Engler, Gabler, Herbst, Hildebrandt, König, Riepp, Silbermann, Stumm, and Trost, almost all of whom were in the business as families. Silbermann, an autonomous genius, blended elements of German, Italian, and French organ art.

CATHOLIC COURT CHURCH, DRESDEN
(built by Gottfried Silbermann of Freiberg, Saxony, 1750−54)

Hauptwerk
C D−d''', 50 keys, middle manual

Principal 16'	Bourdon 16'	Trompete 16'
(tin, façade)	(wood and metal)	(tin)
	Rohrflöte 8'	Trompete 8'
Principal 8'	(metal)	(tin)
(tin, façade)	Terz 1⅗'	
	(tin)	

Octave 4'
(tin)
Quinte 2⅔'
(tin)
Octave 2'
(tin)
Zimbel III
Mixture IV

Kornett V
c' – d''', (tin)

Viola da Gamba 8'
as Spitzflöte (tin)
Spitzflöte 4'
(tin)

Oberpositiv
C D – d''', 50 keys, upper manual

Principal 8'
(tin)
Octave 4'
(tin)
Octave 2'
(tin)
Mixture IV

Gedackt 8'
(metal)
Rohrflöte 4'
(metal)
Nasat 2⅔'
(metal)
Terz 1⅗'
(tin)
Flageolet 1'
(tin, cylindrical)
Echokornett V
(tin)

Vox humana 8'

Quintade 16'
(tin)
Quintade 8'
(tin)
Unda maris 8'

Brustwerk
C D – d''', 50 keys, lower manual

Principal 4'
(tin)
Octave 2'
Quinte 1⅓'
Sifflöte 1'
Mixture III

Gedackt 8'
(metal)
Rohrflöte 4'
(metal)
Nasat 2⅔'
(metal)
Terz 1⅗'

Krummhorn 8'

Pedal
C D – d', 26 keys

Principal 16'
(wood)
Octave 8'
(tin)
Octave 4'
(tin)
Mixture VI
(tin)

Untersatz 32'
(wood)

Posaune 16'
(tin)
Trompete 8'
(tin)
Klarine 4'
(tin)

Couplers: Brustwerk to Hauptwerk; Oberpositiv to Hauptwerk; two tremulants; six bellows; the Trompete 16' is listed as Fagott, but in reality is a genuine Trompete; the Viola da Gamba 8' is a true Spitzflöte; the Unda maris ("wave of the sea") is an undulating stop, similar to the Italian Fiffaro. The organ is preserved. Source: Ernst Flade, *Der Orgelbauer Silbermann*, 2d ed. Leipzig, 1953. (This study is available in English translation in a series of six installments in the *Organ Institute Quarterly*, III – IV, 1953 – 54. [*Translator*])

In the following specifications of instruments built by Silesian masters and masters in southern Germany, we shall distinguish — as we did in the case of Compenius and Fritzsche — between the Principal choir, other labial ranks, and the lingual ensemble.

ABBEY CHURCH OF ST. MARY, GRÜSSAU
(built by Michael Engler the Younger, of Breslau, 1732 – 39)

Brustwerk

Principal 8'	Bourdon 16'
Octave 4'	(wood)
Superoctave 2'	Quintade 16'
Mixture VI	Viola da Gamba 16'
Zimbel II	Salicet 8'
	Unda maris 8'
	Flauto major 8'
	Gemshorn 8'
	Nachthorn 4'
	Gemshornquinte 2⅔'

Rückpositiv

Principal 8'	Quintade 8'	Hautbois 8'
Octave 4'	Flûte allemande 8'	
Quinte 2⅔'	Flauto amabile 8'	
Superoctave 2'		
Sedecime 1'		
Mixture III		

Oberwerk

Principal 8'	Rohrflöte 8'	Trompete 8'
Octave 4'	Flûte traversière 8'	Vox humana 8'
Quinte 2⅔'	Flauto minor 4'	
Superoctave 2'		
Quinte 1⅓'		
Sedecime 1'		
Mixture IV		

Pedal

Majorbass 32' (wood)	Subbass 16' (wood)	Posaune 32' (wood)
Principal 16' (tin)	Violon 16' (wood)	Posaune 16' (wood)
Octave 8' (tin)	Salicet 16' (wood)	Trompete 8' (wood)
Superoctave 4' (tin)	Quintade 16' (wood)	
	Flauto 8' (wood)	

Pedalbasses in chamber pitch

Octave 8'	Subbass 16'
	Quintade 16'
	Salicet 16'

Transposition slide for the Rückpositiv (*Chorton*—then standard organ pitch, half tone higher than today; *Kammerton*, or chamber pitch—then standard orchestral pitch, half tone lower than today); couplers: Rückpositiv to Hauptwerk, Oberwerk to Hauptwerk; Calcant; Exhaust; seven bellows. Source: Ludwig Burgemeister, *Der Orgelbau in Schlesien*, Strassburg, 1925. The organ is preserved.

An Italo-Silesian idiosyncrasy are Principals of 1⅓' and 1' pitches. Reed stops are too sparsely, foundation stops too richly, specified. The South German Josef Gabler built in a similar manner. His large organ in the Monastery at Weingarten, Württemberg, is well known; another of his instruments, the Abbey organ in Ochsenhausen, has been restored very satisfactorily.

ABBEY, OCHSENHAUSEN
(built by Josef Gabler of Ochsenhausen, 1728—34 and 1751—52)

Hauptwerk
C—c''', 49 keys, lower manual

Principal 8' (façade)	Bourdon 16' (wood)	Trompete 8'
Quinte 5⅓'	Violoncell 8'	
Octave 4'	Flauto 8'	
Superoctave 2'	(conical,	
Sesquialtera III—IV	C—f-sharp, wood)	

Mixture IV
Kornett III—V

Koppel 8'
  (covered)
Salicional 8'
  (façade)
Viola 8'
  (wood)
Gamba 8'
Hohlflöte 8'
  (open, wood)
Quintade 8'
  (from c up)
Fugara 4'
Flauto traverso 4'
  (C—b' covered)
Rohrflöte 4'
Piffaro II, 4'
  (C—b' = Gedackt 4'
  + Viola 4'
  c''—c''' = Octave 4'
  + Quinte $2\frac{2}{3}'$)

Rückpositiv

C—c''', 49 keys, middle manual

Principal 4'
  (façade)
Kornett III—IV
Mixture III

Koppelflöte 8'
  (covered, C—F-sharp,
  wood)
Quintade 8'
Unda maris
  (C—B Quintade 4'
  c—b Quintade 8'
  c'—c''' Salicional 8')
Flûte douce 4'
  (wood)
Flageolet 2'
  (conical)

Vox humana 8'
Schalmei 4'

Echowerk

C—c''', 49 keys, upper manual

Principal 8'
  (from c up)
Octave 4'
Doublette 2'
  (as Superoctave)
Zimbel III

Dolcian 8'
  (treble c'—c'''
  as Salicional)
Quintade 8'
Rohrflöte 8'
Violoncell 4'
Flauto 4'
  (C—b' covered)

Hautbois 8'

152

Pedal

C—d, 15 keys

Prestant 16'
(façade)
Octave 8'
Quinte 5⅓'
Mixture III

Subbass 16'
(open, wood)
Violon II
(open, wood 16'+
metal 8')

Posaune 16'
(wood)
Trompete 8'
(wood)

Kuckuck; Rückpositiv tremulant; couplers: Hauptwerk to Pedal; Rückpositiv to Hauptwerk; Echowerk to Hauptwerk. Source: Walter Supper and Hermann Meyer, *Barockorgeln in Oberschwaben.* Kassel, 1941.

By comparison, the tonal concepts of the two famous families König (lower Rhine valley, Eifel) and Stumm (upper Rhine valley, Hunsrück) were more classically oriented:

LIEBFRAUENKIRCHE, COBLENZ
(built by Philipp and Heinrich Stumm of Rhaunen-Sulzbach, 1748—51)

Hauptwerk

Principal 8'
(tin)
Octave 4'
Quinte 2⅔'
Superoctave 2'
Terz 1⅗'
Mixture IV

Gedackt 16'
(wood)
Hohlpfeife 8'
(covered)
Flöte 4'
Kornett IV

Trompete 8'
(bass)
Trompete 8'
(treble)
Klarine 4'
(bass)
Vox angelica 2'
(bass)

Quintade 8'
Viola da Gamba 8'
Salicional 4'

Positiv

Principal 4'
(tin)
Quinte 2⅔'
Octave 2'
Mixture III

Hohlpfeife 8'
(wood; bass
covered)
Rohrflöte 4'

Krummhorn 8'
Vox humana 8'

Salicional 8'
(from c' up)
Flauto traverso 8'
(treble)   153

Echowerk

Principal 4'	Bourdon 8'	Krummhorn 8'
(from c up)	Rohrflöte 4'	Vox humana 8'
Octave 2'		
Quinte 1⅓'		Salicional 8'
		(metal)
		Flauto traverso 8'

Pedal

Principal 16'	Subbass 16'	Posaune 16'
(C−E wood,	(wood)	(wood)
F−d tin)		Kornett 2'
Octave 8'		(metal)
(wood)		
Quinte 5⅓'		
(tin)		
Superoctave 4'		
(metal)		

Couplers: Positiv to Hauptwerk; Hauptwerk to Pedal; Positiv tremulant; Echowerk tremulant; four bellows. Source: original contract in the Staatsarchiv, Coblenz.

The tonal concepts of the König family show great similarities with those of the Stumm family, whose most important representative undoubtedly was Heinrich Stumm.

ST. MAXIMILIAN, DÜSSELDORF
(built by Christian Ludwig König of Cologne, 1753−55)

Hauptwerk
C−d''', 51 keys, middle manual

Prestant 8'	Bourdon 16'	Trompete 8'
(tin, façade)	(bass, metal)	(bass)
Octave 4'	Bourdon 16'	Trompete 8'
(metal)	(treble,	(treble)
Superoctave 2'	metal)	
(metal)	Rohrgedackt 8'	Viola da Gamba 8'
Sesquialtera 2⅔'+1⅗'	(metal)	(metal)
(metal)	Quintgedackt 5⅓'	
Mixture IV	(metal)	
(metal)	Kornett III	
	c'−d'''	

Positiv
C−d''', 51 keys, bottom manual

Principal 4'
(tin)
Quinte 2²/₃'
(metal)
Superoctave 2'
(metal)
Zimbel III

Bourdon 8'
(metal)
Flûte douce 4'
(covered, metal)
Quintflöte 1¹/₃'
(metal)

Vox humana 8'
(metal)
Hautbois 8'
(tin, treble)
Klarine 4'
(tin, bass)

Salicional 4'
(metal)
Flauto traverso 8'
(treble, metal)

Echowerk
C−d''', 51 keys, upper manual

Principal 2'
(metal)
Carillon II
(metal)
Zimbel II
(metal)

Grobgedackt 8'
(metal)
Kleingedackt 4'
(metal)

Vox humana 8'
(tin)
Trompete 8'
(tin,
treble)
Vox angelica 1'
(bass, tin)

Pedal
C−g, 20 keys

Prestant 8'
(tin)
Mixture
(metal)

Subbass 16'
(metal)
Rohrflöte 8'
(metal)

Posaune 16'
(tin)
Trompete 8'
(tin)
Klarine 4'
(tin)

Viola da Gamba 8'
(metal)

Positiv tremulant; Echowerk tremulant; Source: *Zeitschrift für Instrumentenbau*, Breslau, Oct. 1, 1928, article by Sauer.

The following specifications are representative of Italian, English, Spanish, and French organ building. Italy's art of organ building by and large preserved its 15th-century traditions; like the Brabant organ builders, the Italians used spring chests:

S. GIUSEPPE, BRESCIA, ITALY
(built by Graziadio Antegnati, 1581)

Manual
CC−a''

Principal 8'
  (tin, façade)
Octave 4'
Octave 2'
Quinte 1⅓'
  (breaks at 2⅔')
Octave 1'
  (breaks at 2')
Quinte ⅔'
  (breaks at 1⅓')
Octave ½'
  (breaks at 1', 2', and 4')
Quinte ⅓'
  (breaks at ⅔',
  1⅓', and 2⅔')
Octave ¼'
  (breaks at ½',
  1', and 2')

Offenflöte 4'
Offenflöte 2'

Fiffaro 8'
  d−a''
  (undulating stop)

Pedal
(pull-down)

Spring chests; tuning: half tone higher; Principal 8' extends down to 16' range, the remaining stops correspond in the bass range. Source: article by Josef Mertin in *Zeitschrift für Instrumentenbau*. The organ is preserved (see Plate IV). In Italian organ building, the individual stops, as a rule, extend only up to c''''' ⅛', at which point they break by octaves.

English organ building also exhibits very simple designs:

CATHEDRAL, EXETER, ENGLAND
(built by John Loosemore, 1665)

Hauptwerk
GG AA−d'''

First Principal 8'
Octave 4'
Quinte 2⅔'
Superoctave 2'
Sesquialtera III
Kornett III
  c'−d'''

Gedackt 8'

Trompete 8'

Second Principal 8'

Rückpositiv

Principal 4'	Gedackt 8'	Dulzian 8'
Octave 2'	Flöte 4'	

Pedal

G A−a, 14 keys

Principal 16'

The two Principals 8' in the Hauptwerk point toward the old 15th-century tradition of dual Principals. Also, G as low key conforms with this tradition. English organ building of that early period apparently had not yet adopted the practice of breaking mixtures, such as the Zimbel; considerably later, Sesquialtera and Kornett—both with Principal scaling—were accepted as full-fledged mixtures that even contained thirds. Incidentally, it is interesting to note that the South German organ building utilized the Kornett in the same manner.

Spanish organ building, on the other hand, was very diversified.

EPISTLE ORGAN, CATHEDRAL, GRANADA, SPAIN
(built by Leonardo Fernández Dávila, 1746)

Hauptwerk

upper manual, C−c' (bass), c'-sharp−c''' (treble), 49 keys

Principal 16'	Gedackt 8'	⌈ Trompete 8'
(façade; chancel)	Flöte 4' within case	{ Oboe (wood) 8' (treble)
Octave 8' (first)	Nasat (III)	⌊ Violine II (treble)
(façade; chancel)	Hoher Nasat III (bass)	
Octave 8' (second)	Kornett VII (treble)	
(façade; nave)		⌠ Trompete 16' (treble)
Quinte 5⅓'		⎪ Trompete 8' (first)
Octave 4' (first)		⎪ Trompete 8' (second)
Octave 4' (second)	en chamade chorus	⎬ Krummhorn 8'
Quinte 2⅔'	(chancel)	⎪ Holzregal 8' (treble)
Superoctave 2'		⎪ Trompete 5⅓' (treble)
Quinte 1⅓'		⎪ Trompete 4' (bass)
Mixture IV		⌡ Trompete 2' (bass)
Scharf III		
Zimbel III		Querflöte II 8' (treble) 157

Rückpositiv
bottom manual, C−c' (bass), c'-sharp−c''' (treble), 49 keys

Principal 4'	Gedackt 8'	Trompete 8'
(façade)	Kornett V (treble)	(within case; half-
Quinte 2⅔'	Hoher Nasat (bass)	length resonators)
Octave 2'		
Quinte 1⅓'	façade {	Trompete 8' (treble)
Sesquialtera III (treble)		Trompete 4' (bass)
Scharf III		
Zimbel III		

Schwellwerk
playable from lower manual

Principal 2'	Gedackt 4'	Trompetenregal 8'
Scharf III	Kornett V	Trompete 8' (treble)
		Trompete 4' (bass)

Pedal
C−B, 12 keys

Kontrabass 16' (wood)

Manual clutch: Rückpositiv to lower manual, or Schwellwerk to bottom manual (by knee lever); expression shoe for Schwellwerk. Source: James Wyly, *The Pre-Romantic Spanish Organ*, Kansas City, Mo., 1964. The organ is preserved.

The consequent organization in Principal choir, wide-scaled choir, and lingual chorus is to be credited to the influence of Brabant masters, working in Spain, particularly of the Brebos family of Antwerp, working in Madrid. Typically Spanish are the reed choruses added to the Hauptwerk and Positiv as façade ranks (see also Plate III), and the Schwellwerk, which later was to be adopted and logically further developed by Aristide Cavaillé-Coll.

Also related to the Brabant type of organs are the instruments dating from the period of classical French organ building. Although narrow-scaled ranks and stops belonging to the special group were ascetically avoided, and although a division of the Hauptwerk into Principalwerk and Oberwerk is absent, we find beautiful and stylistically pure Principal choirs, wide-scaled labial choirs, and reed choruses. The Récit and Echo division take the place of the Oberwerk and Brustwerk respectively. During the 18th century the Bombard keyboard was added. Precious building materials were used: oak for wood stops; tin not only for Prestant ranks but also for stops mounted within the case. The Pedal compass was extraordinarily large. If the organ type of the Hanseatic cities bespeaks a wealthy bourgeoisie, then the Parisian type is aristocratic by virtue of its solidity and noble restraint.

ST. LOUIS DES INVALIDES, PARIS, FRANCE
(built by Alexandre Thierry of Paris, 1679)

Hauptwerk

C D−c''', 48 keys, second manual from bottom

Principal 16'
  (tin; façade)
Octave 8'
  (tin)
Octave 4'
  (tin)
Superoctave 2'
  (tin)
Mixture V
  (tin; breaks
  by octaves)
Zimbel IV
  (breaks by fifths
  [and fourths])

Bourdon 16'
  (C−b oak;
  c'−c''' metal)
Gedackt 8'
  (C−B oak;
  remainder metal)
Flöte 4'
  (metal;
  C−b covered;
  remainder as Rohrflöte;
  tin)
Gross Terz 3^1/$_5$'
  (metal; covered)
Nasat 2^2/$_3$'
  (metal; conical)
Gemshorn 2'
  (metal; open)
Terz 1^3/$_5$'
  (metal; open)
Sifflöte 1'
  (tin)
Gross Kornett V
  (metal; treble)

Trompete 8'
  (tin)
Vox humana 8'
  (tin)
Klarine 4'

Rückpositiv

C D−c''', 48 keys, bottom manual

Principal 4'
  (tin; façade)
Octave 2'
  (tin)
Mixture III
  (breaks by octaves)
Zimbel II
  (breaks by fifths
  and fourths)

Gedackt 8'
  (C−B oak;
  remainder metal)
Flöte 4'
  (metal; covered)
Nasat 2^2/$_3$'
Terz 1^3/$_5$'
Quintflöte 1^1/$_3$'

Krummhorn 8'
  (tin)

159

Récit
c'−c''', 25 keys

Kornett V (metal; treble)		Trompete 8' (tin)

Echo
c−c''', 37 keys

Zimbel III (breaks by fifths and fourths)	Gedackt 8' (metal) Flöte 4' (metal) Quinte 2²/₃' (metal) Gemshorn 2' (metal) Terz 1³/₅' (metal)	Krummhorn 8' (tin)

Pedal
A₁ C D−f', 30 keys

Weitoctave 8' (oak)		Trompete 8' (tin)

Heavy tremulant; light tremulant; five bellows; the examiners of the organ included among others Nicolas le Bègue and Robert Clicquot. The tuning of the old French organs as compared with today's was one-half tone lower. The extension of the Pedal down to AA, GG or FF was called *ravalement*. See Bach's Fantasia in G Major with BB.

The Echo division of this organ might have served the young Bach as an example for his suggested specification of the Brustwerk in his Mühlhausen organ; incidentally, Jean de Joyeuse designed along the same lines.

The Nineteenth Century and the Present

The 19th century for the most part witnessed mere technical inventions, while tonal aspects were not further developed to the same degree; indeed, they were neglected. Unfortunately German organ building did not pursue the tradition of Scherer, Schnitker, and Silbermann but adopted the concepts of design as practiced by Gabler and Engler. Builders no longer designed instruments according to choruses but favored increasing the number of founda-

160

tion stops. This, however, makes an organ tonally uninteresting. Rückpositiv and Pedal towers, two features which are of great advantage with respect to development and projection of sound, were gradually discontinued. Slider and spring chests, without which beauty, tonal presence, and blend are impossible, were displaced by cheap cone-valve, membrane, and pouch chests. Finally, the *Rollschweller* (Crescendo pedal) was introduced, which made many an organist forget the art of registration. The organ became dynamically oriented, and its classical, splendid wealth of tone colors was lost.

Around the turn of the century, Albert Schweitzer and Emile Rupp emphatically pointed out the significance of slider chests, tracker action, mixtures, mutations, and reed stops. In 1922 the historic and highly significant construction of an organ according to specifications by Michael Praetorius took place in Freiburg, Germany (as a collaboration of Wilibald Gurlitt and Oscar Walcker; see Bibliography: "Reports of Musical Congresses"). At the same time the significance of the Silbermann organ in the Cathedral in Freiburg (Ernst Flade; see Bibliography: "History of the Art of the Organ"), and of the Scherer-Fritzsche-Schnitker organ in St. Jakobi in Hamburg (Hans Henny Jahnn; see Bibliography: "Organ Stops") was recognized. Organ stops, scaling, the art of registration and design in the Gothic, Renaissance, and Baroque periods were described in foundational studies (Christhard Mahrenholz, Hans Klotz; see Bibliography: "Organ Playing and registration"; "Organ Stops"; "Organ Building and Design"). Since then the art of the organ has developed with considerable success toward the goal of regaining a broad, uniform, and colorful concept of building and design.

Surviving Historical Organs

A considerable number of historically important instruments have been preserved, particularly in the Netherlands. In the following selected list, the number of manuals is indicated by Roman numerals, the number of stops by Arabic figures.

Organs with Spring Chests

Instruments with spring chests, which are noted for their beneficial effect on tone quality but which are seldom found, still exist in the following places (see pp. 23 f. for a listing of contemporary organs with spring chests):

Amsterdam (Netherlands): Nieuwe Kerk. Builders: H. W. Schonat of Kitzingen (1650–55) and Jacob Galtusz van Hagerbeer of Haarlem (1668–70); III, 49.

Bologna (Italy): S. Martino. Builder: Giovanni Cipri (1556); I, 11.

Bologna: S. Petronio, first organ. Builder: Lorenzo di Giacomo of Prato (1470–74); 19.

Bologna: S. Petronio, second organ (1596); I.

Borgentreich (Germany): St. Johannis (originally built for the Augustinian Chorherrenstift Dalheim-Sintfeld). Builder: probably Johann Patroclus Möller of Lippstadt (ca. 1732); six double spring chests (the Brustwerk is mounted on a slider chest): III, 45.

Brescia (Italy): S. Giuseppe. Builder: Graziadio Antegnati of Brescia (1581); I, 12. (See Plate IV and specification on p. 156.)

Corvey (near Höxter, Germany): Castle Church. Builder: Andreas Schneider of Höxter (1681); four double spring chests in the Pedal; II, 32.

Florence (Italy): SS. Trinità. Builder: Onofrio Zeffirini di Serafino of Cortona (1571–72); I, 7.

Langwarden (near Nordenham in Oldenburg, Germany): St. Laurentius. Builder: probably Harmen Kröger of Oldenburg (1650–51); II, 21 (three chests).

Lemgo (Germany): St. Marien. Builders: Jorrien Slegel II of Zwolle and Osnabrück (1587), later Hans Scherer; three double spring chests in the Pedal; III.

Mariendrebber (near Diepholz, Germany): Builder: Harmen Kröger (1659); one chest.

Middelburg (Netherlands): Koorkerk (originally built for St. Nikolai, Utrecht). Builders: Peter Gerritsz (Blockwerk, 1479–80); Cornelius Gerritsz (Oberwerk, spring chests, 1547); Bernt uten Eng (Rückpositiv, slider chests, 1579–80); Dirk Petersz de Zwart and Jacob Jansz du Lin (Pedal trumpet, 1601); III, 17.

Salzgitter-Ringelheim (Germany): former Church of the Benedictines, 18th century; two double spring chests in the Pedal; II, 28.

Stade (Germany): SS. Cosmae et Damiani. Builder: Berendt Huess of Glückstadt (1669–73); double spring chest in the Hauptwerk; III, 42.

More than two dozen organs with spring chests of Italian origin and construction (with perpendicularly mounted pallets) can be found in the Swiss cantons Ticino and Southern Grisons; for example in Morcote, Ticino (built around 1600); in Brusio (near Poschiavo), Grisons (built in the middle of the 18th century); in Genesterio, Ticino (18th century); in Solduno, Ticino (built in 1795); in Loco, Ticino (built in 1837); in Losone, Ticino (built in 1856); and in Soazza, Ticino (built in 1894).

Organs with Slider Chests

France

Maursmünster (or Marmoutier, Alsace): Benedictine Abbey. Builders: Andreas Silbermann (1708–10), II, 21; Johann Andreas Silbermann (1745–46); III, 27.

Poitiers: Cathedral. Builder: François Henri Clicquot (1787–90); IV, 43.

St. Maximin (Var): former Church of the Dominicans. Builder: Jean-Esprit Isnard of Tarascon (1772–73); IV, 43.

Netherlands

Alkmaar: Grote of St. Laurenskerk, chancel organ. Builder: Hans Franckens of Coblenz and Amsterdam (1511); I, 7.

Alkmaar: Grote of St. Laurenskerk, large organ. Builders: Germer Galtusz van Hagerbeer (1639–45), II, 39; Frans Caspar Schnitker of Zwolle (1723–26); III, 56.

Arnhem: Grote of St. Eusebiuskerk (originally built for the Hersteld Evangelisch Lutherse Kerk aan de Kloveniersburgwal, Amsterdam). Builder: Johann Stephan Strumphler of Lippstadt and Amsterdam (1794–96); III, 50.

Boxtel: St. Petruskerk. Builder: Franciscus Cornelis Smits of Reek (1841–42); III, 36.

Gouda: Grote of St. Janskerk. Builder: Jean François Moreau of Rotterdam (1732–36); III, 53.

's Gravenhage: Lutherse Kerk. Builder: Johann Hendrik Hartmann Bätz of Utrecht (1762; pupil of Christian Müller).

Haarlem: St. Bavo, large organ. Builder: Christian Müller (1735 to 1738); III, 60.

Helmond: St. Lambertus (originally built for the Abbey in Averbode). Builders: Guillaume Robustel of Liège (1771–73); F. C. Smits of Reek, Brustwerk (replacing the original Récit and Écho) and Pedal, 1862.

Kampen: Boven of St. Nikolaaskerk. Builders: Hans Franckens of Coblenz and Hendrik Niehoff of Amsterdam (1524); Jan Slegel III (1671−76); Albertus Anthonys Hinsz (1742); Frans Caspar Schnitker the Younger (1789).

Leiden: Marekerk. Builders: 16th and 17th centuries, unknown; Rudolph Garrels (1773), pupil of Arp Schnitker.

Maastricht: Liebfrauenkirche, large organ. Builder: Andries Severijn (1652); III, 32.

Maastricht: Waalse Kerk, small organ. Builder: Thomas Weidtmann of Ratingen (1743); I, 10.

Moordrecht (near Gouda): Hervormde Kerk (originally built for Église Wallonne). Builder: Louis de la Haye (1772−73).

Uithuizen: Hervormde Kerk. Builder: Arp Schnitker (1699−1701); II, 28.

Utrecht: University (originally built for Lutherse Kerk, Deventer). Builder: Albertus Anthonys Hinsz (1738); Rückpositiv and Pedal (1962).

Zutphen: Grote of St. Walburgkerk. Builder: Hans Henrich Baader of Unna (1638−43).

Zwolle: Grote of St. Michielskerk. Builders: Arp Schnitker and sons Frans Caspar and Hans Jürgen (1718−21); IV, 64.

Austria

Innsbruck: Hofkirche. Builders: Jörg Ebert of Ravensburg (1556 to 1561); Daniel Herz (1655); II, 16.

Klosterneuburg: Stiftskirche. Builder: Johann Georg Freundt of Passau (1636−42); III, 35.

Vienna: Church of the Franciscans. Builder: Johannes Woeckerl of Vienna (1642); II, 20 (see Plate VII).

Switzerland

Arlesheim: Cathedral. Builder: Johann Andreas Silbermann of Strassburg (1761); III, 32.

Fischingen: Klosterkirche; II, 33.

Muri: Klosterkirche, two chancel organs. Builder: Victor Ferdinand Bossart of Baar (1743−44); Epistle organ: I, 16; Gospel organ: I, 8.

Rheinau: Klosterkirche. Builder: Christoph Leu of Augsburg (1713−15).

Sitzberg. Builder: Friedrich Schmahl (1741); I, 16.

St. Urban: Former Klosterkirche. Builder: Joseph Bossart of Baar (between 1716 and 1721); III, 39.

St. Ursanne: Builder: Jacques Besançon (1776); II, 26.

Sitten (or Sion): St. Valeria. Built in the 14th century; rebuilt by Matthias Carlen (1718); I, 8.

Solothurn: Church of the Jesuits. Builder: Franz Joseph Otter of Ädermannsdorf (1791−94); II, 22.

Stans: Pfarrkirche, chancel organ. Builder: Nikolaus Schönenbühl of Alpnach (1646); I, 8.

Spain and Portugal

Granada: Cathedral, Epistle organ. Builder: Leonardo Fernández Dávila (1746); II, 43 (see specification on p. 157).

Lisbon: São Vincente (ca. 1780).

Madrid: Chapel of the Palacio Nacional. Builder: Jorge Bosch Bernat-Veri of Mallorca (1778); III, 45.

Mafra (40 km. north of Lisbon): former Monastery Church, six one manual organs, the sixth unfinished. Builders: J. A. Peres Fontanes and A. X. Maçhado (1806−07).

Málaga: Cathedral, Epistle organ and Gospel organ of identical size and design. Builder: Julián de la Ordén (1781−82); III, 61.

Salamanca: New Cathedral, Gospel organ. Builder: Pedro Liborna de Echeverría (1744); II, 31.

Toledo: Cathedral, Gospel organ. Builder: Pedro Liborna de Echeverría (1755−58); II, 35.

Germany

Brandenburg: Cathedral. Builder: Joachim Wagner of Berlin (1725); II, 33.

Büren (Westphalia): Pfarrkirche (originally built for the Augustinian Chorherrenstift, Böddeken). Builder: Johann Patroclus Möller (1744); III, 43.

Cappel (near Wursten): Evangelische Pfarrkirche (originally built for the St. Johanniskloster, Hamburg). Builder: Arp Schnitker (1679−80; contains many pipes of 16th century Brabant origin); II, 30.

Freiberg (Saxony): Cathedral of St. Marien. Builder: Gottfried Silbermann (1711−14); II, 44 (see Plate XI).

Fürstenfeldbruck: Church of the Cistercians. Builder: Johann Fux of Donauwörth (1734); II, 25.

Grasberg (Osterholz county): originally built for Hamburg. Builder: Arp Schnitker.

Grüssau: Abbey Church. Builder: Michael Engler, the Younger, of Breslau (1732–39); III, 53 (see specification on p. 150).

Hamburg: St. Jacobi. Builders: Harmen Stüven and Jakob Iversand (1512–16); Dirck Hoyer of Hamburg (1569–70 and 1576–77); Hans Scherer, the Elder, of Hamburg (1588–92 and 1605–07); Gottfried Fritzsche of Hamburg (1635–36); Arp Schnitker of Hamburg (1689–93); IV, 60.

Hilleröd (Denmark): Chapel of the Danebrog Knights in the Frederiksborg (originally built for the Hessen Castle near Wolfenbüttel). Builder: Esaius Compenius (ca. 1605–10).

Kirchheimbolanden: Grosse Kirche. Built in the 18th century by Michael Stumm and/or sons Philipp and Heinrich of Sulzbach near Rhaunen (Idar-Oberstein); III, 38.

Leutesdorf (Neuwied county): Katholische Pfarrkirche. Builder: Michael Stumm of Sulzbach near Rhaunen (Idar-Oberstein; ca. 1735); III, 28.

Lübeck: St. Jacobi. Builder: Friedrich Stellwagen of Lübeck (1636 to 1637; son-in-law of Gottfried Fritzsche); III, 28 (Gothic case).

Lüdingworth (near Hadeln): Evangelische Pfarrkirche. Builders: Antonius Wilde (1598); Arp Schnitker (1682–83); III, 36.

Lüneburg: St. Johannis. Builders: Hendrik Niehoff and Jasper Janszoon of 's Hertogenbosch (1551–53; III, 26, see specification on pp. 141 f.); Matthias Dropa (1712–15; pupil of Arp Schnitker); III, 46.

Marienmünster: Benedictine Abbey. Builder: Johann Patroclus Möller (1736–38); III, 43.

Meisenheim (Glan): Evangelische Schlosskirche. Builders: Philipp and Heinrich Stumm of Sulzbach near Rhaunen (Idar-Oberstein; 1764–67); II, 30.

Ochsenhausen: Abbey Church. Built in 1729–33; IV, 49; rebuilt by Josef Gabler of Ochsenhausen (1751–52); III, 49 (see specification on p. 151).

Ottobeuren: Benedictine Abbey, Epistle ("Trinity") organ and Gospel ("Holy Ghost") organ. Builder: Karl Joseph Riepp of Dijon (1757–66); IV, 48 and II, 27, respectively.

Pellworm (North Sea island): Alte Kirche. Builder: Arp Schnitker (1711); II, 24.

Rötha: St. Georgen. Builder: Gottfried Silbermann of Freiberg (1718–21); II, 23.

Schleiden (Eifel): Katholische Schlosskirche SS. Philippi und Jacobi. Builder: Christian Ludwig König (1770–71); II, 27.

Steinkirchen (Altes Land): Evangelische Pfarrkirche. Builders: Dirck Hoyer (rebuilt 1581); Arp Schnitker (1685–87); II, 28.

Vormbach (Niederbayern): Benediktinerstift. Builder: Ignatius Egedacher of Passau (1734); II, 20.

Weingarten: Benedictine Abbey. Builder: Josef Gabler of Ochsenhausen (1737 and 1750); IV, 63.

Plate IX

Organ of St. Mikkelskirke in Slagelse, Denmark, built in 1961 (three manuals, 33 stops). In the façade are Prestants of the Hauptwerk (8'), Pedal (8'), and Rückpositiv (4'); the Swell (8') is mounted behind the Hauptwerk (top center); the larger pipes of the Hauptwerk Principal are mounted directly in front of the Swell.

Plate X

Organ of St. Georg in Bensheim, Germany; built in 1963 (three manuals, 41 stops). Top center, the Swell division (8′); flanking it on either side, the Hauptwerk (Principal 8′). At the extreme right and left, the Pedal (Principal 16′); front center, the Rückpositiv (Principal 4′).

CHAPTER 7

Some Notes for the Organist

Technique

Technique is the organist's tool. It is wrong to play down technique as compared with musicality, as is occasionally done. Unmusical playing is not the result of technical proficiency; rather, it bespeaks a lack of creative imagination. Bach's enormous technique was proverbial in his time.

Posture

Posture and movements during playing must be relaxed, hands and feet should maintain easy contact with the keyboards; hands and fingers should be gently curved, wrists and elbows in horizontal position, knees together, and feet slightly turned in, so as to facilitate depressing the pedal keys by movement of the ankle toward the inside edge of the foot.[45]

Fingering and Pedaling

Polyphonic textures on the organ often demand extraordinary keyboard fingering; common features of organ fingering include the regular use of the thumb on black keys; crossing under and over the thumb, even with the fifth finger; finger crossing of 4 over 5 and 3 over 4 (right hand ascending, left hand descending) and similar dispositions; thumb glissando from white to white, as well as from white to black keys and vice versa; careful and systematic distribution of the inner voice between both hands is a further requirement. The commonly used all-purpose method of silent substitution should be employed only occasionally, as it has a paralyzing effect on the playing.

Pedal playing with toe and heel, covering intervals of seconds and thirds with one foot, has been emphasized in the methods of Bach pupils and their descendants (Kittel, Ritter, Lemmens, Dupré, and others) and by other teachers (Germani), and rightly

---

[45] This, of course, does not rule out the technique of depressing the pedals with the outside of the foot: the outside edge of the left foot may be used when ascending from d up, and vice versa. [*Translator*]

so; very early Arnold Schlick relied on this technique: three- and four-part pedaling is prerequisite for the performance of some of his works. Another important feature of pedal technique is the glissando from black to black, white to white, and black to white keys.

The preparation for attack is essential: hands and feet must be positioned over the keys prior to the attack (transportation technique); this applies particularly to leaps, manual changes, and heel attack.

Articulation

Clean legato playing is the basic organ touch; staccato has a considerably greater effect on the organ than on the pianoforte, owing to the durational continuity of organ sound; it is, therefore, imperative that the shortening of note values for the purpose of articulation be exactly planned according to durational ratios. Legato may be intensified by minute and variously graded over-lappings; Rameau, Bach, and others indicated this by ties. Similarly, the shortening of note values may be treated more gently in staccato passages and phrase endings.

Touch

Subtle structuring of articulation on the organ is effected by the touch: stresses are achieved by prolonged durations, which in turn are communicated to the listener as stresses. Furthermore, the individual tones may be characterized as "long" and "short" — figuratively speaking — by "horizontal" and "vertical" touch respectively. These nuances may also be simultaneously combined with those of the articulatory stress: "long" and "light," or "short" and "heavy."

Touch and articulation are also employed in the interest of linear clarity. A part played legato-marcato will be clearly discernible as against other parts played portato-leggiero. To be sure, such a concept requires considerable and diligent practice, which, however, will be amply rewarded.

Agogics

Polyphonic music can sustain and does require more relaxed tempos than homophonic music; the same applies to larger vs. smaller rooms; furthermore, a given piece played in a given room would have to be slower in pianissimo or fortissimo than in piano or forte. The choice of tempo should not be dependent on the small note values only, but the large note values must also be taken into consideration: melodic and harmonic rhythm must never stagnate. The tempo relationships between various sections can frequently be determined according to the *proportio sesquialtera*; for example, the value of three eighth notes in the final sections of Bach's *Fugue in E-flat Major* ("St. Anne") and of his Fantasia "Jesu, meine Freude" are to be equated with the value of two quarter notes in the opening sections. Tempos must be especially strict in pieces introducing contrasts of meter, particularly transitions from and to triplets, such as in Sweelinck's Fantasies; Bach's *Passacaglia, Prelude in A Minor*, and the large "Vater unser" (*Clavierübung*, Part III); Mendelssohn's *Prelude in D Minor* and Liszt's *B-A-C-H*. A ritardando should also be measured. All this is by no means to be construed as void, metronomic legalism. Often a sostenendo (rather than an accelerando) may be appropriate in organ playing as an element of enhancement. Entries of themes and final chords have to be prepared with agogic finesse. The final cadence points of Bach's cantus firmi often are sustained organ points with contrapuntally overlapping endings. The final ritardando in such cases should precede rather than follow the cadence point.

On Practicing

There are a number of systematic approaches to practicing, which — while not easy (perhaps rather more difficult) — will ensure success: One should always play so slowly as to be in complete control of every aspect of the performance.

On the first day of practice, one should carefully read through the weekly assignment, analyze it, and painstakingly work out the fingering and the pedaling; then it should be played through once at a slow tempo.

On the following day or two, measure by single measure should be practiced several times in succession; working through the assignment twice in this manner will absorb one practice period.

On the following day or two, one should concentrate on the difficult places: right hand alone, left hand alone, pedal alone; right hand and pedal, left hand and pedal, both hands without pedal; all three parts together. After this, particularly difficult places should be practiced in context with preceding bars; for example, measure 20, then measures 19—20, then 18—20, etc. This method may be applied also to half measures or to even smaller portions. Following this, the same places should be practiced in metric and rhythmic variants.

Finally, the assignment should be practiced in context; the tempo will gradually become more fluent.

The Art of Registration

One should exercise economy in registration.

Desirable is registration in simple, large lines according to the form and texture of a piece; choice of dynamics, color, manual changes, and of trio textures in accordance with musical structure; registration with the fewest possible stops (of course, the organist should draw all stops needed, but not any stops that are unessential to any given registration); as a rule, representation of any one pitch level by one stop only.

One should distinguish between

registrations for polyphonic textures, as needed for toccatas; fugues; passacaglias; simple chorale settings and accompaniments (manual coupler and / or manual change);

and

registrations for textures with single, obbligato parts, such as cantus firmi; single, characteristic counterpoints; the individual parts of duos and trios; melodically important bass lines of accompaniments (to be played on separate, uncoupled manuals).

Here is a listing of registrations for polyphonic textures.

Foundational Registration (Jeux de Fond)

Foundational stop registrations are made up either of single labial stops of 16', 8', or 4' pitch, or of combinations such as 16' + 8'; 8' + 4'; 16' + 8' + 4'.

Examples:
Principal 16'; or Quintade 16'; or Bourdon 16';
Principal 8'; or Gedackt 8'; or Gemshorn 8'; or Salicional 8';
Principal 4'; or Rhorflöte 4'; or Spitzflöte 4';
Bourdon 16' + Gemshorn 8'; or Quintade 16' + Rohrflöte 8';
Quintade 8' + Spitzflöte 4'; or Gedackt 8' + Principal 4';
Quintade 16' + Salicional 8' + Gemshorn 4' and many more possibilities. 173

Foundation stops were used especially by the Italians for the performance of their quiet ricercare in a cappella style, and of their slow toccatas for the Elevation; the Germans and the French used foundational registrations primarily for the accompaniment of solo stops.

The Mixture Plenum (Plein Jeu)
(also *organum plenum; ripieno; lleno; volles Werk*)

The masters of the 15th to the 18th centuries meant by these terms the combination of stops constituting the Principal choir. In the Pedal, reed stops were often called for (Trompete 8', Posaune 16'; especially also for the c.f.). Some authorities advised the doubling of the 16', 8', or 4' levels with Bourdon, Gedackt, or Flöte (Praetorius; 17th-century French masters; Silbermann; Dom Bédos); others rejected this practice (16th-century Netherlands masters; Antegnati; Compenius). Often the 16', 8', or 4' were replaced by Bourdon, Gedackt, or Flöte. Often a small selection only of the stops constituting the Principal choir was drawn *(mezzo ripieno)*.

Examples:
Principal 8' + Octave 4' + Superoctave 2' + Mixture + Scharf (regular plenum)
Gedackt 8' + Flöte 4' + Superoctave 2'
Principal 4' + Octave 2' + Quinte 1⅓' + Scharf
Principal 8' + Octave 4' + Rauschpfeife + Mixture
Bourdon 16' + Principal 8' + Octave 4' + Scharf
Gedackt 8' + Principal 4' + Rauschpfeife and many more possibilities.

The 16' foundation is best used for homophonic rather than polyphonic sections; Gedackt or Flute foundations (in lieu of Principal and Octave) are preferably used in sections assigned to the Positiv.

The Germans and the Italians used the mixture plenum for the performance of toccatas and fugues at the beginning and end of the service; the French used it for the introductions to the *Kyrie, Gloria, Sanctus, Agnus Dei, Hymn,* and *Magnificat,* while Sweelinck played the augmented subjects (Pedal 4') and final sections of his Fantasies with such registrations.

Lingual-Stop Registrations

Lingual stops are used in the following combinations: 8', 16', 16' + 8', 16' + 4', 8' + 4', 16' + 8' + 4'. Optionally, one may draw a labial 8' (Principal, Gedackt, or Quintade), or also two labial stops 8' + 4' (usually Gedackt 8' + Principal 4').

Examples:

Rankett 16' + Krummhorn 8'
Barpfeife 8' + Singendregal 4'
Dulzian 16' + Trompete 4'
Vox humana 8' + Gedackt 8'
Quintade 8' + Geigendregal 4'
Sordun 16' + Trichterregal 8' + Schalmei 4'
Trompete 8' + Gedackt 8' + Octave 4'
Dulzian 16' + Principal 8'

The 17th-century French masters played their *Fugues graves* with reed stops. They did so—quite rightly—for the sake of clarity. Indeed, the inner voices are very distinctly discernible with such a registration, particularly when contrasted to a foundational Pedal registration.

The Reed Plenum (Grand Jeu)

The reed plenum is the combination of the stops contained in the Oberwerk divisions of the classical organs of the Netherlands. It consists of:

Hauptwerk	Positiv
Gedackt 8'	Gedackt 8'
Octave 4'	Principal 4'
Kornett V	Nasat 2⅔'
Trompete 8'	Terz 1⅗'
Trompete 4'	Krummhorn 8'

manual coupler

With such registrations the classical French masters played the final movements of the *Kyrie, Gloria,* and *Agnus Dei* and the *Offertories,* often using the left or right hand for solos on the Hauptwerk, while the other hand accompanied on the Positiv. Not infrequently they also introduced the Kornett of Manual III (Récit) for duo formations between it and the Positiv, or for Trio registrations, with the Pedal (Offenbass 8') serving as the third component. Bach's *Prelude in D Major,* the final movements of the *Partita "O Gott, du frommer Gott,"* and of the *Canonic Variations on "Vom Himmel hoch,"* and several others of his works are similarly conceived. The manual parts of the opening and middle sections of Sweelinck's Fantasies also demand the reed plenum.

Tutti (Grand Choeur)

The old masters did not use reeds in the manual mixture plena; however, in later periods this was done. The resulting tone color and dynamic volume yielded the effect of our present day Tutti.[46] We should make it a rule not to draw all stops indiscriminately; even a Tutti should be the result of selective registration. The audience will be grateful for it.

Here is a listing of the types of registration suitable for solo playing:

Solo Registers

Solo registers include all types of overblown labial stops (such as the Querflöte and Schweizerpfeife); of Farbenzimbels; of Kornetts; and of Carillons.

Single Reed Stops

Single reed stops may be used alone or together with labial ranks of 8' or 4' level respectively (as shown in the examples of registrations for polyphonic textures); they are useful as solo colors in soprano, tenor, and bass ranges.

Mutation Combinations

Especially suitable for mutation combinations are Bourdon 16', Gedackt 8', Flöte 4', Gross Terz 3⅕', Nasat 2⅔', Waldflöte 2', Terz 1⅗', Quintflöte 1⅓', and Sifflöte 1'; furthermore, the Principal choir ranks of 2', 1⅓', and 1' levels; the Sesquialtera and the Terzian; the Carillons; the Kornetts; and, finally, the various types of Zimbels, such as Rauschend Zimbel, Farbenzimbel, and Klingend Zimbel. It is preferable to choose pitch levels for the Principal chorus ranks that are higher than those of the wide-scaled ranks within any given solo combination, for example, Gedackt 8' and Waldflöte 2' and Quinte 1⅓'; or Gedackt 8' plus Flöte 4' plus Terzian; or Rohrflöte 8' and Nasat 2⅔' and Octave 1'. Of course, such stops as Repetierend Septime or Repetierend None are also useful for such combinations.

Duo and Trio Registrations

For duo and trio playing, there are six basic combinations available.

---

[46] The Tutti of the German organ is equivalent to the sforzando pedal in American organs. The Tutti combinations in German instruments of the early decades of our century included not only coupled reed plena but all octave couplers, in addition to unison couplers. [*Translator*]

Basic Duo and Trio Registrations

Combination	1	2	3	4	5	6
Right hand	solo	solo	reed	reed	mutation combination	mutation combination
Left hand	reed	mutation combination	reed	mutation combination	reed	mutation combination

In the combinations under columns 2 and 4 the left hand is registered with relatively low-pitched mutation stops. For combination 6 a principle of registration applies according to which the right hand is assigned brighter and higher pitched stops than the left hand. Furthermore, it is advisable to avoid duplication of pitch levels between the two manuals—excepting, of course, the 8' level, for example:

Right hand: 8' plus 2⅔' plus 1' or 8' plus 2' plus Klingend Zimbel
Left hand: 8' plus 4' plus 1⅗' or 8' plus 4' plus Terzian

Old Masters

The toccatas, fugues, passacaglias, and chorale preludes for one manual only demand one or the other of the aforementioned registrations for polyphonic textures. Manual changes should correspond with the formal sections of a given piece. Within any section, the registration should not be changed; pieces lacking clearly sectional organization are best played without manual changes.

Thus the interpolated fugato sections of toccatas may be played on the Positiv. Buxtehude's *Passacaglia in D Minor* is effectively performed by organizing it in sections of seven variations each that are played successively on Hauptwerk, Unterwerk (Positiv), Oberwerk, and Hauptwerk. Characteristic sectional organization of fugues can be found in Sweelinck's Fantasies, Frescobaldi's types of Canzona and Capriccio, and in the Preludes of Buxtehude, Lübeck, and Bruhns.

Chorale preludes à 2 *claviers et pédale* of the Gothic period (Schlick, Buchner) were preferably registered as soprano solos, even when the cantus firmus was not specifically isolated; rather it was played together with the alto as quasi accompaniment of the soprano. Later on—beginning with Sweelinck—the cantus firmus was played as solo without exception. The solo parts are, 177 of course, to be played with solo registration, and the contrapuntal accompaniment with a properly balanced registration for polyphonic textures, for example:

Solo part	Accompaniment
Kornett V	Gedackt 8'
Krummhorn 8'	Principal 8'
Gedackt 8' + Waldflöte 2'	Barpfeife 8'
+ Klingend Zimbel	
Pedaltrompete 8'	Principal 16' + 8' + Octave 4'
	+ Rauschpfeife + Mixture

Not infrequently, cantus firmi notated in the soprano or alto are best realized in the Pedal with a 4' stop (Choralbass, Trompete), in which case the remaining parts are, of course, to be assigned to the hands.

Johann Sebastian Bach

All of the aforesaid applies, of course, also to the performance of Bach's organ works, with the following additional observations: In his Sonatas one has to decide on one of two options. Either all three movements are played with identical registration — a tonal organization that is eminently characteristic of the sonata — or the middle movement is played with a registration contrasting with that of the outer movements, a practice reminiscent of the concerto and justified by Bach's choice of three (concerto) rather than four (sonata) movements. The omission of 16' Pedal stops is frequently of good effect. Since the left hand never descends into the low octave, the performance on only one manual with a 4' registration is possible (left hand plays one octave lower). A number of Bach's Preludes and Fugues should be played without manual changes, among them II, 1, in C Major; II, 2, in G Major; III, 10, in E Minor; IV, 1, in C Major; IV, 5, in C Minor and others.[47] The Brustwerk should be assigned only such episodes as are written exclusively for manual. The Hauptwerk and Positiv of Bach's organ are dynamically equal and may, therefore, share the same Pedal registration.

The *Prelude in D Major* is written in French style, introducing sections of dialog between left hand and pedal. The Preludes and

---

[47] The Roman numerals refer to the volume, the Arabic figures to the specific composition in the Peters edition. [*Translator*]

Fugues in C Major (III, 7) and in C Minor (IV, 5) were written originally in E Major and D Minor respectively. The *Eight Little Preludes and Fugues* are surely not composed by Bach but likely by Krebs, father or son. The *Trio in D Minor* (IV, 14) and the *Aria in F Major* (IX, 5) were probably intended as middle movements for the Preludes and Fugues in C Major (II, 1) and in G Major (II, 2) respectively.

Chorale preludes not marked *à 2 claviers* should generally be played on no more than one manual. Five-part pieces marked *à 2 claviers* sound good in the *Grigny-registration* (left hand: Krumm-horn 8'; right hand: Kornett V). In the chorale variations it is necessary to examine each variation as to its cantus firmus possibility, since Bach did not always mark them *à 2 claviers*. In some of the *Canonic Variations on "Vom Himmel hoch"* the pedal part consistently crosses the left hand; these pedal parts must be realized only on an 8' basis. In the four-stanza variation (reed plenum) the trio section is intended for Kornett and Positiv (Krummhorn); the forte for the Hauptwerk with the accompaniment on the Positiv; and the diminuzione and stretti entirely for the coupled Hauptwerk.

The Question of Dynamics

Modern organ music relies on dynamic gradations far more heavily than does the classical, gradations not only in the sense of alternation between forte and piano but also of crescendo and diminuendo. Baroque organ building offered manual changes, coupling, the Schwellwerk (Spain), combination pedals (Italy), and wind trunk ventils (Germany and France) as means of dynamic gradation. Later generations of organ builders improved these means, which was good. Unfortunately they also felt it necessary to add a few more that should, however, be rejected (automatic piano-pedal; fixed combinations labeled *pp, p, mf*, etc.; Echo organs; octave couplers; crescendo pedal [*Rollschweller*]).

Dynamics on the organ must correspond to the formal structure of a piece without affecting the tonal character. The use of the expression pedal must be so effected as to leave the audience unaware; it must trace the musical line rather than suggest sentimentality. In a good organ, the crescendo leads from the closed Schwellwerk over the Positiv to the coupled Hauptwerk under gradual opening of the shutters and with the manual changes being effected according to the individual parts of the music; the Pedal follows in correspondence with the musical significance of its part. For such manual changes (according to the parts of the music), the successive entries of counterexpositions in Reger's works — not infrequently marked carefully by the composer in this sense — lend themselves particularly well; for example in the Fugues in E-flat Major, Op. 40, No. 1; in B-flat Major, Op. 46; in D Minor, Op. 135 b; and particularly in E Minor, Op. 63, No. 10.

Franck and Recent French Organ Music

Ever since the middle of the 17th century French organists have been in the habit of giving detailed instructions concerning registration. Some of the most common terms are listed below:

G. or G. O.	Grand Orgue	Hauptwerk
P. or Pos.	Positif	Positiv, Rückpositiv
R. or Ré.	Récit	Schwellwerk
Péd.	Pédalier, Pédale	Pedal
	Accouplement	Coupler (usually manual coupler)
	Tirasse	Pedal coupler
G. P. R.		Hauptwerk with Positiv and Schwellwerk coupled to it
	Fonds	Labial foundation stops
	Mixtures	Labial stops of 2⅔' and higher, as well as mixtures and compound stops
	Anches	reeds; usually referring to the reeds and mixtures of the *Appel* (wind-trunk ventil button)
	Anches préparées	Reeds and mixtures drawn (prepared), but not yet engaged by the corresponding "Appel"
	Boîte ouverte	box open
	Boîte fermée	box closed
	Claviers accouplés	manuals coupled
	Claviers séparés	manuals uncoupled
	mettre or ajouter	draw or add
	ôter or retrancher	cancel or disengage
	récit	solo, usually for the right hand
	dessus	solo for the right hand
	en taille	solo in the tenor for the left hand or for pedal
	basse	solo for the left hand
	ensemble	both hands
	montre	Principal

préstant	Octave 4', Choralbass 4', Principal 4'
doublette	Superoctave 2', Octave 2', Principal 2'
flûte harmonique	Querflöte 8'
flûte octaviante	Querflöte 4'
octavin	Querflöte 2'
bombarde	Posaune 16' or Trompete 16'
clairon	Trompete 4'
cornet séparé	Kornett of solo manual (récit)
jeu doux pour un cornet	soft stop as accompaniment for Kornett solo
plein jeu	mixture plenum (Principals 8' 4' 2', Mixture, and Scharf)
grand jeu	reed plenum (tierce [see below] + Kornett V + Trompete 8' and 4')
tierce	Gedackt 8' + Flöte 4 + Nasat $2^2/_3$' + Flöte 2' + Terz $1^3/_5$'
dialogue	grand jeu (when occurring without qualifying adjunct)

The consoles of Aristide Cavaillé-Coll show a number of accessories, such as couplers, expression shoe, and studs for the wind-trunk ventil. In order for the Hauptwerk to sound, it must be coupled to its manual (G. O. sur machine); reed stops and mixtures are mounted on separate chests and will sound only when the wind-trunk ventils are open (Appel des anches G. O.; Anches Péd., etc.); occasionally the foundation stops of the Pedal are governed by a separate Appel (Fonds Péd.). The scores of Franck, Widor, Tournemire, Dupré, Messiaen, and of other French composers usually bear careful Appel markings.

With couplers and Appels engaged, naturally only stops that are drawn will sound; thus the tutti will vary accordingly. Of course, crescendo and diminuendo may also be confined to proper manual changes and to the expression pedal. The Appels affect reeds and mixtures (separately or together) only, but an additional degree of variety can be achieved by changing the order of usage within a piece. This flexibility of the organ's crescendo is utilized especially in contemporary French organ music (Messiaen). It is also important to remember that the dynamic indications pp, p, mf, and f in French organ music usually refer to the position of the expression pedal; sugary registrations are almost nonexistent in French organ music. The indication pp often means approximately the following (with closed shutters):

Schwellwerk	Principal 8' + Gedackt 8' + Octave 4' + Superoctave 2' + Mixture + Trompete 8' + Trompete 4'
Positiv	Gedackt 8' + Principal 4' + Flöte 4'
Hauptwerk	Principal 8' + Gedackt 8' + Octave 4'

The full ensemble of the organ *(Grand Choeur)* is often indicated by *fff*.

Reger and Recent German Organ Music

The most important German organ master after Bach was Max Reger. The first truly great master of the post-Bach era, his musical training centered on the organ, and to it he devoted an essential part of his creative work. Through his efforts organ music has again attained the highest stature. At the same time, Reger represents the link to Bach within the broken chain of great organ traditions, for he recreated the large forms of toccata, prelude, fantasy, passacaglia, fugue, chorale variation, and chorale fugue.

In performing Reger's music, one must keep in mind that his dynamic indications are only of relative significance: neither the numerous indications of *ppp, ff, mp*, etc., nor his direction *Organo pleno* must be interpreted literally. Reger's dynamic indications meet the tendencies of the organ building of his time, which strove for musical expression by means of a constant rise and fall in dynamics, a concept totally opposed to the character of the organ. His real goal, however, was a "soulfully animated performance" (Straube); this objective can be realized on the organ only by touch, agogics, and articulation. With regard to character and volume of sound, the registration must be suggested primarily by the musical form; only such criteria will yield full expressive effects. Not infrequently Reger performed his own works in this manner — deviating from his written dynamic indications — and he emphatically approved of Straube's interpretation of his works, which were conceived in that manner.[48]

Naturally, the concept which holds that registration changes are proper only in pieces that show clearly sectional organization applies also to the performance of many of Reger's works. These include a large number of pieces of toccata character containing alternating fugato and free sections; fugues such as the tertiary

---

[48] See Karl Straube, *Briefe eines Thomaskantors*, Stuttgart, 1952, pp. 172 and 233; and Straube's Preface to Reger's *Fantasy: Ein feste Burg ist unser Gott*, Op. 27, Leipzig, 1938.

Fuge über den Namen B-A-C-H, Op. 46; another work in tertiary form, the *Fugue in D Minor*, Op. 135b; and a large work, organized in six sections, the *Fugue in E Minor*, Op. 127; his works in variation technique such as the Chorale Fantasies *Wie schön leuchtet der Morgenstern*, Op. 40; and *Wachet auf! ruft uns die Stimme*, Op. 52; and the *Variations on an Original Theme in F-sharp Minor*, Op. 73. In pieces of uniform structure, such as the *Fugue in D Major*, Op. 65; F-sharp Minor fugue in Op. 73; and many more, we must limit ourselves, for the most part, to manual changes that must be carefully planned, occasionally even by departure from Reger's directions. Of course, such manual changes can be so devised by strict conformity to the structural implications of the music that the resulting dynamic development represents a crescendo of large dimensions.

The following works demand solo registrations: *Variations on an Original Theme in F-sharp Minor*, Op. 73, p. 14 (alternately obbligato solo and trio texture); *Gigue in D Minor*, Op. 80; *Pastorale in F Major*, Op. 59; *Pastorale in A Major*, Op. 65 (trio textures); the *Melodies in B-flat Major*, Op. 59 and 129; *Moment musical in D Major*, Op. 69 (cantus in soprano with contrapuntal accompaniment, in *Moment musical* alternating with plenum sections); *Prelude in B Minor*, Op. 129 (trio sections alternating with plenum sections).

Reger's tempo indications must be interpreted on the slow side. His metronome markings are usually half again as high as his actual intention. Karl Straube, Reger's good friend and great interpreter, has indicated the correct tempos in his editions of Reger's organ works; for example, molto sostenuto in place of Reger's con moto; allegretto grazioso in place of vivacissimo; moderato e tranquillo in place of vivace, etc. In the correspondence with his count, Reger clearly stated that in the state of transport while composing, he marked the tempos too fast. At the occasion of the Reger Festival in Dortmund in 1910, he admonished Gerard Bunk, organist of St. Reinoldi: "Young man, let's not play my things too fast; play everything quite deliberately, even though it's notated faster!" He himself "commenced his fugues quite slowly and gradually enhanced them by way of their architectural development rather than through agogic acceleration; an incredible quietude was, indeed, the specific quality of his playing" (Karl Hasse). Furthermore, in performing his works, he modified the tempos not infrequently and introduced fermatas and small pauses. As a rule of thumb for the choice of the correct basic tempo, Reger's metronome indications may be reduced by one third, for example, a quarter note = 90 may be reduced to a quarter note = 60.

Reger's return to the old, genuine forms of organ music has inspired a strong following by other contemporary composers, and his striving for clarity in the application of these forms has set a worthy example. This return, however, must not be construed as slavish imitation, since Reger as well as his successors (Kaminski, Hindemith, Raphael, and others) have further developed and adapted the old forms to their contemporary idiom, each according to his own idiosyncrasies. The interpretation of such contemporary German organ music is, of course, subject to the basic requirement of thorough formal analysis as the logical criterion for the choice of registration.

Accompanimental Organ Playing

The following rules apply to accompanimental organ playing.

1. The choir or soloist to be accompanied must stand in front of the ranks used for accompaniment. If they stand below or behind the accompanimental stops, they will hear too little and the congregation too much of the accompaniment.

2. Neither the organist nor the choir nor the soloist can decide on the suitability of a given combination of accompanimental stops. It is necessary for the organist to consult with a knowledgeable listener in the nave as to proper balance of the registration, or—even better—to listen himself from the nave.

3. Principally, foundation stops are used for accompaniment. Single obbligato motifs may be set off by similar, but slightly stronger stops. For a continuous obbligato part, an unobtrusive solo combination, possibly on the Rückpositiv, is advisable. Bach's organ accompaniments have almost always an obbligato bass, which must be played with separate registration.

The accompaniment—or more correctly, the leading—of congregational singing makes far greater demands on the abilities of the organist than is generally assumed. It does not merely consist of playing a given hymn correctly in four-part harmony. The registration should be selected from foundation stops of 8' and 4' levels in the manual, and of 16', 8', and 4' levels in the pedal. Of these, ranks with relatively rich harmonics are preferable in the manual; the pedal should always be registered proportionately strong. The hymn melody may be played in women's and men's range (an octave lower) at the same time, but always legato. The accompanimental parts, however, must be realized in a sensitively balanced alternation between legato and non legato, in accordance with the rhythmic delineation of the tune. The correct application of this rule demands much artistic finesse. The so-called fermatas cannot everywhere be treated identically. Here again, it is not easy to find the right mean. Much can be learned from watching a congregation sing without accompaniment. Upon adoption of a mode of treating the fermatas in a given hymn, one must adhere to it consistently. Precise releases at the conclusion of hymn phrases will facilitate the congregation's beginning the following phrases punctually and together. Authentic harmonization of chorales poses particularly tricky problems. Undoubtedly it is wrong to harmonize every melody note. Even though this may be a time-honored tradition, it is no less faulty for it. A good harmonization is conditioned by the style and the rhythmic character of the tune: the harmonic rhythm evolves in coordination with the rhythmic centers of gravity. Whenever possible, anacruses should be assigned the harmony of the preceding rhythmic focal point. The volume of registration has to be adjusted to the number of singers, to the particular character of the liturgical season or occasion, and to the character of the hymn. We must further take into account the degree of the congregation's familiarity with a given tune.

———————————

All these suggestions are offered as practical hints, derived from practical experience and intended to help answer some of the technical questions of organ playing.

The most important aspect of an organist's job is his own interpretation of it. Charles-Marie Widor has most aptly defined it:

ORGAN PLAYING MEANS REVEALING A WILL IMBUED WITH THE VISION OF ETERNITY.

Plate XI

Console of the organ of St. Marien Cathedral in Freiberg (Saxony), Germany; built by Gottfried Silbermann, 1711—14. Lower manual, Brustwerk; middle manual, Hauptwerk; upper manual, Oberpositiv. Pedal range is C, D—c'. Stop knobs are arranged vertically, which is preferable to a horizontal layout. Lower and upper manuals can be coupled to the middle manual by appropriate positioning of the keyboards.

Plate XII

Console of the organ in the Church of the Carthusians in Cologne, Germany; built in 1960. Drawknobs arranged vertically and angled toward the organist; general and divisional setter pistons. Pedal levers—preferable to push buttons—are used to engage couplers and pistons.

APPENDICES

BIBLIOGRAPHY

List of Abbreviations

Archives	Guilmant, Felix Alexandre, comp. *Archives des maîtres de l'orgue,* 10 vols. Paris: Durand, 1893—1909.
BV	Bärenreiter-Verlag, Heinrich Schütz Allee 29, Kassel-Wilhelmshöhe, Germany.
B&B	Bote & Bock, Sonnenbergerstrasse 14, Wiesbaden, Germany.
B&H	Breitkopf & Härtel, Burgstrasse 6, Wiesbaden, Germany.
Bib Org	*Bibliotheca Organologica, Facsimiles of Rare Books on Organ and Organ Building,* Vols. I—VIII, XVIII, XIX, XXV to date. Amsterdam: Frits Knuf, 1962—.
Born	Bornemann, 15 rue de Tournon, Paris 6^e, France.
CEKM	*Corpus of Early Keyboard Music,* ed. Willi Apel, Vols. I—XII, XV, XXVII to date. American Institute of Musicology, 1963—.
DDT	*Denkmäler deutscher Tonkunst,* Folge I, new ed., ed. H. J. Moser, 65 vols. Wiesbaden: Breitkopf & Härtel, 1958—59.
DTB	*Denkmäler der Tonkunst in Bayern / Denkmäler deutscher Tonkunst,* Folge II, many eds., 38 vols. Many publishers, 1900—38.
DTO	*Denkmäler der Tonkunst in Oesterreich,* 115 vols. to date. Wien: Oesterreichischer Bundesverlag, 1894—.
EP	Edition Peters, Forsthausstrasse 101, Frankfurt, Germany. 373 Park Avenue South, New York, New York.
Han	Wilhelm Hansen Verlag, Eschersheimer Landstrasse 12, Frankfurt, Germany.
HE	Hinrichsen Edition, 10 Baches Street, London N. 1, England.
K&S	Kistner & Siegel, Luisenstrasse 8, Lippstadt, Germany.
Leduc	Alphonse Leduc, 175 rue St. Honoré, Paris 1er, France.
Lem	Henry Lemoine, 17 rue Pigalle, Paris, France.
LO	Liber Organi, ed. E. Kaller, H. Klotz, and others, 11 vols. to date. Mainz: Schott, 1931—.
MeV	Merseburger Verlag, Alemannenstrasse 20, Berlin, Germany.
Organum	*Organum. Ausgewählte ältere vokale und instrumentale Meisterwerke,* Reihe IV, ed. M. Seiffert & H. Albrecht, 22 vols. Lippstadt: Kistner & Siegel, 1925—.
Ric	G. & C. Ricordi, Via Berchet 2, Milano, Italy. G. Ricordi, 16 West 61st Street, New York, New York.
Sch	Schott, Weihergarten 5, Mainz, Germany. 48 Great Marlborough Street, London W. 1, England.
Schult	C. L. Schultheiss, Tübingen, Germany.

SDM   Willy Müller, Süddeutscher Musikverlag, Hauptstrasse 85,
           Heidelberg, Germany.

SDOB   *Süddeutsche Orgelmeister des Barock,* ed. R. Walter, 6 vols. to
           date. Altötting: Coppenrath, 1956–.

Ugr   Ugrino, Elbchausée 499a, Hamburg, Germany.

UE   Universal Edition, Karlsplatz 5, Wien, Austria.

Selected List of Organ Music

Historical Collections and Performance Editions

Achtzig Orgelintonationen, ed. H.-A. Metzger. [Schult] n. d.

Alte italienische Meister des Orgelspiels, ed. M. E. Bossi. (EP) 1936.

Les anciens maîtres espagnols, ed. P. Piédelièvre. Paris: Schola Cantorum, n. d.

Anthologia Antiqua. Classic Works for the Organ, 8 vols. New York: J. Fischer, 1935–52.

Anthologie des maîtres classiques de l'orgue, ed. M. Dupré & R. Falcinelli, 72 vols. to date. (Born) 1942–.

Auler, Wolfgang, ed. *Spielbuch für Kleinorgel. Werke alter Meister,* 2 vols. (EP) 1951.

Biggs, E. Power, ed. *Treasury of Early Organ Music.* New York: Music Press, 1947.

Bonnet, Joseph, ed. *Anthology of Early French Organ Music.* New York: H. W. Gray, 1942.

Bossi, Marco Enrico, ed. *Sammlung von Stücken alter italienischer Meister für die moderne Orgel.* (EP) 1936.

Butcher, Vernon, ed. *English Organ Music of the Eighteenth Century,* 2 vols. (EP) 1951.

Buxheimer Orgelbuch (ca. 1460–70), facsimile, ed. B. Wallner, (BV) 1955. Transcription, ed. B. Wallner, Vols. XXXVII–XXXIX of *Das Erbe Deutscher Musik.* (BV) 1958–59.

Choralbearbeitungen und freie Orgelstücke der deutschen Sweelinck-Schule, ed. H. J. Moser & T. Fedtke, 2 vols. (BV) 1954–55.

Choralbuch zum Evangelischen Kirchengesangbuch, ed. Ch. Mahrenholz & R. Utermöhlen. (BV) 1965.

Choralvorspiele für den gottesdienstlichen Gebrauch, ed. A. Graf. (BV) 1939.

Clementi, Muzio, ed. *Clementi's Selection of Practical Harmony, for the Organ or Pianoforte,* 4 vols. London: Clementi, Banger, Hyde, Collard & Davis, 1811–15.

Commer, Franz, ed. *Kompositionen für Orgel aus dem 16., 17. und 18. Jahrhundert,* 6 vols. Leipzig: Leuckart, 18–.

Corpus of Early Keyboard Music, ed. W. Apel, Vols. I–XII, XV, XXVII to date. American Institute of Musicology, 1963–.

Dietrich, Fritz, ed. *Elf Orgelchoräle des siebzehnten Jahrhunderts.* (BV) 1932.

Dreissig Choralintonationen, ed. F. Zipp. (Schult) n. d.

Eslava y Elizondo, Hilarion, ed. *Museo organico español.* Madrid: Salazar, 1856.

Freie Orgelstücke alter Meister, ed, A. Graf. (BV) 1950.

Guilmant, Felix Alexandre, ed. *Archives des maîtres de l'orgue,* 10 vols. Paris: Durand, 1893—1909.

Hawke, William, ed. *Elkan-Vogel Organ Series,* 5 vols. Philadelphia: Elkan-Vogel, 1947—48.

Jeppesen, Knud, ed. *Die italienische Orgelmusik am Anfang des Cinquecento.* Copenhagen: Munksgaard, 1943 (second edition, 1960).

Kastner, Santiago, ed. *Silva Ibérica. De musica para tecla de los siglos XVI, XVII, y XVIII.* (Sch) 1954.

Keller, Hermann, ed. *Achtzig Choralvorspiele deutscher Meister des 17. und 18. Jahrhunderts.* (EP) 1937.

————, ed. *Orgelvorspiele alter Meister in allen Tonarten,* 2d ed. (BV) 1964.

Kraus, Eberhard, ed. *Cantantibus Organis,* 14 vols. to date. Regensburg: Pustet, 1958—.

Liber Organi, ed. E. Kaller, H. Klotz, and others, 11 vols. to date. (Sch) 1931—.

Locheimer Liederbuch, Das, in *Jahrbücher für Musikalische Wissenschaft II.* Leipzig: B&H, 1867. Facsimile reprint, ed. K. Ameln; Berlin: Wölbing, 1925.

Lüneburger Orgeltabulatur, ed. M. Reimann as Vol. XXXVI of *Das Erbe Deutscher Musik,* Litolff Verlag, 1957.

Masterpieces of Organ Music, ed. N. Hennefield, 67 vols. New York: Liturgical Music Press, 1944.

Moser, H. J., ed. *Frühmeister der deutschen Orgelkunst.* Leipzig: B&H, 1930.

Muset, Joseph, ed. *Early Spanish Organ Music.* New York: G. Schirmer, 1948.

Musica Sacra. Sammlung der besten Meisterwerke des 16., 17. und 18. Jahrh. Berlin: B&B, 1839—. Vol. I is *Sammlung . . . für die Orgel.* Reedition by H. Redlich in 1931.

Neue Choral-Vorspiele, ed. H.-A. Metzger. [Schult] n. d.

Neue Orgelvorspiele, ed. H. Haag & W. Hennig. (MeV) 1961.

Neues Choralbuch zum Evangelischen Kirchengesangbuch, ed. K. Gerok & H.-A. Metzger. (BV) 1956.

Old English Organ Music, ed. J. E. West, 36 vols. London: Novello, n. d.

Organum. Ausgewählte ältere vokale und instrumentale Meisterwerke, Reihe IV, ed. M. Seiffert & H. Albrecht, 22 vols. to date. (K&S) 1925—.

Die Orgel. Reihe I, *Werke des 20. Jahrhunderts,* 7 vols. to date. Reihe II, *Werke alter Meister,* 20 vols. to date. (K&S) 1949—.

Orgelbuch zum Evangelischen Kirchengesangbuch, ed. O. Brodde, 21 vols. to date. (BV) 1954 — .

Orgelbuch zum Evangelischen Kirchengesangbuch, ed. H. Grabner. (MeV) 1955.

Orgelchoräle des 17. und 18. Jahrhunderts, ed. W. Senn. (BV) n. d.

Orgelmeister des 17. und 18. Jahrhunderts, ed. K. Matthaei. (EP) n. d.

Orgelmusik im Gottesdienst, 2 vols. Zürich: Eulenburg (New York: C. F. Peters), 1964.

Orgelstücke altfranzösischer Meister, ed. W. Lutz. (Schult) 1943.

Orgelvorspiele zum Evangelischen Kirchengesangbuch, ed. H. M. Poppen, Ph. Reich & A. Strube. (MeV) pref. 1953

Orgelwerke altböhmischer Meister, ed. R. Quoika, 3 vols. (B&H) 1949.

Orgue et liturgie, ed. C. Gay, 60 vols. to date. Paris: Schola Cantorum, 1956 — .

Pedrell, Felipe, ed. *Hispaniae schola musica sacra. Opera varia (Saecul. XV, XVI, XVII, et XVIII).* Barcelona: Pujol, 1894 — 98.

Peeters, Flor, ed. *Oudnederlandse Meesters voor het Orgel,* 3 vols. (Lem) 1938 — 48.

Raugel, Felix, ed. *Les maîtres français de l'orgue aux XVIIᵉ et XVIIIᵉ siecles,* 2 vols. Paris: Schola Cantorum, 1925.

Schering, Arnold, ed. *Alte Meister aus der Frühzeit des Orgelspiels.* Leipzig: B&H, 1913.

Stevens, Denis, ed. *Altenglische Orgelmusik.* (BV) 1954.

Straube, Karl, ed. *Alte Meister. Eine Sammlung deutscher Orgelkomponisten aus dem XVII. und XVIII. Jahrhundert.* (EP) 1929.

_____. *Alte Meister des Orgelspiels, neue Folge,* 2 vols. (EP) 1929.

_____. *Choralvorspiele alter Meister.* (EP) 1907.

Süddeutsche Orgelmeister des Barock, ed. R. Walter 6 vols. to date. Altötting: Coppenrath, 1956 — .

Tallis to Wesley. English Organ Music from the Sixteenth to the Nineteenth Century, ed. G. Phillips, 34 vols. to date. (HE) 1956 — .

Thomas, Paul, ed. *The Church Organist,* 3 vols. to date. St. Louis: Concordia, 1965 — .

Torchi, Luigi, ed. *L'arte musicale in Italia,* Vol. III, *Composizioni per organo e cembalo secoli XVI, XVII e XVIII.* (Ric) 1897 — 1908.

Weman, Henry, ed. *Organ Pieces of the Eighteenth and Nineteenth Centuries,* 3 vols. *(Han) 1949 — 57.*

Individual Composers

This section does not include American composers for reasons of space; for a selective listing of organ music inclusive of English and American composers, the reader is referred to Index II of Gerhard Krapf's *Organ Improvisation,* Minneapolis, 1966.

Ahrens, Joseph (1904—)
Orgelwerke. (Sch) 1935—52.

Alain, Jehan (1911—1940)
Choral dorien et choral phrygien. (Leduc) 1938; *Trois pièces* (Leduc); *Introduction, Variations, Scherzo et Choral.* (Leduc) 1942; *Prélude et fugue* (Leduc) 1942; *Trois danses.* (Leduc) 1942; *Intermezzo.* (Leduc) 1935; *Douze petites pièces.* (Leduc) 1942; *L'oeuvre d'orgue* (Leduc) 1959—.

d'Andrieu, Jean François (1682—1738)
Premier livre de pièces d'orgue (1739). Archives VII, 1.

Bach, Johann Sebastian (1685—1750)
Werke. Leipzig: Bach-Gesellschaft, 1851—1947; *Compositionen für Orgel,* 9 vols., ed. F. Griepenkerl, F. Roitsch. (EP) 1844—1904; *Neue Ausgabe sämtlicher Werke* (BV) 1954, Organ works in Series IV; *Complete Organ Works,* ed. C. M. Widor & A. Schweitzer. New York: G. Schirmer, 1912—68; *Organ Works,* ed. W. T. Best, revised A. E. Hull. 10 vols. London: Augener, 1914; *Oeuvres complètes pour l'orgue,* ed. M. Dupré. 6 vols. (Born) 1940; *Prelude and Fugue in B Minor,* ed. G. Kinsky. (UE) 1923; *Fantasia super "Komm, heiliger Geist,"* ed. P. Wackernagel. (MeV) 1949.

Barbe, Helmut (1927—)
Sonate für Orgel (1964). Stuttgart-Hohenheim: Hänssler, 1967.

Bender, Jan (1909—)
Tabulatura Americana, Op. 22, 2 vols. St. Louis: Concordia, 1961—63; *Twenty Short Organ Pieces.* St. Louis: Concordia, 1956; *Festival Preludes on Six Chorales,* Op. 26. St. Louis: Concordia, 1963.

Böhm, Georg (1661—1733)
Sämtliche Werke, Vol. I, *Klavier und Orgelwerke,* ed. J. Wolgast. (B&H) 1927 (Reprint, Wiesbaden, 1952, 1964); *Selected Organ Works. Organum,* 4.

Bornefeld, Helmut (1906—)
Intonationen (BV). *Choralpartiten* (BV). *Choralvorspiele* (BV). *Begleitsätze.* (BV) 1950—.

Brahms, Johannes (1833—1897)
Sämtliche Orgelwerke. (B&H) 1928; *Complete Organ Works,* ed. W. Buszin & P. Bunjes. (EP) 1964.

Bruhns, Nikolaus (1665—1697)
Orgelwerke, ed. F. Stein. (EP) 1939; *Selected Organ Works. Organum,* 8.

Brunner, Adolf (1901—)
Pfingstbuch. (BV) n. d.

Buchner, Hans (1483—1538)
Fundamentbuch, ed. C. Paesler, in *Vierteljahresschrift für Musikwissenschaft,* V (1889).

Burkhard, Willy (1900–)
Werke für Orgel. (BV) 1954–58.

Buxtehude, Dietrich (1637–1707)
Werke für Orgel, ed. Ph. Spitta & M. Seiffert. (B&H) 1876; *Selected Organ Works,* ed. H. Keller, 2 vols. (EP) 1938–39.

Cabanilles, Juan (1644–1712)
Opera omnia, ed. H. Anglés. Barcelona: Biblioteca Central, 1927– .

Cabezón, Antonio de (1510–66)
Claviermusik, ed. S. Kastner. London, 1951; *Pièces pour orgue,* ed. C. Gay. Paris: Schola Cantorum, 1956– .

Cavazzoni, Girolamo (1520–1560)
Orgelwerke, ed. O. Mischiati, 2 vols. (Sch) 1959–60.

Cavazzoni da Bologna detto d'Urbino, Marcantonio (ca. 1490–ca. 1570)
Recherchari, motetti, canzoni, libro primo (1523), in *Die italienische Orgelmusik am Anfang des Cinquecento,* ed. K. Jeppesen. Copenhagen: Munksgaard, 1943 (second edition, 1960); another edition, ed. G. Benvenuti, in *I Classici musicali italiani,* Vol. VI. Milan: Società anonima notari la Santa, 1919–21.

Clérambault, Louis Nicolas (1676–1749).
Livre d'orgue, ed. A. Guilmant, *Archives,* III, 3. (Sch) 1903; ed. F. Raugel. Paris: Schola Cantorum, 1952.

Coelho, Manuel Rodrigues (1583–ca. 1623 or after)
Flores de musica para o instrumento de tecla & arpa (1620), ed. S. Kastner, Vols. I and III of *Portugaliae Musica.* Lisbon: Fundação Calouste Gulbenkian, 1959–61.

Correa de Arauxo, Francisco (ca. 1575–1663)
Libro de tientos y discursos . . . de organo intitulado Facultad organica, in Vols. VI & XII of *Monumentos de la musica espanola,* ed. S. Kastner. Barcelona: Instituto espanol de musicologia, in progress.

Couperin, François (1668–1733)
Livre d'orgue (1690), in *Archives,* V, 2, *Oeuvres complètes,* ed. M. Cauchie, 12 vols. Paris: L'oiseau lyre, 1932–33, organ works in Vol. VI.

David, Johann Nepomuk (1895–)
Choralwerk; Choralvorspiele, Partiten, Toccaten, Fantasien, Passacaglien; and other works for organ (B&H) 1932– .

Degen, Helmut (1911–)
Weihnachtsmusik "Kommet, ihr Hirten." (BV) n. d.; *Konzert für Orgel und Orchester.* (Sch) 1943.

Distler, Hugo (1908–1942)
Veni Redemptor; Wachet auf; Kleine Choralbearbeitungen, Op. 8 (BV) 1958–60; *Spielstücke für die Kleinorgel; Orgelsonate.* (BV) pref. 1939.

Driessler, Johannes (1921–)
Orgelsonaten durch das Kirchenjahr, Op. 30. (BV) 1954–56; *Toccata und Hymnus.* (B&H) 1964.

Drischner, Max (1891–)
Tokkata und Fuge (Schult); *Nordische Kanzonen* (Schult); *Norwegische Variationen* (Schult); *Sonnenhymnus* (Schult). n. d.

Du Mage, Pierre (1676–1751)
Livre d'orgue (1708), Archives, III, 4: ed. F. Raugel. Paris: Schola Cantorum, 1952.

Dupré, Marcel (1886–)
Symphonie-passion, Op. 21. (Leduc) 1921; *Trois préludes et fugues*, Op. 35. (Born) 1938; *Le tombeau de Titelouze*, Op. 38. (Born) 1942; *Le chemin de la croix*, Op. 29. Paris: Durand, 1931–32.

Erbach, Christian (1573–1635)
Acht Kanzonen für Orgel oder andere Tasteninstrumente, ed. A. Reichling, Vol. XXIII of *Veröffentlichungen der Gesellschaft der Orgelfreunde.* (MeV) 1965. (Complete ed. in preparation in CEKM.)

Fasolo, Giovanni Battista (17th century)
Annuale (Venice, 1645), ed. R. Walter. (SDM) 1965.

Fischer, Johann Kaspar Ferdinand (ca. 1670–1746)
Ariadne musica (1702), ed. E. Kaller (*LO 7*); *Musikalischer Blumenstrauss, SDOB*, 1 (1965); *Sämtliche Werke für Klavier und Orgel*, ed. E. von Werra Leipzig, 1901.

Franck, César (1822–90)
Six Pièces. Paris: Durand, 1860–62; *Trois Pièces*. Paris: Durand, 1878; *Orgelwerke*, ed. O. Barblan. (EP) 1921.

Frescobaldi, Girolamo (1583–1643)
Orgel- und Klavierwerke, Gesamtausgabe, ed. P. Pidoux. (BV) 1949–55; *Selected Organ Works*, 2 vols., ed. H. Keller. (EP) 1943; *Sonate*, in *I Classici musicali italiani*, ed. G. Benvenuti, Vol. XII. Milan: Società anonima notari le Santa, 1919–21.

Froberger, Johann Jacob (1616–67)
Orgel- und Klavierwerke, in *DTO*, vols. VIII, XIII, XXI (1897–1903), reprint, Graz, 1960; *Selected Works, Organum*, 11.

Gabrieli, Andrea (ca. 1510–86)
Canzoni alla francese, ed. P. Pidoux. (BV) 1953; *Intonationen*, ed. P. Pidoux. (BV) 1959; *Ricercari*, ed. P. Pidoux. (BV) 1952.

Gabrieli, Giovanni (ca. 1555–1612)
Gabrieli composizioni per organo, ed. S. D. Libera. (Ric) 1957.

Geiser, Walther (1897–)
Fantasie I, Op. 17a. (BV) 1931; *Fantasie II*, Op. 28. (BV) 1939; *Sonatine*, Op. 26. (BV) 1939; *Konzertstück für Orgel und Kammer-Orch.*, Op. 30. (BV) 1941.

Grabner, Hermann (1886–)
Media vita in morte sumus, Die Orgel, Reihe I, 2. (K&S) 1957; *Pater noster*. Leipzig: Kahnt, n. d.; *Christ ist erstanden* (K&S); *Sonate* (K&S); *Erhalt*

uns, Herr, bei deinem Wort (K&S), n. d.

Grigny, Nicolas de (1672 – 1703)
  Premier livre d'orgue. Archives, V, 1.

Handel, Georg Frideric (1685 – 1759)
  Works, ed. F. Chrysander, 100 vols. Leipzig: Deutsche Händelgesell-
  schaft, 1858 – 83. Reprint by Gregg Press, Ridgewood, N. J., 1965 –.
  (Organ Concerti in Vol. XXVIII); *Sechs Orgelkonz.,* Op. 4, ed. S. de Lange.
  (EP) 1953; *Concerti per l'organo et altri stromenti,* Op. 4, ed. K. Matthaei.
  (BV) 1948; *Concerti per organo,* Op. 4, ed. H. Walcha. (Sch) 1940 – 42;
  Orgelkonz., Op. 4 & Op. 7, ed. M. Seiffert. (B&H) 1924 – 28; *Seize con-
  certos,* ed. M. Dupré, 3 vols. (Born) 1937.

Hessenberg, Kurt (1908 –   )
  Choralpartiten, Op. 43. (Sch) 1952; *Trio-Sonata.* (Sch) 1952.

Hindemith, Paul (1895 – 1963)
  Konzert. (Sch) 1928; *Orgelsonate I.* (Sch) 1937; *Orgelsonate II.* (Sch) 1937;
  Orgelsonate III. (Sch) 1940; *Concerto for Organ and Orchestra.* (Sch) 1962.

Hofhaimer, Paul (1459 – 1537)
  Gesammelte Tonwerke, Anhang to H. J. Moser, *Paul Hofhaimer.* Berlin:
  Cotta, 1929.

Kaminski, Heinrich (1886 – 1946)
  Tokkata über "Wie schön leuchtet der Morgenstern." (UE) 1923; *Choral-
  sonate.* (UE) 1926; *Drei Choralvorspiele* (UE) 1928; *Toccata und Fuge.*
  (BV) 1939; *Andante.* (BV) 1939; *Orgelchoral.* (BV) 1947.

Karg-Elert, Sigfrid (1877 – 1933)
  Sechsundsechzig Choral-Improvisationen, Op. 65, 6 vols. (B&H) 1909;
  3 Impressions, Op. 72. London: Novello, 1911; *Diverse Pieces,* Op. 75.
  London: Novello, 1910; *Chaconne and Fugue Trilogy,* Op. 73. London:
  Novello, 1912; *Passacaglia and Fugue on B-A-C-H,* Op. 150. (HE) 1933.

Kerll, Johann Kaspar (1627 – 93)
  Selected Works. DTB, II, 2 (1901); *Modulatio organica* (1686). *SDOB,* 2
  (1956).

Kickstat, Paul (1893 –   )
  Zehn Postludien für die Festtage des Kirchenjahres. (MeV) n. d.

Kluge, Manfred (1928 –   )
  Fantasie in drei Rhythmen. (B&H) 1957; *Vater unser im Himmelreich.*
  (B&H) 1963.

Kötschau, Joachim (1906 –   )
  Sonata in C Minor, Op. 24. Mehner; *Kleines Choralbuch,* Op. 26. (B&H)
  1952.

Krebs, Johann Ludwig (1713 – 80)
  Gesammtausgabe der Tonstücke für Orgel, ed. C. Geissler. Magdeburg:
  Heinrichshofen, 18 –; *Orgelwerke,* ed. W. Zöllner. (EP) 1938.   195

Krieger, Johann Philipp (1649—1725)
  Ausgewählte Orgelstücke, ed. M. Seiffert. (K&S) 1930.

Liszt, Franz (1811—1886)
  Musikalische Werke, ed. Franz Liszt-Stiftung, 31 vols. (B&H) 1908—36;
  Negy orgonamii, ed. S. Pecsi. Budapest: Zenemiikiado Vallalat, 1961.

Lublin, Johannes de (16th century)
  Tablature of Keyboard Music, ed. J. R. White, 6 pts. *CEKM*, VI.

Lübeck, Vincent (1654—1740)
  Vier Praeludien und Fugen für Orgel, ed. M. Seiffert, in *Organum*, 9;
  Musikalische Werke, ed. G. Harms. (Ugr) 1921; *Orgelwerke*, ed. H. Keller.
  (EP) 1941.

Mendelssohn-Bartholdy, Felix (1809—47)
  Compositionen für die Orgel, ed. F. A. Roitzsch. (EP) n. d. *Oeuvres pour
  orgue*, ed. M. Dupré. (Born) 1948.

Merulo, Claudio (1533—1604)
  Canzonen, 1592, ed. P. Pidoux. (BV) 1954.

Messiaen, Olivier (1908—   )
  Apparition de l'église éternelle. (Lem) 1934; *L'ascension*. (Leduc) 1934;
  Le banquet céleste. (Leduc) 1934; *La nativité du Seigneur*. (Leduc) 1936;
  Les corps glorieux. (Leduc) 1942; *Livre d'orgue*. (Leduc) 1953; *Messe le la
  Pentecôte*. (Leduc) 1951.

Micheelsen, Hans Friedrich (1902—   )
  Musik für Orgel. (BV) 1947—54.

Mozart, Wolfgang Amadeus (1756—91)
  Drei Stücke für ein Orgelwerk in einer Uhr, ed. Brinkmann. (BV) n. d.

Muffat, Georg (1653—1704)
  Apparatus musico-organisticus (1690), ed. S. de Lange. (EP) 1888; *Apparatus musico-organisticus. SDOB*, 3 (1957).

Murschhauser, Franz Xaver Anton (1663—1738)
  Octi-tonium novum organicum. SDOB, 6 (1961).

Nielsen, Ludvig (1910—   )
  Variationen, Op. 2; Fantasie, Op. 4.

Nivers, Guillaume Gabriel (1632—1714)
  Premier livre d'orgue (1665), ed. N. Dufourcq, 2 vols. (Born) 1963; *Troi-
  sieme livre d'orgue*, ed. N. Dufourcq,Vol. I/14 of *Publications de la société
  française de Musicologie* (1958).

Pachelbel, Johann (1653—1706)
  94 Kompositionen, ed. H. Botstiber & M. Schneider, in *DTO, XVI* (1901).
  Selected Organ Works. Organum, 12—14; ed. K. Matthaei, 4 vols. (BV)
  1934—49.

Pachelbel, Wilhelm Hieronymus (1686—1764)
  Complete Edition of Extant Organ Works, ed. H. J. Moser and T. Fedtke.
  (BV) 1957.

Paumann, Conrad (ca. 1415—73)
Fundamentum organisandi, facsimile ed., ed. K. Ameln. Berlin, 1925; "Das Locheimer Liederbuch nebst der Ars organisandi von Conrad Paumann," ed. F. Arnold & H. Bellermann, in *Jahrbücher für musikalische Wissenschaft*, II (1867), 1—234.

Peeters, Flor (1903—)
Toccata, Fugue et Hymne "Ave maris stella." (Lem) 1936; *Zehn Orgel-choräle*. (Sch) 1937; *Passacaglia und Fuge*. (Sch) 1938; *Drei Präludien und Fugen*. (Sch) 1951; *Lied-Symphony*. (EP) 1950; *Hymn Preludes for the Liturgical Year*, 24 vols. (EP) 1966—69.

Pepping, Ernst (1901—)
Konzerte. (Sch) 1942; *Fugen*. (Sch) 1949; *Grosses Orgelbuch*, 3 vols. (Sch) 1941; *Kleines Orgelbuch*. (Sch) 1941; *Partitas*, 3 vols. (BV) 1953; *Hymnen*. (BV) 1954; *Böhmisches Orgelbuch*. (BV) 1953—; *12 Choral-vorspiele*. (BV) 1957.

Praetorius, Michael (1571—1621)
Sämtliche Orgelwerke, ed. K. Matthaei. Wolfenbüttel: Kallmeyer-Möseler, 1930.

Raphael, Günter (1903—60)
Orgelwerke. (B&H) 1930—47.

Reda, Siegfried (1916—)
Orgelmusik, 4 vols. (BV) 1953—57.

Reger, Max (1873—1916)
Complete Organ Works, ed. H. Klotz, Vols. XV—XVIII of *Complete Works*. (B&H) 1954.

Easy compositions:
Passacaglia in D Minor (B&H); *Fünf leichte Präludien und Fugen*, Op. 56. (UE) 1904; *Dreizehn leichte Choralvorspiele*, Op. 79b. Langensalza: Beyer, 1904; *Vier Präludien und Fugen*, Op. 85. (EP) 1905; *Dreissig kleine Choralvorspiele*, Op. 135a. (EP) 1928; *Sieben Stücke*, Op. 145. (B&H) 1938.

Chorale Preludes and Chorale Fantasies:
Zweiundfünfzig Choralvorspiele, Op. 67. (UE) 1908; *Ein feste Burg ist unser Gott*, Op. 27. (EP) 1934; *Freu dich sehr, o meine Seele*, Op. 30. (UE) 1904; *Wie schön leuchtet der Morgenstern*, Op. 40, No. 1 (UE) 1910; *Straf mich nicht in deinem Zorn*, Op. 40, No. 2. (UE) 1910; *Alle Menschen müssen sterben*, Op. 52, No. 1. (UE) 1910; *Wachet auf, ruft uns die Stimme*, Op. 52, No. 2. (UE) 1912; *Halleluja! Gott zu loben*, Op. 52, No. 3. (UE) 1910.

Preludes, Fugues, Canons, Bassi Ostinati, Passacaglias, and other forms:
Zwölf Stücke, Op. 59. (EP) 1901; *Zwölf Stücke*, Op. 65. (EP) 1902; *Zwölf Stücke*, Op. 80. (EP) 1904; *Monologe*, Op. 63. (UE) 1908; *Zehn Stücke*, Op. 69. (B&B) 1908; *Neun Stücke*, Op. 129. (B&B) 1913; *Suite in G Minor*, Op. 92. Leipzig: Forberg, 1906.

Larger Works:

Sonata in F-sharp Minor, Op. 33 (UE) 1904; *Sonata in D Minor*, Op. 60. Leipzig: Leuckart, 1902; *Fantasie und Fugue B-A-C-H*, Op. 46. (UE) 1904; *Fantasie und Fuge* (D Minor), Op. 135b. (EP) 1928; *Symphonische Fantasie und Fuge*, Op. 57. (UE) 1904; *Variationen und Fuge über ein Originalthema* (F-sharp Minor), Op. 73. (B&B) 1909; *Introduktion, Passacaglia und Fuge* (E Minor), Op. 127. (B&B) 1913.

Practical Performance Edition:
Präludien und Fugen, selected from Op. 59, 65, 80, and 85, ed. Straube, 4 vols. (EP) 1929.

Reincken, Jan Adam (1623–1722)
Complete Works. CEKM, XVI (1967).

Reubke, Adolf (1805–75)
Sonate (Der 94. Psalm), ed. H. Keller. (EP) 1958.

Roberday, François (ca. 1624–ca. 1680)
Fugues et Caprices. Archives, III, 1

Roeseling, Kaspar (1894–1960)
Ostinato grave. (Sch) 1935; *Choralvorspiele.* (SDM) 1960

Rössler, Ernst (1909–   )
Introductio. (BV) 1959; *Passionsmusik.* (BV) 1954.

Sandberg Nielsen, Otto (1900–41)
Präludium, Trio und Ciacona "Auf meinen lieben Gott." Edition Dania. n. d.

Scheidemann, Heinrich (ca. 1596–1663)
Chorale Preludes, ed. G. Fock. (BV) 1967.

Scheidt, Samuel (1587–1654)
Tabulatura Nova (1624), ed. M. Seiffert, in *DDT,* 1 (1892), reprint, revised by H. J. Moser, Wiesbaden, 1958; *Werke,* ed. G. Harms, 7 vols. (Ugr) 1923–53; *Ausgewählte Werke für Orgel und Klavier,* ed. H. Keller. (EP) 1939; *Das Görlitzer Tabulaturbuch,* ed. Ch. Mahrenholz. (EP) 1941.

Schlick, Arnold (ca. 1460–after 1521)
Tabulaturen etlicher Lobgesäng (1512), ed. G. Harms. Klecken, 1924. Second edition. (Ugr) 1957.

Schroeder, Hermann (1904–   )
Werke für Orgel, 6 vols. (Sch) 1931–60.

Schumann, Robert (1810–56)
Werke, ed. C. Schumann. (B&H) 1881–93; *Oeuvres pour orgue,* ed. M. Dupré. (Born) 1948.

Schwarz-Schilling, Reinhard (1904–   )
12 Choralvorspiele. (BV) 1953; *Präludium und Fuge.* (BV) 1949; *Concerto per organo.* (MeV) 1959.

Seeger, Josef Ferdinand Norbert (1716–82)
Selected Works. Organum, 22.

Speuy, Hendrik (ca. 1575–ca. 1625)
Psalm Preludes, ed. F. Noske. Amsterdam: Heuwekemeijer, 1963.

Stanley, Charles John (1713–86)
Voluntaries for the Organ, facs. ed., ed. D. Vaughan, 3 vols. London: Oxford University Press, 1957.

Stockmeier, Wolfgang (1931–)
Konzert für Orgel und Streichorchester. Wolfenbüttel: Möseler, 1962; *Sonata.* Wolfenbüttel: Möseler, 1961.

Sweelinck, Jan Pieterszoon (1562–1621)
Werken voor Orgel en Clavicimbal, ed. M. Seiffert. (B&H) 1894. Reprint, Amsterdam, 1943; Selected Works, ed. D. Hellmann, 2 vols. (EP) 1957.

Tallis, Thomas (ca. 1505–85)
Complete Keyboard Works, ed. D. Stevens. (HE) 1953.

Tagliavini, Luigi Ferdinando (1929–)
Passacaglia on a Theme of Hindemith. Padua: Zanibon, 1929.

Telemann, Georg Philipp (1681–1767)
Musikalische Werke, ed. T. Fedtke. (BV) in progress (Organ Works in Vol. 13); *Zwölf leichte Choralvorspiele,* ed. H. Keller. (EP) 1936.

Titelouze, Jehan (1563–1633)
Oeuvres completes. Archives, I.

Tournemire, Charles (1870&1939)
L'orgue mystique. Paris: Heugel, n. d.; *Suite évocatrice.* (Born) 1938; *Cinq improvisations pour orgue,* ed. M. Duruflé. Paris: Durand, 1958.

Tunder, Franz (1614–67)
Complete Chorale Preludes, ed. R. Walter. (Sch) 1956.

Viderø, Finn (1904–)
Passacaglia in D Minor. Copenhagen, n. d.

Walther, Johann Gottfried (1684–1748)
Gesammelte Werke für Orgel, ed. M. Seiffert, in *DDT,* Vols. XXVI & XXVII. Reprint, revised by H. J. Moser, Wiesbaden, 1959; *Selected Works for Organ. Organum,* 15; *Selected Organ Works,* ed. W. Buszin. St. Louis: Concordia, 1948; *Selected Chorale Preludes,* ed. Th. Beck. St. Louis: Concordia, 1964.

Weber, Heinrich (1901–)
Choralvorspiele, Op. 10. Schwann; *Passacaglia in E Minor,* Op. 8. Schwann; *Fünf kleine Stücke.* Böhm; *Variationen und Fuge.* Böhm; *Toccata "Haec dies."* Böhm; *Triptychon.* Viersen; *Choral, Variations et Fantasie* (Leduc), n. d.

Weckmann, Matthias (1621–74)
Gesammelte Werke, ed. G. Ilgner, in Series II, No. 4 of *Erbe Deutscher Musik.* Leipzig, 1942; *Selected works for Organ. Organum,* 3.

Widor, Charles-Marie (1844–1937)
4 Symphonien, Op. 13. Paris: Hamelle, 1901; *4 Symphonien,* Op. 42. Paris: Hamelle, 1901; *Gotische Symphonie,* Op. 70, No. 9. (Sch) 1895; *Romantische Symphonie,* Op. 73, No. 10. Paris: Hamelle, 1900.

Zimmermann, Heinz Werner (1930–)
Orgelpsalmen. (MeV) 1958.

Zipp, Friedrich (1914–)
Freie Orgelstücke. (MeV) 1962.

Organ Playing and Registration

Aldrich, Putnam
Ornamentation in J. S. Bach's Organ Works. New York: Coleman-Ross, 1950.

Bédos de Celles, Dom François
"Les principaux mélanges ordinaires des jeux de l'orgue," *L'Art du facteur d'orgues* (Paris, 1766–78), reprint, ed. Ch. Mahrenholz. (BV) 1963. II, 523–36.

Bunk, Gerard
Liebe zur Orgel, Vol. XVIII of *Veröffentlichungen der Gesellschaft der Orgelfreunde,* 3d ed. Dortmund: Ardey, 1958.

Bruggaier, Eduard
Studien zur Geschichte des Orgelpedalspiels in Deutschland bis zur Zeit Johann Sebastian Bachs. Ph. D. dissertation, Goethe-Universität, Frankfurt a. M., 1959 (available from BV-Antiquariat).

Dallman, Wolfgang
"Die Kunst des Übens," *Der Kirchenmusiker,* XVIII (1964), 97.

––––––. "Lockerheit beim Orgelspiel," *Württembergische Blätter für Kirchenmusik,* XXV (1958), 57.

Dietrich, Fritz
Elemente der Orgelchoralimprovisation. (BV) 1935.

Dolmetsch, Arnold
The Interpretation of the Music of the Seventeenth and Eighteenth Centuries Revealed by Contemporary Evidence. London: Novello, 1916; rev. in 1946.

Donington, Robert
The Interpretation of Early Music. London: Faber & Faber, 1963.

Dupré, Marcel
Cours complet d'improvisation à l'orgue, 2 vols. (Leduc) 1925–37.

––––––. *Exercises préparatoires a l'improvisation.* Paris: Herelle, 1937.

––––––. *Méthode d'orgue.* (Leduc) 1958.

Enright, Richard
Introduction to Organ Playing. Nashville, Tenn.: Abingdon Press, 1964.

Ferand, Ernst Thomas
Improvisation in Nine Centuries of Western Music. Cologne: Arno Volk, 1961. (This is an anthology with historical introduction.)

Fischer, Martin
Die organistische Improvisation im 17. Jahrhundert. (BV) 1929.

Geer, Ezra Harold
Organ Registration in Theory and Practice. Glen Rock, N. J.: J. Fischer, 1957.

Germani, Fernando
Metodo per organo. Method for the Organ, new ed. Rome: De Santis, 1960.

Gleason, Harold
Method of Organ Playing, 5th ed. New York: Appleton-Century-Crofts, 1962.

Guilmant, Alexandre
"La musique d'orgue," *Encyclopédie de la musique et dictionnaire du conservatoire,* ed. A. Lavignac & L. de la Laurencie, II parts in 11 vols. Paris: Delagrave, 1913−31. II/2, 1125−1180.

Hluchán, Jan
Kleine Schule des Pedalspiels. Prague: Artia, 1962.

Huré, Jean
La Technique de l'orgue. Paris: Sénart, 1917.

———. *L'Esthétique de l'orgue.* Paris: Sénart, 1923.

Johnson, David N.
Instruction Book for Beginning Organists. Minneapolis: Augsburg, 1964.

Kee, Cor
Honderd adviezen betreffende orgelimprovisatie. n. d.

Keller, Hermann
Phrasing and Articulation; a Contribution to a Rhetoric of Music, Trans. L. Gerdine. New York: W. W. Norton, 1965. Translation of *Phrasierung und Artikulation.* (B&H) 1955.

———. *Schule der Choralimprovisation.* (EP) pref. 1939.

———. *Schule des klassischen Triospiels.* (BV) 1928. Fourth edition, 1955.

Koch, Johannes H. E.
"Vorübungen zur Improvisation auf der Orgel," *Kirchenmusik, Vermächtnis und Aufgabe, 1948−1958. Festschrift zum zehnjährigen Bestehen der Westfälischen Landeskirchenmusikschule in Herford,* ed. W. Ehmann. Darmstadt: Tonkunst-Verlag, 1958. 86−99.

Klotz, Hans
Fünfzehn Übungsstücke für das Orgelpedal, 2d ed. (BV) 1964.

———. "Orgelspiel," *Die Musik in Geschichte und Gegenwart,* ed. F. Blume, 14 vols. to date. (BV) 1949−. X, 385−96.

———. *Über die Orgelkunst der Gotik, der Renaissance und des Barock.* (BV) 1934. (This is an exposition of the classical principles of registration and of organ design.)

Krapf, Gerhard
Organ Improvisation: A Practical Approach to Chorale Elaborations for the Service. Minneapolis: Augsburg, 1966.

Matthaei, Karl
  Vom Orgelspiel, 2d ed. (B&H) 1949.

Messiaen, Olivier
  The Technique of My Musical Language, trans. J. Satterfield, 2 vols.
  (Leduc) 1944—66.

Peeters, Flor
  Ars organi [organ method in four languages], 3 vols. (Sch) 1952—53.

Rameau, Jean Philippe
  "De la mécanique des doigts sur le clavecin, à observer pareillement
  sur l'orgue," *Pièces de clavecin* (1724), ed. E. Jacobi. (BV) 1958, rev.
  ed. 1961, 16—21.

Rössler, Ernst Karl
  Klangfunktion und Registrierung. (BV) 1952

Senn, Kurt Wolfgang
  "Zu den Fragen künstlerischer Interpretationskunst," *Musik und
  Gottesdienst,* V/3 (1951); 81.

Tell, Werner
  Improvisationslehre für die Orgel. Berlin: Pro Musica, 1954.

———. *Schule des gottesdienstlichen Orgelspiels,* 3d. ed. (MeV) 1964.

———. *Von der Orgel und vom Orgelspiel.* Berlin: Evangelische Verlags-
  anstalt, 1949. 2d ed. 1956.

Thalben-Ball, George
  Variations on a Theme by Paganini: A Study for the Pedals. London:
  Novello, 1962.

Tournemire, Charles
  Précis d'exécution de registration et d'improvisation à l'orgue. Paris: Eschig;
  New York: Associated, 1936.

Veldcamps, Aeneas Egbertus
  "Instructie van het gebruyk van alle de Registers van het Nieuwe
  Orgel der Stadt Gouda, 1736," *Bouwstenen van de Vereniging voor
  Nederlandse Musiekgeschiedenis,* 1965.

Viderø, Finn
  School of Organ Playing. (Han) 1963.

Walcha, Helmut
  "Zum Choralvorspiel," *Musik und Kirche,* V/5 (1933), 237—51; VI/6
  (1934), 310—18.

Organ Stops

Audsley, George Ashdown
  Organ Stops and Their Artistic Registration. New York: H. W. Gray, 1921.

Bunjes, Paul George
  "A Classification of Basic Organ Voices," *Church Music 67.1.* St. Louis:
  Concordia, 1967.

Goebel, Joseph
  Theorie und Praxis des Orgelpfeifenklangs. Intonieren und Stimmen.
  (BV-Antiquariat) 1967.

Hunt, Noel Aubrey Bonavia, and H. W. Homer
  The Organ Reed. New York: J. Fischer, 1950.

Irwin, Stevens
  Dictionary of Pipe Organ Stops. New York: G. Schirmer, 1962.

Jahnn, Hans Henny
  "Die Registernamen und ihr Inhalt," *Beiträge zur Organistentagung
  Hamburg-Lübeck*, 1925, ed. G. Harms. (Ugr) 1925.

Locher, Carl
  *Erklärung der Orgel-Register mit Vorschlägen zu wirksamen Register-
  mischungen.* Bern: Nydegger & Baumgart, 1887; Rev. ed., *Die Orgelregister, ihr Klang und ihr Gebrauch*, ed. P. Smets. Mainz, 1943; Translation
  from the fourth edition, *Dictionary of the Organ; Organ Registers, Their
  Timbres, Combinations, and Acoustic Phenomena*, trans. C. Landi. New
  York: E. P. Dutton, 1914; Reprint of the fifth edition, *Die Orgel-Register
  und ihre Klangfarben*, ed. J. Dobler (Bern, 1912), in preparation. Hil-
  versum: F. Knuf. *Bib Org*, XII.

Mahrenholz, Christhard
  Die Orgelregister, ihre Geschichte und ihr Bau, 2d ed. (BV) 1968.

Schneider, Thekla
  *Die Namen der Orgelregister. Kompendium aller Registerbezeichnungen
  aus alter und neuer Zeit.* (BV) 1958.

Sundberg, Johan
  Mensurens betydelse i oppna labialpipor, Vol. III of *Acta universitatis
  Upsaliensis studia musicologica Upsaliensia nova series.* Uppsala: 1966.

The Organ in the Liturgy

Gotsch, Herbert
  "The Organ in the Lutheran Service of the Sixteenth Century," *Church
  Music 67.1.* St. Louis: Concordia, 1967.

Klotz, Hans
  "Die kirchliche Orgelkunst," *Leiturgia, Handbuch des evangelischen
  Gottesdienstes*, IV (1961), 759—804.

Krapf, Gerhard
  Liturgical Organ Playing. Minneapolis: Augsburg, 1964.

Mehl, Johannes G.
  Die Aufgabe der Orgel im Gottesdienst der Lutherischen Kirche. Munich:
  Lempp, 1938.

Rietschel, Georg
  Die Aufgabe der Orgel im Gottesdienste bis in das achtzehnte Jahrhundert.
  Leipzig, 1893.

Senn, Kurt Wolfgang
"Pfarrer und Organist," *Musik und Kirche*, XXI (1951), 134–38.
Türk, Daniel Gottlob
Von den wichtigsten Pflichten eines Organisten. Bib Org, V, 1966.

History of the Art of the Organ

Antegnati, Costanzo
L'Arte organica (Brescia, 1608), reprint, ed. R. Lunelli. Mainz: Rheingold, 1938.

Apel, Willi
Die Geschichte der Klaviermusik bis 1700. (BV) 1967.

Arbus, Marie Réginald
Une merveille d'art provencal, le grand orgue de la basilique de St.-Maximin-la-Ste-Baume et l'histoire generale de l'orgue. Aix-en-Provence, 1956.

Armstrong, William H.
Organs for America. Philadelphia: University of Pennsylvania Press, 1967.

Banchieri, Adriano
Conclusioni nel suono dell'organo (Bologna, 1609), facs. reprint. Milan: Bollettino bibliografico musicale, 1934.

Bösken, Franz
Die Orgelbauerfamilie Stumm aus Rhaunen-Sulzbach und ihr Werk. Mainz: Verlag des Mainzer Altertumsvereins, 1960.

Bouman, Arie
Nederland—Orgelland. Leiden: Spruyt, Van Mantgem & de Does, 1964.

Burgemeister, Ludwig
Der Orgelbau in Schlesien. Strassburg: Heitz, 1925.

Clutton, Cecil, and Austin Niland
The British Organ. London: Batsford, 1963.

Dähnert, Ulrich
Der Orgel- und Instrumentenbauer Zacharias Hildebrandt. (B&H) 1960.
_____. *Die Orgeln Gottfried Silbermanns in Mitteldeutschland.* Leipzig: Koehler & Amelang, 1953.

Deschrevel, Antoon
"Historische terugblik op het orgel in West-Vlaanderen. Ieperinternational centrum van Orgelbouw en orgelcultuur in de Loop der tijden (familie Langhedul [Languedeuil] en Jacobus van Eynde)," *West-Vlaanderen,* XI (1962), 23.

Dreimüller, Karl
"Beiträge zur niederrheinischen Orgelgeschichte," *Beiträge zur rheinischen Musikgeschichte,* XIV (1955), 17–51.

Dufourcq, Norbert
Documents inédits relatifs à l'orgue français, 2 vols. Paris: Droz, 1934–35.

_____. *Esquisse d'une histoire de l'orgue en France du XIIIe au XVIIIe siecle.* Paris: Larousse, 1935.

_____. *Jean de Joyeuse et la pénétration de la facture d'orgues parisienne dans le Midi de la France au XVIIme siècle.* Paris: Picard, 1958.

_____. *La musique d'orgue française de Jehan Titelouze a Jehan Alain.* Paris: Librairie Floury, 1949.

_____. *Le grand orgue de la chapelle Saint Louis du prytanée militaire de la flèche.* Paris: Picard, 1964.

_____. *Les Cliquot; facteurs d'orgues du Roy.* Paris: Floury, 1942.

Eberstaller, Oskar
Orgeln und Orgelbauer in Oesterreich. Graz: Bählaus, 1955.

Eggebrecht, Hans Heinrich
Die Orgelbewegung. Stuttgart: Musikwissenschaftliche Verlags-Gesellschaft, 1967.

Erici, Einar
"Eine kurze schwedische Orgelgeschichte im Lichte des heutigen Bestandes," *Musik und Kirche,* XXVI (1956), 97—104, 176—86.

_____. *Inventarium over bevarade aldre kyrkorglar i Sverige tillkomna fore mitten av. 1800-talet nagra ock mellan aren 1850 och 1865 och ett par annu senare, men dock stilistiskt sammanhorande med de aldre.* (BV-Antiquariat) 1965.

Fellot, Jean
A la recherche de l'orgue classique. Paris: l'auteur, 1961.

Fischer, Johannes
Das Orgelbauergeschlecht Walcker in Ludwigsburg. (BV) 1943.

Flade, Ernst
Gottfried Silbermann: ein Beitrag zur Geschichte des deutschen Orgel- und Klavierbaus im Zeitalter Bachs, 2d ed. (B&H) 1953. English translation, in *Organ Institute Quarterly,* III/3, 32—47; III/4, 26—34; IV/1, 36—61; IV/2, 38—57; IV/3, 38—51; IV/4, 28—41 (1953—54).

Friis, Niels
Orgelbygning i Danmark; Renaissance, Barok og Rokoko. Copenhagen: Friis, 1949.

Frotscher, Gotthold
Geschichte des Orgelspiels und der Orgelkomposition, 2d ed., 2 vols. (MeV) 1959.

_____. *Orgeln* [includes phono-record]. (BV-Antiquariat) 1968.

Gurlitt, Wilibald
"Der Kursächsische Hoforgelmacher Gottfried Fritzsche," *Festschrift Arnold Schering.* Berlin: Glas, 1937.

Haacke, Walter
Die Entwicklungsgeschichte des Orgelbaus im Lande Mecklenburg-Schwerin

von den Anfängen bis ins ausgehende 18. Jahrhundert. Wolfenbüttel: Kallmeyer, 1935.

Hedar, Josef
Dietrich Buxtehudes Orgelwerke. Stockholm: Nordiska Musikförlaget, 1951.

Hess, Joachim
Dispositien van de merkwaardigste Kerk-orgeln. Gouda: Vander Klos, 1774.

Hickmann, Hans
Das Portativ. (BV) 1936.

Hinrichsen, Max, ed.
Music Book VIII: The Organ of Bach . . . and matters related to this subject. (HE) 1956.

————. *Music Book X: Organ and Choral, Aspects and Prospects.* (HE) 1958.

Hoppe, Alfred
Die Orgel der Kirche zu Himmelpforten. Stade, 1952.

Hulverscheidt, Hans
"Die rheinische Orgellandschaft," *Jahrbuch der rheinischen Denkmalpflege* XXV (1965).

Kalkoff, Artur
Das Orgelschaffen Max Regers im Lichte der Deutschen Orgelerneuerungsbewegung. (BV) 1950.

Kaufmann, Walter
Die Orgeln des alten Herzogtums Oldenburg. Oldenburg: Stalling, 1962.

Keller, Hermann
Die Orgelwerke Bachs, (EP) 1948. English translation, *The Organ Works of Bach,* trans. H. Hewitt. (EP) 1967.

Kirby, F. E.
A Short History of Keyboard Music. New York: The Free Press, 1966.

Klotz, Hans
"Gedanken zur Orgelmusik Max Regers," Mitteilungen des Max-Reger-Instituts, VII (1958)

Loewenfeld, Hans
Leonhard Kleber und sein Orgeltabulaturbuch als Beitrag zur Geschichte der Orgelmusik im beginnenden 16. Jahrhundert. Berlin, 1897; reprint. (BV-Antiquariat) 1968.

Lunelli, Renato
Der Orgelbau in Italien in seinen Meisterwerken vom 14. Jahrhundert bis zur Gegenwart. Mainz: Rheingold, 1956.

————. *L'arte organaria del rinascimento in Roma e gli organi di S. Pietro in Vaticano dalle origini a tutto il periodo Frescobaldiana,* Vol. X of *Historiae musicae cultores biblioteca.* Florence, 1958.

Merklin, Alberto
  Organologia. Madrid: Asilo de huérfanos del S. C. De Jesus, 1924.

Meyer, Hermann
  Karl Joseph Riepp, der Orgelbauer von Ottobeuren. (BV) 1939.

Norman, Herbert, and H. John
  The Organ Today. London: Barrie and Rockliff, 1966.

"Les orgues de France," *Bulletin des monuments historiques de la France,* nouvelle serie, VIII/2—3 (1962). Introduction by J. Verrier. Contributions by various authors.

Perrot, Jean
  L'orgue de ses origines hellénistiques a la fin du XIIIᵉ siècle. Paris: Picard, 1965.

Phelps, Lawrence I.
  "A Short History of the Organ Revival," *Church Music 67.1.* St. Louis: Concordia, 1967.

Quoika, Rudolf
  Das Positiv in Geschichte und Gegenwart. (BV) 1957.

———. *Die altösterreichische Orgel der späten Gotik, der Rennaissance und des Barock.* (BV) 1953.

———. *Vom Blockwerk zur Registerorgel. Zur Geschichte der Orgelgotik, 1200—1520.* (BV) 1966.

Reuter, Rudolf
  Orgeln in Westfalen. (BV) 1965.

———. *Altbayern als Orgel-Landschaft,* ed. W. Supper. (MeV) 1954.

Riedel, Friedrich Wilhelm
  Quellenkundliche Beiträge zur Geschichte der Musik für Tasteninstrumente in der zweiten Hälfte des 17. Jahrhunderts, Vol. X of *Schriften des Landesinstitutes fur Musikforschung, Kiel.* (BV) 1960.

Ritter, August Gottfried
  Zur Geschichte des Orgelspiels, vornehmlich des deutschen, im 14. bis zum Anfange des 18. Jahrhunderts, 2 vols. Leipzig: Hesse, 1884.

Rokseth, Yvonne
  La musique d'orgue au XVᵉ siècle et au début du XVIᵉ. Paris: Librairie E. Droz, 1930.

Rücker, Ingeborg
  Die deutsche Orgel am Oberrhein um 1500. Freiburg: Albert, 1940.

Rupp, Emile
  Die Entwicklungsgeschichte der Orgelbaukunst. Einsiedeln: Benziger, 1929.

Schierning, Lydia
  Die Überlieferung der deutschen Orgel- und Klaviermusik aus der ersten Hälfte des 17. Jahrhunderts. (BV) 1961.

Schmieder, Wolfgang
  Thematisch-systematisches Verzeichnis der musikalischen Werke von Johann Sebastian Bach (BWV). (B&H) 1950.

Schneider, Thekla
  "Die Orgelbauerfamilie Compenius," *Archiv für Musikforschung*, II (1937), 8—76.

Seiffert, Max
  Geschichte der Klaviermusik, Vol. 1: *Die ältere Geschichte bis um 1750* (all published). (B&H) 1899.

Sigtenhorst Meyer, Bernhard van den
  Jan Sweelinck en zijn instrumentale muziek. Den Haag: Servire, 1946.

Sponsel, Johann Ulrich
  Orgelhistorie (Nürnberg, 1771), reprint, ed. P. Smets. (BV) 1931; reprint, *Bib Org*, XVIII, 1968.

Stahl, Wilhelm
  Geschichte der Kirchenmusik in Lübeck. (BV) 1931.

———, ed., and others. *Orgelmonographien*, 36 vols. Mainz: Rheingold Verlag, 1942—56.

Stein, Fritz Wilhelm
  Thematisches Verzeichnis der im Druck erschienenen Werke von Max Reger. (B&H) 1953.

Stockmeier, Wolfgang
  Die deutsche Orgelsonate der Gegenwart. Ph. D. dissertation, Cologne, 1958.

Supper, Walter, and Hermann Meyer
  Barockorgeln in Oberschwaben. (BV) 1941.

'T Kruijs, M. H. van
  Verzameling van Disposities der verschillende Orgels in Nederland. *Bib Org*, I, 1962.

Vente, Maarten Albert
  Bouwstoffen tot de Geschiedenis van het Nederlandse Orgel in de 16de Eeuw. Amsterdam: Paris, 1942.

———. *Die Brabanter Orgel*. Amsterdam: Paris, 1958.

———. *Proeve van een repertorium van de Archivalia betrekking hevvende op he Nederlandse Orgel en zijn makers tot omstreeks 1630*. Brussels: Académie royale de Belgique, 1956.

Walcker, Oscar
  Erinnerungen eines Orgelbauers. (BV) 1948.

Wester, Bertil
  Gotisk Resning i Svenska Orglar. Stockholm: Generalstabens litografiska, 1936.

Williams, Peter F.
  The European Organ, 1450—1850. London: Batsford, 1966.

Wilson, Michael
The English Chamber Organ: History and Development, 1650—1850.
Columbia, S. C.: University of South Carolina Press, 1968.

Wörsching, Joseph
Der Orgelbauer Karl Riepp. Mainz: Rheingold, 1939.

_____. *Die Orgelbauerfamilie Silbermann in Strassburg im Elsass,* 2 vols.
Mainz: Rheingold, 1944—47.

Wyly, James
*The Pre-Romantic Spanish Organ; its Structure, Literature, and Use in
Performance.* Ph. D. dissertation, University of Missouri, 1964.

Organ Building and Design

Adlung, Jacob
Musica mechanica organoedi (Berlin, 1768), reprint, ed. Ch. Mahrenholz.
(BV) 1961.

Andersen, Poul Gerhard
Orgelbogen; Klangteknik, Arkitektur og Historie. Copenhagen: Munksgaard, 1956.

Arnaut, Henri
Orgeltraktat (1450), trans. & ed. K. Bormann. (MeV) 1965.

Audsley, George Ashdown
The Art of Organ-Building, 2 vols. New York, 1905; reprint, New York:
Dover Publications, 1965.

Barnes, William Harrison
The Contemporary American Organ, 7th ed. Glen Rock, N. J.: J. Fischer
& Bro., 1959.

Bédos de Celles, Dom François
L'Art du facteur d'orgues (Paris, 1766—78), reprint, ed. Ch. Mahrenholz.
(BV) 1963.

Bendeler, Johann Philipp
*Organopoeia, oder Unterweisung wie eine Orgel nach ihren Hauptstücken
als Mensuriren, Abtheilung derer Laden, Zufall des Windes, Stimmung
oder Temperatur &c.* Frankfurt & Leipzig: Calvisii, ca. 1690.

Bermudo, Juan
Declaracion de instrumentos musicales (Ossuna, 1555), reprint, ed.
S. Kastner. (BV) 1957.

Bunjes, Paul George
The Praetorius Organ. Ph. D. dissertation, University of Rochester,
N. Y., 1966.

Cellier, Alexandre and Henri Bachelin
L'orgue. Paris: Librairie Delagrave, 1933.

Bornefeld, Helmut
Das Positiv, 2d ed. (BV) 1947.

————. *Orgelbau und neue Orgelmusik.* (BV) 1952.

Elis, Carl
Orgelwörterbuch. (BV) 1933.

Ellerhorst, Winfrid
Handbuch der Orgelkunde. Einsiedeln: Benziger, 1936; *Bib Org,* VII, 1966.

Fesperman, John
The Organ as Musical Medium. New York: Coleman-Ross, 1962.

Glatter-Götz, Josef von
"Die physikalischen und physiologischen Grundlagen der mechanischen Spieltraktur," *Altbayerische Orgeltage,* ed. W. Supper. (MeV) 1958. 34.

Hopkins, Edward J., and Edward F. Rimbault
The Organ, Its History and Construction. London, 1855; *Bib Org,* IV, 1965.

Hunt, Noel Aubrey Bonavia
The Modern British Organ, rev. ed. London: Weekes, 1950.

Jamison, James Blaine
Organ Design and Appraisal. New York: H. W. Gray, 1959.

Lange, Martin
Kleine Orgelkunde. (BV) 1955.

Mahrenholz, Christhard
Die Berechnung der Orgelpfeifen-Mensuren vom Mittelalter bis zur Mitte des 19. Jahrhunderts, 2d ed. (BV) 1968.

Mersenne, Marin
"Des Orgues," *L'Harmonie universelle* (Paris, 1636), reprint, 3 vols. Paris: Centre nationale de la recherche scientifique, 1963. III, 309–412.

Praetorius, Michael
De Organographia, Vol. II of *Syntagma musicum* (Wolfenbüttel, 1619), reprint, ed. W. Gurlitt. (BV) 1958–59.

Praetorius, Michael, and Esaias Compenius
Orgeln Verdingnis, ed. F. Blume. Wolfenbüttel-Berlin: Kallmeyer, 1936.

Schlick, Arnold
"Gutachten über Orgelbau" (1491), *Quellen und Bausteine zur Geschichte der Musik und des Theaters im Elsass (500–1800),* ed. M. Vogeleis. Strassburg, 1911.

————. *Spiegel der Orgelmacher und Organisten* (Speyer, 1511), reprint, ed. E. Flade. (BV) 1951; reprint, ed. P. Smets. Mainz: Rheingold, 1959; trans. excerpts in *Organ Institute Quarterly,* VII, 4–X, 4 (see below, "Journals and Yearbooks").

Schlimbach, G. C. Fr.
Über die Struktur, Erhaltung, Stimmung, Prufung etc. der Orgel. Bib Org, VIII, 1966.

Seidel, Johann Julius
    Die Orgel und ihr Bau. Bib Org, II, 1962.

Sorge, Georg Andreas
    Der in der Rechen- und Messkunst wohlerfahrene Orgelbaumeister (Lobenstein, 1773), ed. P. Smets. Mainz: Smets, 1932.

Sumner, William Leslie
    The Organ: Its Evolution, Principles of Construction, and Use, 3d ed. London: MacDonald, 1962.

Supper, Walter
    Der Kleinorgelbrief, 2d ed. (BV) 1949.

———. *Die Orgeldisposition: eine Heranführung.* (BV) 1950.

———. *Fibel der Orgeldisposition.* (BV) 1946.

Töpfer, Johann Gottlob
    Lehrbuch der Orgelbaukunst (Leipzig, 1855; 2d ed., Weimar, 1888), new revised ed., ed. P. Smets, 4 vols. Mainz: Rheingold, 1955—60.

Werckmeister, Andreas
    Andreae Werkmeisters . . . erweiterte und verbesserte Orgelprobe (Quedlinburg, 1698), reprint. (BV) 1927.

Wolfram, Johann Christian
    Anleitung zur Kenntniss, Beurtheilung und Erhaltung der Orgeln. Bib Org, III, 1962.

Internationales Regulativ für Orgelbau. Entworfen und bearb. von der Sektion für Orgelbau auf dem 3. Kongress der internationalen Musikgesellschaft, Wien, 1909. Vienna: Artaria, 1909.

Case and Façade

Blanton, Joseph Edwin
    The Organ in Church Design. Albany, Tex.: Venture, 1957.

———. *The Revival of the Organ Case.* Albany, Tex.: Venture, 1965.

Brunzema, Daniel
    Die Gestaltung des Orgelprospektes im friesischen und angrenzenden Nordseeküstengebiet bis 1670 und ihre Bedeutung für die Gegenwart, Vol. XXXV of *Abhandlungen und Vorträge zur Geschichte Ostfrieslands.* Arich: Verlag Ostfriesische Landschaft, 1958.

Freeman, Andrew
    Church Organs and Organ Cases. London: Society for Promoting Christian Knowledge, 1942.

Hill, Arthur George
    Organ Cases and Organs of the Middle Ages and Renaissance. London: Whittingham, 1891, reprint. Bib Org, VI.

Kaufmann, Walter
    Der Orgelprospekt in stilgeschichtlicher Entwicklung, 3d ed. Mainz: Rheingold, 1949.

Werner, David
  Gestaltungsformen des modernen Orgelprospekts. (BV) 1952.

Physics

Gravesaner Blätter, ed. H. Scherchen, IV/11–12 (1958).

Klangstruktur der Musik. Neue Erkenntnisse musik-elektronischer Forschung, ed. F. Winckel. Berlin: Verlag für Radio-Foto-Kinotechnik, 1955.

Lottermoser, Werner and Jürgen Meyer
  Orgelakustik in Einzeldarstellungen, Vol. XVI of *Fachbuchreihe Das Musikinstrument.* Frankfurt a. M.: Das Musikinstrument, 1966.

Journals and Yearbooks

American Guild of Organists Quarterly. New York: AGO, 1956–67, absorbed by *Music, A. G. O. Magazine.*

Ars organi: Mitteilungsblatt der Gesellschaft der Orgelfreunde. (MeV) 1953–.

Association F. H. Clicquot. Poitiers.

Bach-Jahrbuch. (B&H) 1905–.

Church Music. St. Louis: Concordia, 1966–.

Clavier. Evanston, Ill., 1961–.

De Praestant: Tijdschrift voor Orgelcultur in de Nederlanden. Antwerp: Tongerlo, 1952–.

Der Kirchenmusiker. (MeV) 1950–.

Het Orgel. Steenwijk: Nederlandsche organistenvereeniging, 1903–.

Het Orgelblad: Maandblad voor Orgelliefhebbers. Leiden.

Instrumentenbau-Zeitschrift. Siegburg: Schmitt, 1946–.

I. S. O.-Information [triannual of the *International Society of Organbuilders.* Josef von Glatter-Götz, editor in chief; Lawrence I. Phelps, editor for U. S. A. and Canada; in preparation]. Lauffen a. N., 1969–.

Journal of Church Music. Philadelphia: Fortress Press, 1958–.

Mitteilungen des Max-Reger-Instituts. Bonn, 1954–.

Music: The A. G. O. Magazine [absorbed the *A. G. O. Quarterly*], New York, 1967–.

Music Ministry. Nashville, Tenn.: Abingdon Press, 1959–.

Musik und Gottesdienst. Zürich: Zwingli, 1947.

Musik und Kirche. (BV) 1929–.

Organ Institute Quarterly. Andover, Mass., 1951–.

Organist en Eredienst: Maandschrift van de Gereformeerde Organistenvereniging.

L'Organo: Rivista di cultura organaria e organistica. Bologna, 1960–.

L'Orgue. Paris: L'Association des amis de l'orgue, 1929–. Reprint. (BV) 1967.

Response—In Worship—Music—the Arts. St. Paul: Lutheran Society for

Worship, Music, and the Arts, 1959—.

Sacred Music [continuing *Caecilia*], publ. by Church Music Association of America. St. Paul, Minnesota, 1874—.

The American Organist. Staten Island, N. Y., 1918—.

The Diapason. Chicago, 1909—.

The Musical Heritage of the Lutheran Church. St. Louis: Concordia, 1944—.

The Organ. Luton, Beds.: Musical Opinion, 1921—.

Reports of Musical Congresses

Bericht über die Freiburger Tagung für deutsche Orgelkunst vom 27. bis 30. Juli 1926, ed. W. Gurlitt. (BV) 1926.

Bericht über die dritte Tagung für deutsche Orgelkunst in Freiberg (Sachsen) 2.—7. Oktober 1927, ed. Ch. Mahrenholz. (BV) 1928.

Bericht über die Tagung in Ochsenhausen 30. Juli—5. August 1951, ed. W. Supper, (MeV) 1952.

Bericht über den internationalen Kongress für Kirchenmusik in Bern 1952. Bern: Schweiz. musikforschende Gesellschaft, 1953.

Bericht über den Zweiten internationalen Kongress für Kirchenmusik in Bern 1962. Bern: Schweiz. musikforschende Gesellschaft, 1964.

Reference Works

Graaf, G. A. C. de
Literatur over het Orgel. Literature on the Organ. Amsterdam: de Graaf, 1957.

Heyer, Anna H. ed.
Historical Sets, Collected Editions and Monuments of Music: A Guide to Their Contents. Chicago: American Library Association, 1957.

Lohmann, Heinz
Handbuch der Orgelliteratur. (B&H) n. d.

Lukas, Viktor
Orgelmusikführer. Stuttgart. Reclam, 1963.

Münger, Fritz
Choralbearbeitungen für Orgel. (BV) 1952.

Die Musik in Geschichte und Gegenwart, ed. F. Blume, 14 vols. to date. (BV) 1949—.

Probst, Cécile
Literatur für Kleinorgel. Zürich, 1964.

Sauer, Franz
Handbuch der ˏOrgel-Literatur. Vienna: Wiener philharmonischer Verlag, 1924.

Weigl, Bruno, ed.
Handbuch der Orgelliteratur. Leipzig: Leuckart, 1931.

Westerby, Herbert
The Complete Organ Recitalist. London: "Musical Opinion" and "The Organ" office, 1934.

INDEX OF NAMES

[The abbreviation *OB* stands for *organ builder*]

INDEX OF PLACES

* specification

Unna 164
Utrecht 164

Verden 35
Vienna 110, 164
Vormbach 167

Weiler in den Bergen 24

Weingarten 151, 167
Wolfenbüttel 146
Wolfsburg 114

Zutphen 164
Zwolle 163, 164

GEOGRAPHICAL INDEX

SUBJECT INDEX

223